C000054405

FEMALE SUICIDE BOMBINGS

A Critical Gender Approach

As media coverage of terrorism and terroristic acts has increased, so too has the discussion about the identities, motives, and gender of the perpetrators. Over the past fifteen years, there have been over 150 reported suicide bombings committed by women around the world. Because of its prominence in media reporting, the phrase "female suicide bomber" has become weighted with gendered notions and assumptions that elicit preconditioned responses in the West.

Female Suicide Bombings critically examines and challenges common assumptions of this term. Tanya Narozhna and W. Andy Knight introduce female suicide bombings as a socio-political practice and a product of deeply politicized, gendered representations. Drawing on a combination of feminist and postcolonial approaches as well as terrorism studies literature, the authors seek to transcend ideological divisions in order to enhance our understanding of how gender, power, and academic practices influence our perceptions of female suicide bombings.

TANYA NAROZHNA is an associate professor of global politics at the University of Winnipeg.

W. ANDY KNIGHT is a professor in the Department of Political Science at the University of Alberta.

Female Suicide Bombings

A Critical Gender Approach

TANYA NAROZHNA AND W. ANDY KNIGHT

UNIVERSITY OF TORONTO PRESS

Toronto Buffalo London

© University of Toronto Press 2016
Toronto Buffalo London
www.utppublishing.com

ISBN 978-1-4875-0007-8 (cloth)   ISBN 978-1-4875-2004-5 (paper)

Library and Archives Canada Cataloguing in Publication

Narozhna, Tanya, 1976–, author
Female suicide bombings : a critical gender approach / Tanya Narozhna
and W. Andy Knight.

Includes bibliographical references and index.
ISBN 978-1-4875-0007-8 (cloth). – ISBN 978-1-4875-2004-5 (paper)

1. Women suicide bombers. 2. Women terrorists. 3. Terrorism – Social
aspects. 4. Terrorism – Political aspects. 5. Feminism. I. Knight,
W. Andy, author   II. Title.

HV6431.N37 2016   363.325082   C2016-901510-6

University of Toronto Press acknowledges the financial assistance to its
publishing program of the Canada Council for the Arts and the Ontario
Arts Council, an agency of the Government of Ontario.

Canada Council   Conseil des Arts
for the Arts   du Canada

ONTARIO ARTS COUNCIL
CONSEIL DES ARTS DE L'ONTARIO
an Ontario government agency
un organisme du gouvernement de l'Ontario

Funded by the   Financé par le
Government   gouvernement
of Canada   du Canada

For Vasyl
   – T.N.

Contents

Acknowledgments

On 8 September 2004, we published an opinion editorial in the *Globe and Mail* titled "Women Who Terrorize," which debunked some of the assumptions about "black widows" and posited a controversial but compelling thesis on female agency in a number of high-profile female suicide terrorist attacks. Little did we know, then, that this article would generate so much interest that eventually we would consider the possibility of writing a book on the subject. So we should first thank the *Globe and Mail* for giving our initial thoughts on this subject national and global exposure.

To undertake the sweeping research needed for case study examination of the female face of terror, we applied to the Social Sciences and Humanities Research Council (SSHRC) of Canada for funding. We acknowledge the generous financial support from this funding agency, realizing that the research for this book would not have been possible without it.

We would also like to thank a number of people who helped to make this book possible. First, we are indebted to an army of research assistants at the University of Winnipeg (Adelina Vouriot, Laura Metcalfe, Bojan Pirnat, Mladen Kojic, and Ksenia Prints) who collected primary and secondary source material instrumental in helping us ensure that the manuscript was as up to date as possible. A class of graduate students in the Department of Political Science at the University of Alberta, who were taking an Advanced International Relations Theory course, provided critical comments on various iterations of the draft manuscript. We are grateful for their feedback and criticisms. Second, participants in a conference on female suicide bombings (Alistair Edgar, Margaret Gonzalez-Perez, Paige Eager, David Cook, Laura Sjoberg,

Francine Banner, Tami Jacoby, Andrew Mack, Jayne Huckerby, and Marc Imbeault) held at the University of Winnipeg in 2013 played an important role in helping us refine our ideas. Their input, questions, and vital commentary were very much appreciated and in many ways forced us to take into consideration certain nuances in the debate over structure and agency in our attempt to understand certain women's role in the perpetuation of violence. Third, we are thankful for being given the opportunity to present our ideas at the International Studies Association (ISA) annual meetings (San Francisco, 2013, and New Orleans, 2010), the Canadian Political Science Association (CPSA) conference at the University of Alberta (2012), the Comparative Interdisciplinary Studies Section of the ISA conference in Potsdam (2009), and at a major international conference "Towards the 'Dignity of Difference': Neither the 'Clash of Civilizations' nor the 'End of History'" held at the University of Alberta (2009). Panelists and members of the audience in each case provided useful suggestions on individual chapters that were presented.

The quality of any academic book is highly dependent on the blind reviews of other academics. We benefited enormously from the comments and constructive criticisms of four anonymous reviewers. The final product was vastly improved as we meticulously tried to grapple with their suggestions. Daniel Quinlan, Wayne Herrington, and Ian MacKenzie played a pivotal role in helping us convert the idea for the book into reality. We very much appreciated their patience and prodding at various stages of the production process.

Despite the contributions, comments, critiques, and suggestions from those mentioned above, we acknowledge our own personal responsibility for any errors or omissions in the final outcome resulting in this book. Finally, we would be remiss if we did not acknowledge the love and sacrifices of our respective families when we pursue difficult and tedious research projects like this one. We thank them from the bottom of our hearts.

Tanya Narozhna
University of Winnipeg

W. Andy Knight
University of Alberta

FEMALE SUICIDE BOMBINGS

A Critical Gender Approach

Introduction

Setting the Context

Female suicide bombers entered the stage of modern political violence nearly three decades ago. Their arrival generated a broad range of reactions, from deep shock over and condemnation of uncharacteristic violent performance by women to sensationalizing and glorifying such violence. Their persistent reappearance in Afghanistan, Cameroon, India, Iraq, Israel, Lebanon, Nigeria, Pakistan, Palestine, Russia, Somalia, Sri Lanka, Syria, Turkey, and Uzbekistan mesmerized immediate and distant audiences, became crucial to dominant stories of modern political violence, and in some places achieved a shroud of legitimacy. The seeming novelty and contentious nature of this violent role played by women defied almost ubiquitous cross-cultural belief in the notion of female peacefulness and compelled uneasy reconsiderations of multiple social, historical, and political orthodoxies with their attendant power dynamics and boundaries.

Female suicide bombings are a challenging object of inquiry. Their number being relatively small,[1] they have acquired a liminal yet significant status within contemporary debates on political violence. Each act of female suicide bombing typically puts the spotlight on the individual bombers and prompts the urge to find out more about them: who they were, how they lived, and what drove them to commit their final acts. With their pictures and stories in every major news outlet, we often feel as if we are intimately familiar with the protagonists of these stories. Yet they remain curiously puzzling, threatening, intriguing, and shocking. Their impact is amplified by the fact that more often than not their final acts remain the only public statements they have made.[2] For the most part, we cannot hear from female suicide bombers in their own words, cannot ask them why they committed their violent acts or what the meanings of these acts were. Empirical information about them is second hand at best – pieced together from interviews with those who knew them, scant, with questionable cred- ibility, and often dismissive of contextual socio-political and cultural specificity. These limitations are extremely consequential, for in the absence of reliable empirical information, widely accepted knowledge about female suicide bombers and the meanings of their final acts are, in fact, the product of the prevalent modes of representation constructed by those in a position to speak and make authoritative claims about them. While many of these representations fixate on individual perpe- trators, critical questions about power, knowledge, identity, violence, legitimacy, and meaning go unasked.

In this book, we are concerned with how female suicide bombings are studied, made sense of, and represented within Western academia. Convinced that the process through which female suicide bombings come to connote particular meanings is inherently political, gendered, and gendering, we inquire about the ethical and political ramifications of such knowledge. We question dominant discourses and common understandings of female suicide bombings, ask about the modes of representation excluded from mainstream practices of knowledge pro- duction, and explore the ways in which conventional knowledge is intertwined with existing power relations and social hierarchies. In this respect, our book is, in part, deconstructive. Our analysis offers critical insights into the ways in which female suicide perpetrators, their acts of violence, as well as broader collective struggles of which they are part become, through discursive framing, feminized, i.e., depoliticized, delegitimized, and devalorized (Peterson 2010).

In the process of shedding light on the biases and strengths in mainstream research, we also work towards a reconceptualization of female suicide bombings, drawing on a combination of feminist and postcolonial approaches. We present an alternative reading of female suicide bombings that employs the analytical category of gender criti- cally, i.e., as a socially constructed identity and a set of discourses that function as an ordering principle of all social relations. Understood in this way, gender is simultaneously reproductive of and reproduced through social relations (Sjoberg and Gentry 2007; Connell 1995). Our reading conceives of the acts of female suicide bombings, the contexts within which they took place, their discursive representations, as well as the immediate and long-term policy measures in response to such violence as interconnected and, therefore, crucial for understanding violence in global politics. We develop a series of theoretical arguments about women, gender, violence, knowledge, and power. We argue that mainstream scholarship is inextricably linked to the political agendas of hegemonic masculine states and validates a very limited spectrum of viewpoints. Despite its claims to objectivity, knowledge about female suicide bombings produced by mainstream scholars is not neutral. Rather, it is politicized, gendered, and gendering. It draws on the particular configurations and relational properties of masculinity and femininity to recreate systems of meaning through which the violence itself, as well as subjects and objects of female suicide bombings, can be rendered intelligible. It also mobilizes dominant modes of masculinity and femininity to ascribe superiority to the idealized Western rationalist hypermasculinity and to relegate a variety of "inferior" femininities and masculinities to the margins. Such discursive deployment of gender hierarchy and sexual difference has practical effects across socio-political life, not least of which are discursive reproduction of gendered power relations globally through ideological reification of Western hegemony, as well as legitimation of coercive counterterrorism and structural violence.

Our analytical focus is specifically and unapologetically on women, rather than men or all suicide bombers. We chose this focus self-consciously to study marginalized agents and their strategies. We therefore inquire about the representations of politically violent women, their agency and victimhood within specific social relations, and the effects of their final acts across multiple places and contexts. In our analysis, we address the issue of traditional women's invisibility and/or insignificance in political violence, even – or perhaps especially – when they are at the forefront of such violence. We do not seek to provide moral justification for women who engage in suicide bombings or communities that support or even glorify their violence as a legitimate response against occupation, oppression, or non-military forms of violence.[3] Rather, we engage extensively with the issue of complex gendered constructions of female suicide bombings in order to reveal multiple ways in which mainstream representations of this political violence build on the assumption of essential differences between male and female bombers, stereotypically contrast female suicide perpetrators with their male counterparts, and consistently depoliticize violence of the former, despite the fact that their acts have been perpetrated in the larger context of socio-political struggles. These representations, as mentioned above, rest upon and reify deeply entrenched, recognizable discourses of masculinity and femininity. Therefore, our analytical focus on women is both warranted and justified for a simple reason that it is women bombers who are misrepresented and backstaged by having their agency and political motivations marginalized or denied on the basis of gender.

Indeed, in the course of our research we found that the expert reviews that followed the emergence of female suicide bombers were disappointingly reductive and of little depth. Some early accounts of the nature, advantages, causes, and lessons learned about female suicide bombings (see Victor 2003; Davis 2003) advanced claims about the irrationality and/or psychopathology of female suicide perpetrators, tendentially emphasizing personal issues and individual psychology, and effectively engaging in what Bloom (2008) called "psychological autopsy."[4] For example, Barbara Victor (2003) focused on the personal motives of four Palestinian female suicide bombers and ex post facto reconstructed their life stories in order to uncover individual problems that may have caused these women to embrace violence. In her investigation, she discovered that all female suicide bombers, as well as those who failed to complete their missions, had personal problems that made their lives untenable in their society and culture. In her work, Victor made specific references to mental illness, acute emotional distress, and psychological predispositions as potentially playing a role in individual women's decisions to carry out suicide attacks.

In these early publications, female suicide bombers were portrayed, by and large, in conformity with social and cultural stereotypes about women and femininity. Conventional wisdom holds that women, as bearers of life, lack the natural inclination for carrying out violent acts. These gender stereotypes made it difficult to conceive of female suicide bombers as agents of violence in their own right. In some instances, they were represented as oppressed, deceived, irrational, and/or ignorant "romantic dupes," manipulated into their destructive role by men; and in others, they were framed as "feminist warriors" embracing the violence of suicide bombings as the only venue available to them for achieving gender equality (Ness 2008c, 3). On occasion, the relevance of gender was dismissed altogether, despite its centrality in analysing, explaining, and representing the acts of female suicide bombings. As Skaine (2006, 10) boldly put it, "Gender importance of a bomber is largely a Western concept. Militarily, a bomber is a bomber."

Dominant Representations

Within Western academy much analytical engagement with female suicide bombings took place in the field of terrorism studies. A number of core texts and experts[5] approached this topic in instrumental terms, eschewing earlier psychodynamic explanations of female suicide bombings in favour of a more complex rationalist approach.

Terrorism studies scholars developed two synergistic sets of self-reinforcing instrumental explanations: one within the matrix of nation states, especially Western nation states gendered as masculine, (inter) national security, and counterterrorism; and another one with the focus on the internal and external dynamics of the organizations behind the bombings.

On the former point, terrorism studies scholars a priori relegated the violence of female suicide bombings to the realm of states and (inter) national security, rendering it illegitimate on the grounds that this violence is directed against states and reducing it to a limited number of variables, i.e., threat, risk, coercion, strategy, tactic, etc.[6] More specifically, they identified female suicide bombings from the perspective of sovereign states understood in the Weberian sense as the only entities in global politics that successfully claim the monopoly on the legitimate use of violence. Female suicide bombings, from this perspective, by default represent an illegitimate form of violence directed against sovereign states and a threat to (inter)national security. Having conflated the normative meaning of violence with the nature of actors engaging in it, i.e., state actors / legitimate violence, non-state actors / illegitimate violence, these scholars, then, offered a set of presumably neutral and effective instruments intended to enable states to meet their security objectives and counter the violence of female suicide bombings. That is, in order to understand and explain acts of female suicide bombings, this scholarship is concerned explicitly with how states "view, treat, and strategize against them" (Ness 2008c, 1), as well as with the ways in which these strategies can be improved (Zedalis 2008; Bloom 2007, 2011; Cragin and Daly 2009; Qazi 2011). Terrorism studies scholars share their preoccupation with counterterrorism with earlier journalistic accounts of female suicide bombings. Skaine, for example, is explicit about her concern with counterterrorism when she quotes Jennifer Hardwick, a senior director of the Terrorism Research Center Inc.: "My most pressing concern is that the U.S. is completely unprepared for suicide bombings, especially by a woman" (2006, 7). Thus, terrorism studies literature on female suicide bombings presents itself as an objective scholarship, while focusing centrally on the Western and specifically U.S. counterterrorism agenda. Counterterrorism concerns and effectiveness of counterterrorism measures became the key guiding criteria, influencing every aspect of terrorism studies works – from methodological commitments and collection of empirical data to epistemological positions and substantive analyses.

Effectiveness, however, as David Mutimer (1998, 100) observed, is a relative term that cannot be understood without the "goals, standards and interests against which [it is] ... judged." Terrorism studies scholars treated these goals, standards, and interests as objective and unproblematic, thus eclipsing an alternative understanding, namely that, in the process of selecting and using "neutral" and "effective" security instruments, states uphold and reproduce certain social, political, and strategic practices. Far from being analytically objective and gender-neutral, terror and counterterror practices carry with them a set of meanings laden with assumptions about femininity and masculinity that are constitutive of the actions, identities, relations, and interests of those involved. Terrorism studies scholars focus on the terrorist methods and their security impact without engaging with or at least making the gendered politics of terrorism and counterterrorism explicit (Brown 2011, 201).

Interestingly, terrorism studies scholars do not view the two commitments – to objectivity and U.S. counterterrorism – as contradictory. The logic and language of instrumental rationality enables them to draw meaning from function without recognizing that the particular understanding of terrorism and counterterrorism measures, the very criteria by which their effectiveness is determined, and social contexts that shape intersubjective meaning of the particular functions these measures perform are all contingent on the "interpretive frame operative at particular moments in particular places" (Euben 2007, 130). Different social positions of suicide bombers, their immediate victims, societies, and states they target condition distinct views. Therefore, no single explanation of suicide bombings and counterterrorism measures can or should be universally applicable (Brown 2011, 210). At the same time, refusal to acknowledge the contestability of their vantage point leads all terrorism studies scholars to integrate Western biases via U.S. counterterrorism concerns (Brunner 2007, 968). The mere fact that female suicide bombings became the object of serious inquiry in the West only after Palestinian women began to blow themselves up in Israel in 2002 speaks to this bias. Prior to 2002, females committed suicide bombings in places of little strategic and geopolitical importance to the West. It is only after this practice erupted in the context of Israeli-Palestinian conflict and posed a direct security threat to Israel that Western nations began to take notice of it. As Ness (2008c, 3) put it, following the 2002 female suicide attacks in Israel, "the idea that females were capable of inflicting unapologetic carnage, and subsequently, were of great strategic importance to terrorist operations across the globe, was indelibly lodged in the Western subconscious." This idea became stronger with the launching in 2001 of the Global War on Terror, followed by an increased number of female suicide bombings in Iraq that threatened or directly targeted Western troops.

The privileging of the Israeli-Palestinian and Iraqi theatres of violence in the disproportionate number of terrorism studies publications persists to this day. Integral to much of this literature is the tendency to conjure a depoliticized image of an essentialized, irrational Palestinian/ Muslim/Arab female suicide bomber, which is then used as an archetype for generic explanations. Equally important is tendential blending of Israel and the West into a single political and strategic space, with an implication that Muslim/Arab female suicide bombers posit a threat to the West and international security. As Bloom (2007, 173) put it, quoting from Scheuer, "Right or wrong, Muslims are beginning to view the United States as a colonial power with Israel as the surrogate, and with a military presence in three of the holiest places in Islam, the Arabian Peninsula, Iraq …, and Jerusalem." Female suicide bombings are thus conjecturally represented as part of the globalization of terrorism, having major strategic impact on the United States as the leader of the Global War on Terror (Zedalis 2008, 53). Ideological bias towards the American counterterror agenda persists either through the employment of biographical narratives (Davis 2003), or by stripping female suicide bombers of their agency and framing their acts of political violence as a revolt against orientalized Third World patriarchy (Bloom 2007) – an issue that we discuss at length in chapter 5.

The second set of instrumental explanations focused primarily on the strategic and tactical advantages of the organizations that deploy female suicide bombers and recognized multiple, mixed, and context-specific individual motivations. Terrorism studies literature framed female suicide bombings as an innovative tactic complementing regular insurgent methods and bringing benefits to (or misfiring against) the organizations faced with stronger, well-armed adversaries within asymmetric conflict (Bloom 2007, 2011; Cragin and Daly 2009). Hence the terminological preference for "female suicide bombers" or "female suicide terrorists," as opposed to "female martyrs" – a term that is more likely to be used by the supporters or sympathizers. Suicide bombers, as Pape (2005) put it in explicitly gendered terms, are the weapons of the weak, an extreme form of "the rationality of irrationality" in which the weaker side becomes stronger through "irrational" individual acts of self-sacrifice in pursuit of a "rational" coercive strategy designed to achieve specific political objectives. Presumably, insurgent organizations gain a number of benefits on different levels, given the tactical and coercive efficiency of these attacks, difficulties in deterring them, their symbolic value, media coverage, as well as popular and financial support generated by suicide bombings framed as martyrdom. By now, there is an established consensus that the benefits are greater if *female* suicide bombers are employed (Zedalis 2008; Cragin and Daly 2009; Bloom 2011; Stone and Pattillo 2011; Qazi 2011; Berko 2012; Davis 2013). Female suicide perpetrators maximize tactical advantage, media coverage, and psychological impact because they violate traditional understandings of women, femininity, and violence. In other words, gender stereotypes make female suicide perpetrators effective and expedient instruments in the hands of terrorist groups. Women, as Christine Sixta (2008, 268) put it, "are used as an exploitable resource … [and] thought of as throw away artillery."

Accounts centred on the organizational level, however important, cannot explain why some groups choose to use female suicide bombers, while others refrain from this violent tactic. Therefore, while retaining the focus on internal group dynamics, targets, tactics, strategies, and motivating ideologies, terrorism studies scholars were compelled to acknowledge the simplicity of mono-causal explanations and called for the recognition of the embeddedness of suicide bombings in the broader historical, socio-political, and cultural contexts. They stressed the combination of "the logic of terror and oppression" and complexity of individual motives, i.e., belief in a cause, history of abuse, various grievances, shared experiences of humiliation, culture of martyrdom, family relationships, and coercion in driving individuals to become suicide bombers (Bloom 2011, 28–30). Analyses of the strategic cost-benefit calculations by the sponsoring organizations were often supplemented by discussion of women's individual motives, as well as considerations of the role of community and culture in moulding the perpetrators' mindset. On this latter point, terrorism studies works consistently emphasized that women's willingness and readiness to engage in suicide bombings in various contexts was often linked to societal and cultural pressures, especially those related to some women being viewed as "damaged goods" (i.e., sexually compromised, unmarriageable, unable to have babies, or subject to honour codes) (Schweitzer 2008, Bloom 2010; Bloom, Thayer, and Hudson 2010/11; Berko 2012). As Bloom (2011, 31) put it, "In too many cases of women's involvement, the woman has been *abused, victimized,* or *targeted* in ways that leave her little choice but to join the terrorists in hope of reclaiming her honor." In other words, suicide bombings represented a rational alternative to women implicated in various sorts of social and cultural transgressions, real or alleged.

As we demonstrate in this book, this rationalist explanatory model set the boundaries of conventional knowledge about female suicide bombings, determining what we know about the perpetrators, how we approach and understand their violence, and what kind of responses we support. It produced a range of meanings behind state counterterrorism practices and "forced many to verbally negotiate and assert who they are, who they are allied with, and who they are against" (Bhatia 2005, 7). Effectively, terrorism studies scholars made important authoritative and political claims about how the subjectivities of female suicide bombers and their societies are constructed, social relations are reproduced, as well as certain political and ethical outcomes are made possible.

Indeed, amidst terrorism studies literature one finds remarkably little serious reflection on the ways in which the framing of the problem in line with the positivist logic of instrumental rationality produced a highly politicized, gendered, and gendering knowledge of female suicide bombings and precluded critical reflexivity in the study of this violent social practice. As Claudia Brunner (2005, 46) noted insightfully, "Suicide bombings seem to be irrational in their genesis, but hardly any kind of physical violence is as rational as it pretends to be." Brunner's observation suggests that behind any group's rational calculations to employ a suicide bomber, and the individual's decision to become one, lie powerful collective emotions and intersubjective meanings that create a "world" fundamentally different from the one in terrorism studies analyses. Terrorism studies' reliance on rational choice explanations makes them ill-equipped to account for the sociology and social psychology of structural violence or to treat critically the impact of gender and discursive violence in the analysis of female suicide bombings.

As Shapiro (2007) observed, rational choice theories operate well at the individual level, making them a good source for explaining strategic calculations behind individual decisions to deploy suicide bombers or not to. However, rational choice literature is less helpful when it comes to explaining the group dimension of collective resistance. And, as Leila Khaled, a Palestinian female terrorist known for her role in the two airplane hijackings in 1969 and 1970, stated in one of her interviews, "Armed struggle is not an individual choice. It's a people's choice for the cause that they are struggling for" (Gentry 2011a, 122).

We do not refute the idea that understanding strategic objectives and practices is important for explaining, combating, and preventing female suicide bombings. On the contrary, we appreciate the arguments about strategic behaviour of those who recruit, train, and deploy female suicide bombers. We agree, however, with Shapiro that the rationalist approach is inherently limited in its ability to account for group solidarity and other complex dynamics of collective support for suicide bombings perceived as martyrdom and sends us instead "in search of selective incentives to get individuals to contribute to the provision of collective goods" (Shapiro 2007, 136). The treatment of general conditions as "selective incentives" enables terrorism studies scholars to view socio-economic, demographic, political, and other conditions as secondary to the strategic side of this violent practice. Constrained by security-as-state-survival logic, this approach precludes any meaningful engagement with violences that are not centred on the states, fall outside the war/peace dichotomy, or are non-military in character – what Shepherd (2009, 209) called "the violences of the in-between times … and the violences inherent to times of peace that are overlooked in the study of war."[7]

Contra Shapiro, we find that rational choice theory does not operate very well on the individual level either, in that, despite its self-professed universality, this theory is predicated analytically and normatively on masculine assumptions and values. The individual that rational choice theory attempts to explain is implicitly gendered male. In other words, rational choice theory is necessarily partial, as its explanatory framework builds exclusively on men's historical experiences and leaves out women's violence. Rational choice theory, as Sjoberg and Gentry (2007, 178) observed, "is *gendered* both by omission (women) and by commission (the partiality of its theoretical insight)." Rational choice theorists analyse motivations and assign responsibility for individual violence, both male and female, on the basis of dominant gender norms, thus failing to provide adequate explanations for violence by either men or women (189). Indeed, as a result of the gendered nature of their explanatory framework, terrorism studies scholars invest female suicide bombers with absolutism and essentialism, exceptionalize their final acts, and treat them as a prefixed, homogeneous, gendered category that overemphasizes commonalities and downplays differences. This explains why references to female suicide bombers within terrorism studies literature are often made in a singular form.[8] This approach reifies artificially constructed gender stereotypes and divisions, creates silences, and reinforces dominant masculinist universalisms. It renders gender, specific geo-political space, deeply held religious beliefs, cultural norms, and moral commitments either marginally relevant or irrational. Yet as Euben (2007, 130) observed, these "norms, ideas, and beliefs do not simply reflect or obscure a set of given conditions, constraints, and choices, but rather determine how and in what terms they are understood. Explaining the function of any particular practice or tactic thus requires close examination of the complex interactions among material conditions, strategic choices, multiple and at times overlapping contexts, and the very beliefs and commitments these studies set aside, along with other 'incentives' whose content is largely incidental."

Therefore, explanations of female suicide bombings centred on instrumentalism and rationality should not be taken for granted or treated as self-evident and unproblematic. Rather, they should be seen as power-laden social constructs that build on the established interpretive dispositions, cultural templates, and practical orientations within Western societies, all of which essentialize male agency and female victimhood in violence.

In this book, we offer a critical gender approach to understanding and explaining female suicide bombings. This approach is particularly helpful in demonstrating incompleteness of explanations focused exclusively on instrumental rationality, revealing crude inadequacy of the rational-emotional binary drawn on the basis of gender, and providing important insights into the ways in which terrorism studies literature taps into prevalent intersubjective understandings in Western societies to construct gendered images of others, while obscuring its own ideological assumptions and political goals. Taking seriously the effects of gender on the day-to-day lives of individuals provides the starting point of our critical intervention and leads us to a more meaningful and nuanced analysis of the violence of female suicide bombings. It also allows us to reveal the contestability of the foundational assumptions in terrorism studies analyses. We challenge the reductionist treatment of gender, culture, religion, race, socio-economic and political conditions as "incentives," and treat them as complex "interlocking system[s] of meanings" that define identities, provide interpretive frameworks, create collective memory, determine the limits of acceptable practices (Euben 2007, 129–33), and render the very idea of reconciling a specific counterterrorism agenda with objective analysis of female suicide bombings incongruous.

A Critical Gender Approach

Significantly, terrorism studies' engagement with the violence of female suicide bombings has been marked by an uncritical deployment of the analytical category of gender, manifested most explicitly in the strong gendering of female perpetrators vis-à-vis their male counterparts. As mentioned above, gendering, or social differentiation on the basis of assumed socially constructed group characteristics (Sjoberg and Via 2010; Sjoberg and Gentry 2007, 2011; Tickner 2001), enabled terrorism studies scholars to represent female suicide bombers as a group phenomenon and render them exceptional in view of the relatively low frequency of attacks and small number of women perpetrators. This happened without much substantiation and despite the uniqueness of each individual case. Female suicide bombers were analysed and portrayed first and foremost as women (Sjoberg and Gentry 2007; Ness 2008a; Sjoberg 2009; Rajan 2012).[9] A mere necessity to specify "female" highlighted their "historical rarity and symbolic position as unconventional" (Alison 2004, 447) and "disturbing" (Cragin and Daly 2009, 1) figures. U.S. President George Bush clearly demonstrated the difficulty of reconciling female violence and gender stereotypes in the president's radio address on 6 April 2002 when referring to the third Palestinian female suicide bomber: "When an 18-year-old Palestinian girl is induced to blow herself up and in the process kills a 17-year-old Israeli girl, the future is dying."[10] In his statement, Bush implied that an act of female suicide bombing is qualitatively different from male suicide bombing, thus showing that female suicide bombings became the site where the boundary between femininity and masculinity was reproduced and reaffirming the inviolability of the "natural" gender order.

Terrorism studies scholars acknowledged that gender matters but treated it as a stable descriptor of identity, effectively collapsing gender into sex, naturalizing and reinforcing a rigid gender hierarchy (see Berko 2012; Bloom 2007, 2010, 2011; Weinberg and Eubank 2011). Terrorism studies scholars often ask what motivates female suicide bombers. Unlike their male counterparts, female suicide bombers are said to be driven by personal motives.[11] Considering that the practice of suicide bombings is political, Rose (2004) is correct to remind us that the question of motives of female suicide perpetrators is loaded in and of itself. The answer to this question is not contingent on the extent of the empirical information one can collect about the individual bombers – it is predetermined by the stereotypical understandings of femininity and female roles. The answer as such may be irrelevant, despite the fact that it seems important and attracts great attention. It is the question that is both intriguing and unsettling in that it alludes to the possibility of establishing a direct causal relationship between specific motives and the actual acts of bombings on the basis of sex. Terrorism studies scholarship tends to assume the existence of such a relationship, to make unsubstantiated assertions about the nature of motives, and to create differences between male and female suicide bombers without explicating underlying gendered assumptions of such uncorroborated claims.

Terrorism studies authors perceive women as being motivated by very personal reasons often shaped by social/cultural pressures, while attributing men's decisions to become suicide bombers to the politics of nationalism and/or religion. The stark distinction between different motivations behind male and female suicide bombings is problematic in many respects. For one thing, individual motivations are difficult to know and easy to misperceive. Even when perceptions are accurate, analytical focus on motivations suggests the possibility of neatly and objectively disentangling the social from the political, and embed women perpetrators of violence within the former while positioning their male counterparts within the latter. It also implies the possibility of separating the personal from the political, denying the inherently political character of personhood and inseparability of individuals and political communities. As we will demonstrate in our analysis, the gendered and gendering effects of mainstream analyses are pervasive and far-reaching. Drawing on gender dichotomy enables terrorism studies scholars to insidiously reproduce multiple forms of domination without questioning the very assumptions that allow them to think in terms of inclusions and exclusions, visibilities and erasures, norms and exceptions. This can be seen in a strong tendency to reiterate a deeply entrenched androcentric view that the realm of political violence is a man's world where the "terrorist" is "a subject gendered male by definition" (Sjoberg 2009, 69). By this logic, women's involvement in terrorism can be explained only in instrumental, utilitarian terms as "damaged goods" / expedient resources in the hands of men and masculine terrorist organizations.

The paradoxical effect of such gendering of female suicide bombers within a rationalist explanatory approach has been exclusion through inclusion. Despite the identical nature of their final acts, male suicide bombers were attributed presumably natural and idealized centredness: they were privileged over female suicide bombers and granted higher status because the perpetrators' sex was used to determine differences in their motivations (Sjoberg 2009, 69). Female suicide perpetrators were included in the gendered, pre-existing framework of suicide bombings, but only as a marginal category, an exception. Even though the acts of suicide bombings committed by women were analysed as part of the rational calculations by the organizations behind the attacks (inclusion), female perpetrators were, nonetheless, excluded from the rationality attributed to male suicide bombers and denied further meanings associated with masculinity, i.e., purposefulness, agency, power, autonomy, strength, control, social status, leadership, etc. They remained the devalued shadow of male suicide perpetrators – present, yet erased and inescapably weak, lacking in capacity, emotional, unpredictable and dangerous.

Against this backdrop, a burgeoning body of literature emerged, working from feminist perspectives[12] and offering fresh and more fine-grained analytical insights into women's involvement in political violence.[13] These scholars do not always agree on the specific definition of feminism or meaning of gender. Yet they all concur with Peterson's (1999, 37) view that gender analysis is "an imperative starting point" in the study of all social and political experiences, identities, and practices, and consciously undertake such study from the perspective of the socially subordinated. Feminist scholars agree that gender is personal, political, and international at the same time and challenge state-centrism of the mainstream/malestream scholarship by focusing on real people and everyday places. They approach the study of political violence from the myriad individual and collective experiences – social, physical, emotional – and expose multiple ways of gender subordination within political conflict. They challenge mainstream/malestream orthodoxy by revealing the gendered nature of its analyses and demonstrating how gender works as a fundamental power relationship, a systemic "governing code" based "on the signifying system of masculine-feminine differentiations" (Peterson 2010, 18). Gender ascribes certain identities and features to objects and subjects and positions them at the opposite ends of domination and subordination. It predetermines victims and perpetrators, peaceful and violent, powerful and powerless, normal and aberrant. As a formative social process and embedded structural attribute of politics, gender is of great significance to understanding violence and security. It functions at once as a "constitutive category which defines (and is defined by) international actors' understandings of their security as well as those left out of security analyses ... [and as] a causal variable, which causes (or is caused by) states' security-seeking behaviour" (Sjoberg 2010, 5).

Inspired by this scholarship, our book seeks to analyse Western mainstream academic representations of female suicide bombings in order to unearth complex ways in which these discourses are intertwined with gender, knowledge, and power. A critical gender approach can and does stimulate new lines of inquiry into political violence. It opens up venues for a more nuanced analytical engagement with female suicide bombings that contests the parameters of the discussion established by terrorism studies and departs in important respects from the mainstream take on this issue. Our goals are to expand and deepen understanding of female suicide bombings and to contribute to a genuine debate over accepted knowledge, as well as the political ramifications of such knowledge by offering careful examination and systematic analysis of mainstream representations and their contestations, as well as by reconstructing female suicide bombings using a critical gender approach. While embarking on this task, we follow what Christine Sylvester (2013, 3) has called "an exemplary text methodology" built around the idea that "all traditions of analysis have knowledges to share and to reconfigure" (13). This methodology underscores the fact that female suicide bombings are not purely a type of political violence, but, importantly, are deeply entangled with scholarly knowledge production. It enables us to engage with contending perspectives on female suicide bombings without reifying boundaries between or prematurely dismissing alternative understandings.[14] Indeed, this methodology leaves open the possibility for knowledge sharing and effectively sustains the environment of enhanced intellectual reflexivity (Lapid 1989) in which scholarly communication, critique, and ingenuity thrive, even if they do not result in consensus and synthesis. We utilize a discourse analysis[15] of the secondary texts as our key methodological tool for unearthing how different meanings of female suicide bombings are carefully constructed through the use of gendered assumptions and metaphors, what these particular practices of representation achieve, and which political actions they enable or preclude. Discourse analysis sheds light on how female suicide bombings serve as a site where gendered identities and power relations are discursively reproduced at the same time as different conceptions of gender are employed to construct alternative understandings of female suicide bombings and their perpetrators, of which only some come to dominate thinking about this violent social practice in international relations (IR) and beyond. Our methodological approach, in other words, explicitly acknowledges connections between the competing practices of knowledge production and distribution, the politics of representation, and power relations and hierarchies that configure social reality.

Since we set out to critically analyse key discourses on female suicide bombings in Western academia, we limited our analysis to scholarly publications in English because this language is representative of Western academia. Many, if not all, notable academic works on female suicide bombings have been published in or translated into English, even though their authors have different national backgrounds and are affiliated with various English and non-English language academic institutions in the West. Two key criteria guided our selection of texts: (1) alternative conceptions of gender (discussed in chapter 1) that inform analyses of female suicide bombings; and (2) related to that, different theoretical/ideological perspectives on female suicide bombings and women's political violence, more generally.[16] For example, scholarly works by Bloom, Pape, and Schweitzer utilize essentialist conceptions of gender and illustrate the mainstream terrorism studies approach, while publications by Ahall, Gentry, and Sjoberg employ post-structuralist and constructivist understandings of gender and represent feminist security studies / critical terrorism studies approaches.

The result of using "an exemplary text methodology," we believe, is a more honest and balanced analysis that transcends intellectual iso-lationism and parochialism sustained by ideological divisions, avoids both muffling dogmatism and condescending indifference/ignorance, and encourages substantive discussion across different theoreti-cal perspectives instead of prematurely foreclosing it. We take Ken Booth's (2013, xvi) caution "to resist the temptation of being drawn into … academic tribal rivalry" seriously and, despite principled disagreements, engage with the mainstream literature in a respectful dialogical manner (Jackson, Breen Smyth, and Gunning 2009). Achieving genuine dialogue while vigorously challenging fundamental assumptions and thoroughly scrutinizing knowledge claims of the others is not an easy task, however preferable to monologue it may be. But ensuing discussion enables us to critically reflect not only on the limitations of the conventional knowledge, but also on its merits. We acknowledge that there is a lot to learn from dialogical engagement with the terrorism studies scholarship, as it speaks to important audiences and "exerts enormous 'causal weight'" (Booth 2013, xvi). On their own terms, terrorism studies works represent an impressive and coherent scholarship. We disagree, while still appreciating its relative strengths, especially on the organizational dimension of female suicide bombings, which we discuss extensively in chapter 4. We also recognize that turning our backs on terrorism studies' explanations removes the potential to contest, refute, or transcend them.

At the same time, we are aware that no theoretical approach is ever complete and that knowledge produced by mainstream scholarship has its own blind spots. We therefore undertake to scrutinize mainstream terrorism studies texts on female suicide bombings, drawing on a combination of feminist and postcolonial approaches. That is, through discourse analysis we challenge dominant gendered assumptions and ontologically privileged knowledge claims generated by mainstream scholarship, as well as the socio-political practices such knowledge sustains. In doing so, we look for communication, rather than "schoolism" (Booth 2013, xvii) and "intellectual identity politics" (Sylvester 2013, 9). We agree with Biersteker (2010, 605) that it is in the interest of better analysis to seek the ways of bringing opposite knowledge-generating perspectives together, to look "for order out of disorder, and pursue what the dialectical analyst would describe as 'the unity of opposites.'" In this sense, both terrorism studies works and feminist security studies literature provide an inter-textual context for our own analysis. Convinced that the most interesting ideas are to be found across rather than within intellectual borders, we insist that these works should be read not only against each other, but alongside *and* against each other. This integrative and synergistic approach allows for mutual learning and enhances our understanding of the complex intertwinement of gender, power, and practices of knowledge production in the explanations of female suicide bombers and their societies.

Overview of the Book

Analysis presented in this book takes the reader beyond the simplistic images of female suicide bombers, their violence and societies – a task that requires shedding light on the gendered biases in the interest-driven mainstream research that can be best described as "problem-solving" in orientation. Problem-solving literature tends to sustain existing gendered social relations and power structures, rather than provide a broader critical framework for understanding the violence of female suicide bombings as a social practice of resistance against domination and oppression. This analysis offers the reader, instead, an alternative framework for examining female suicide bombings. We make the case for the utilization of a critical gender approach that offers a social relational explanation of this violence and engages in fundamental reassessment of the counterterrorism measures proposed by problem-solving authors as a way of addressing female suicide bombings.

To this end, the book is organized into six chapters. Drawing on Robert Cox's (1996) distinction between critical and problem-solving theories, chapter 1 outlines a basic conceptual framework for organizing research on female suicide bombings and for thinking about this violence in social relational terms. In particular, we demonstrate how a critical gender approach can provide means for uncovering gendered biases in the mainstream literature on female suicide bombings, including, among other things, exclusive focus on rationality and instrumentalism in conceptualizing female suicide bombings, unsubstantiated gendered assumptions about perpetrators, their violence and societies, contestable terminology, fragmented knowledge, and contradictions among the epistemological and normative commitments. More importantly, this conceptual framework opens up room for alternative viewpoints and allows us to reconceptualize female suicide bombings as a bodily social practice of violent resistance. We elaborate a critical gender approach that enables us to elucidate multiple gendered and gendering effects of this violence, to shift the analytical lens away from rationality and instrumentalism inherent in problem-solving understandings of female suicide bombings and to highlight the importance of gender in understanding symbolic dimension of this violence.

To place specific acts of female suicide bombings in the broader historical and socio-political contexts, chapter 2 provides an overview of the origins and nature of specific conflicts, the guiding ideologies of the organizations behind female suicide bombings, societal dynamics, as well as individual circumstances – where information is available – that affected women's decisions to engage in acts of violence that were represented in the West as suicide bombings. This chapter documents acts of female suicide bombings within specific historical circumstances. It offers a holistic view of this complex violent social practice by explaining how it evolved, how societies reacted to it, whether the practice was legitimized, under what circumstances specific groups made the decisions to resort to it, whether female suicide bombings were directed against military or civilian targets, and how the practice spread from one geopolitical context to another. Re-embedding female suicide bombings in their respective contexts takes us beyond the essentialized image of an Arab/Muslim/oppressed female bomber and restores various identities to the perpetrators.

In chapter 3, we provide a careful examination of mainstream discursive representations of female suicide bombings, with a special focus on the individual perpetrators, their agency, and structural constraints enabling or facilitating their agential capacities. The two structuralist images produced by the problem-solving scholarship that portray female suicide bombers either as victims or feminist warriors tend to frame these women as always/already victims of their nature and culture. Generally, these images reinforce raced/gendered othering of female suicide perpetrators while denying their agency. Using a critical gender approach we demonstrate that while mainstream analyses extensively document gender inequality that conditions much of the social reality of female suicide perpetrators, they tend to overlook the centrality of the discourses of gender in shaping their explanations of this violence. Effectively, problem-solving authors distinguish between female and male suicide bombers on the basis of socially prescribed but largely unsubstantiated gender stereotypes. We argue that it is important to recover the critical analytical potential of gender, reconceptualize the gendered notion of agency within relational structure-agency framework, and recognize complex interactions between gender and other signifiers of identity. Relational understanding of structure and agency allows us to overcome structural determinism of problem-solving accounts and to see female suicide bombers as purposeful agents of political violence.

Chapter 4 explores organizational aspects of female suicide bombings that are planned, organized, and often claimed by concrete militant groups. Against the historical backdrop of female involvement in modern terrorist activities, we trace the gradual expansion of women's roles and responsibilities within gendered militant groups. Detailed analysis of the organizational dimension of female suicide bombings reveals partial consensus between competing perspectives, providing an opportunity for dialogue and mutual learning. We agree with some problem-solving scholars that even though women increasingly participate in political violence as perpetrators and assume diverse and multiple roles, stereotypical perception of female terrorists as insignificant actors persists largely because their gender and relatively young age relegate women terrorists to the margins of highly gendered terrain of most militant groups. We also note that women's general invisibility within terrorist organizations and common gender stereotypes offer terrorist organizations employing female suicide bombers some tactical advantages. However, while maintaining that terrorist organizations provide hostile environments to women, we observe that the excessive emphasis in the problem-solving literature on the coercive recruitment of female cadres solidifies "women-as-victims" constructions and obscures remarkable agential properties exhibited by women terrorists. Moreover, gender analysis of the terrorist organizations reveals that they are caught up in a gender paradox where they sustain highly masculine values and rules inside the group while finding themselves locked on a feminized end of a gendered relationship with sovereign states. The latter "damages" their masculinity, prompting these groups to remasculinize through violence. Therefore, employing gender as a category of analysis certainly offers a richer understanding of terrorist groups and the ways in which gender influences their internal structure and functioning, as well as their interactions with broader societies and sovereign states.

In chapter 5 we shift the analytical lens to the gendered politics of cultural difference that underscores problem-solving representations of female suicide bombings. We argue that mainstream literature utilizes discourses of race, sex, gender, and religion to produce a reductive, unidimensional understanding of female suicide bombers as an attribute of putatively oppressive orientalized patriarchy. Problem-solving discourses are built on Western-centric terms of reference that entail gendered articulation and hierarchical ordering of cultural difference. Drawing on the constructions of orientalized patriarchy and Islamic essentialism, these discourses produce and stabilize the categories of the "modern liberal Western Self" and the "backward oppressive Oriental Other" and view their relationship in antagonistic and hierarchical terms. Knowledge produced by mainstream scholarship on female suicide bombings is complicit in justifying and sustaining gendered power dynamics based on domination and inequality globally. Coming from a critical gender approach, we question a strong tendency in the problem-solving literature to feminize female suicide bombers, their violence and societies, to reduce religion to Islam, and to confuse race with religion. We emphasize the importance of recovering the specificity of socio-historical contexts as a means of gleaning a more nuanced understanding of female suicide bombings.

In the final chapter, we provide a reading of problem-solving scholarship that highlights the political thinking of mainstream authors, especially their overwhelming concern with Western counterterrorism. We examine the implications of problem-solving analyses for sustaining a particular set of coercive counterterrorism policies. The analysis in this final chapter clearly reveals the ways in which gendered statist conceptualizations of security in the problem-solving works determine not only the referent object and scope of security but also the type of normative understanding of the issues pertaining to identity, authority, legitimacy, and power. Concerned with the limited effectiveness of the counterterrorism approach proposed by the problem-solving scholars, we look for ways to address weaknesses in the counterterrorism strategy embraced by the West in the Global War on Terror. The search for alternatives has led us to propose a different vision of security based on the broad, critical conceptualizations of "human security." This vision of security is gender-sensitive, and it brings to the forefront the insecurities not only of victims of female suicide bombings but also of the perpetrators. Engaging with these insecurities has a better chance of addressing the violence of female suicide bombings than the dominant state-centric counterterrorism approaches. We conclude our book by scrutinizing a 2013 female suicide bombing in Volgograd, Russia, in order to demonstrate multiple genderings in mainstream representations of this act of violence and to shatter stereotypical explanations based on essentialist conceptions of gender. Our critical gender approach highlights the fact that the subjects, dynamics, and contexts of violence are always gendered and gendering. Being attentive to gender is therefore an imperative if we are to understand and respond more effectively to the violence known in the West as female suicide bombings. It is an approach that certainly deserves further study, and we hope that you, the reader, will contemplate on it.

Chapter One

Mapping the Framework:
Key Terms and Concepts

Introduction

This chapter lays out a conceptual framework within which contending accounts of female suicide bombings can be critically explored and our own approach articulated and positioned. We proceed from the recognition of an intrinsic connection between discursive representations and analytical categories with socio-political hierarchies and power dynamics, and pay close attention to what different texts achieve analytically, normatively, and politically, how they do it, and what they leave out when constructing explanations of female suicide bombings. We draw on Robert Cox's (1996, 85–123) distinction of problem-solving and critical theories so as to demonstrate that terrorism studies' engagement with the violence of female suicide bombings has thus far been significantly determined by an instrumentalist, rationalist, positivist problem-solving approach. We use Cox's classification with two cautionary notes. First, just as in any dichotomy, this categorization is both imperfect and incomplete in that it purports to neatly separate all theories into one category or another, whereas many theories fall somewhere in between. Second, we acknowledge that the opposition between these two categories has been overdrawn and exaggerated – a point we expand on later in this chapter. Despite these caveats, we find Cox's distinction useful for the purpose of illuminating ontological, epistemological, and methodological foundations of what we perceive as contending approaches to analysing female suicide bombings, and of revealing normative and practical implications of these approaches.

Problem-solving research represents an important and ambitious attempt to explain the socio-political practice of female suicide bombings in rationalist terms. This approach has been extremely effective in producing an intelligible, parsimonious, and policy-friendly account of the violence of female suicide bombings and a singular, homogeneous category of female suicide bombers. On the other side, the problem-solving approach also erased heterogeneity and complexity within the practice of female suicide bombings and the category of female suicide bombers, and reinforced the politics of inequality and domination. This is precisely where critical interventions can offer substantive correctives.

Approaching acts of violence conventionally known in the West as female suicide bombings from a critical theoretical perspective presents a number of questions: What is the explanatory power of the rationalist model? What kinds of explanations of female suicide bombings does it offer? How does this model account for gender, race, religion, and other markers of identity? Where does this model position the violent practice of female suicide bombings in terms of gender? How does the body of knowledge generated by problem-solving authors define common understandings of female suicide bombings, as well as their communities? What modes of representation are excluded from and silenced in the problem-solving practices of knowledge-production? How does problem-solving knowledge relate to existing power relations and structures?

One may object that Cox did not engage with gender and women's issues in his work and therefore has little to no relevance in examining the representations of female suicide bombings. We are not concerned with the substantive focus of Cox's theory, even though we share with Cox a broader foundation for inquiry in that, just like his, our approach is social relational. Directing our analytical glance towards social relations, rather than either structures or agency, enables us to avoid essentializing the social practice of female suicide bombings and allows for a more nuanced understanding of this violence and its perpetrators. More importantly, we find Cox's categorization of theories helpful for examining and critiquing mainstream Western academic representations of female suicide bombings, demonstrating that this body of scholarship functions as an epistemic community, and unearthing the role of this scholarship in sustaining knowledge/power relations. We also find it analytically useful for illustrating how a more nuanced and holistic understanding of female suicide bombings can be gained by applying a critical gender approach.

We begin with a brief overview of Cox's distinction of theories on the basis of distinct sets of ontological, epistemological, methodological, and research commitments. While acknowledging the importance of all philosophical, method- and research-related issues, we nonetheless highlight epistemological differences because positivist claims to objectivity within the problem-solving approach allow for self-proclaimed superiority in knowledge outcomes and provide a basis for dismissing or marginalizing alternative explanations. We then focus on unresolved terminological and definitional issues within the problem-solving literature on female suicide bombings and its failure to produce consensus on the terms used and definitions offered. Finally, we elaborate a critical gender approach to understanding female suicide bombings as a bodily social practice of violent collective resistance and detail its gendered character and gendering effects.

Problem-Solving and Critical Theoretical Approaches

Cox's oft-quoted statement reminds us that "theory is always for someone and for some purpose" (1996, 87). The purpose of theory, according to Cox, is either to provide a guide for solving specific problems within a particular history-bound perspective, or to reflect upon its initial perspective and attempt to transcend the institutional and relational parameters within which a particular theory has originated. Accordingly, all theories can be categorized as "problem-solving" or "critical." Problem-solving theories are conservative and ahistorical. They are predicated on an implicit assumption of fixity with regard to existing socio-political order and treat the context of their origin as an objective, immutable condition with existing institutions and structures of power as the natural order of things. The objective of problem-solving analysis and praxis is to maintain the institutional and power-relational status quo by confronting any destabilizing pressures within the international system. Such pressures are usually seen as possible sources of disruption of the systemic equilibrium, which explains why problem-solvers are eager to overcome these pressures in order to maintain smooth functioning of the system.

The objective of problem-solving scholarship profoundly influences its methodology. Without questioning the general form and practice of existing institutional and power relations, problem-solvers end up compartmentalizing specific "problems," limiting them to clearly defined areas in which these "problems" presumably arise. Other areas of social reality are considered unaffected by the "problems" outside their limits. Consequently, problem-solving theorists focus narrowly on the fragments of arbitrarily divided social reality, ignoring Cox's caution that "a conventional cutting up of reality is at best just a convenience of the mind" (1996, 85). In time, the pressures of an evolving social reality necessitate the adjustment or even rejection of old concepts (87). Despite relying on historically specific concepts and categories, problem-solving authors present their theories as neutral or value-free. Yet again, as Cox (89–90) notes, problem-solving theory "is value-free [only] insofar as it treats the variables it considers as objects … but it is value-bound by virtue of the fact that it implicitly accepts the prevailing order as its own framework." Therefore, the assumption of fixity reveals both the shortcoming of method and ideological bias of problem-solving theorizing.

The problem-solving mode of reasoning is not without merit. Reducing any issue to a manageable set of parameters allows for a fairly quick and precise examination of the "problem." This, in turn, opens up the possibility for producing parsimonious explanations and circumscribed recommendations for immediate policy measures to be undertaken in tackling the "problem" in question. However, without questioning central normative assumptions and scrutinizing dominant ontological, epistemological, and methodological commitments, problem-solving theorists produce only fragmented knowledge and offer short-term managerial solutions to the particular "problems." They cannot provide holistic understandings or comprehensive, long-term solutions.

Unlike problem-solving scholarship, critical theories are concerned with the larger picture of the socio-political order and *longue durée* historical change. We do not suggest that critical theory is monolithic in any way. On the contrary, we acknowledge that this broad and sweeping category is remarkably heterogeneous, bringing together theories that share fundamental intellectual commitments:

Epistemologically, critical theorists question positivist approaches to knowledge, criticizing attempts to formulate objective, empirically verifiable truth statements about the natural and social world. Methodologically, they reject the hegemony of a single scientific method, advocating a plurality of approaches to the generation of knowledge while highlighting the importance of interpretive strategies. Ontologically, they challenge rationalist conceptions of human nature and action, stressing instead the social construction of actors' identities, and the importance of identity in the constitution of interests and action. And normatively, they condemn value neutral theorizing, denying its very possibility, and calling for the development of theories explicitly committed to the exposure and dissolution of structures of domination. (Price and Reus-Smit 1998, 261)

All critical theories reject dogmatic assertions of universal truths and stress the importance of self-reflexivity in establishing regularities in social processes. While embracing a historically conditioned perspective as their point of departure, critical theorists engage in in-depth reflections on the normative framework of their origin and give serious consideration to alternative scenarios of the socio-political order. Unlike problem-solving theorists, who end up objectifying their initial perspective, critical theorists recognize the relativity of their own perspectives.

Within the discipline of International Relations, critical and problem-solving theories have been widely perceived as irreconcilable as the result of differences in the levels of abstraction, epistemological, ontological, and methodological orientations, and programmatic agendas. Such dichotomy is a by-product of a particular appropriation of Cox's initial categorization by mainstream academe in its attempt to set the limits to acceptable knowledge-generating practices. Implicit in this dichotomous juxtaposition is the idea that some theories focus on the real world issues and are, therefore, more "useful," while other offer critique for the sake of critique, representing nothing but a negative project (Duvall and Varadarajan 2003). Such disconnect between problem-solving and critical IR theories is grossly overdrawn. The problem-solving/critical binary is rightly criticized for imposing dubious categorizations and simplifying all research as either "policy relevant" or having no bearing on policymaking at all, for all theory is political and normative (81). That is, at the most basic level, all theoretical research bears implications for practical political action in distinct ways for different actors.

More importantly, differences between problem-solving and critical theories make them complementary, rather than opposite. What distinguishes problem-solving and critical theoretical perspectives is the nature of their relationship to the centres and exercise of power and social practices through which power is reproduced (Duvall and Varadarajan 2003). Problem-solving IR theorists (be they realists, liberal institutionalists, or mainstream constructivists) share a common commitment to positivist epistemology, which determines the way in which they view their knowledge about existing institutions and power structures, and makes them ideal for reinforcing the power-relational status quo. The practical relevance of problem-solving theories to those in positions of power is self-evident.

In contrast, critical theorists, from modernist to post-structural forms, consider any disruptions and challenges to stability as potential indicators of the need for systemic change. Critical theorists generally concern themselves with the inequalities produced and sustained by the structures, practices, and discourses of power. They contest the naturalness of the entrenched social relations of domination and subordination and "speak, therefore, not to those in positions of power, but to those who seek to resist and challenge them" (Duvall and Varadarajan 2003, 81). Critical theories, in other words, are distinguishable from problem-solving theories by their concern with emancipation – understood as feasible alternatives for transforming the existing order "with a view of freeing people, as individuals and collectivities, from contingent and structural oppressions" (Booth 2005, 181).

It is worth reiterating a point we made in the Introduction, namely that the parameters of analytical engagement with female suicide bombings within terrorism studies have been self-imposed by a commitment, implicit or otherwise, to produce policy-relevant research that offers governments practical recommendations for countering terrorism. In this sense, this literature represents a problem-solving approach. As mentioned earlier, we do recognize that not all of terrorism studies research fits squarely into the problem-solving category and not all of the terrorism studies works that we classified as problem-solving seamlessly overlap or are the same in all respects. They do, however, share important similarities of concern to us, namely the commitment to positivist epistemology, concern with Western counterterrorism, and essentialist understanding of terrorism and gender. Cumulatively, terrorism studies literature on female suicide bombings is broadly representative of the problem-solving approach. It certainly provides a practical "toolbox" guide for policymakers. But the problem-solving approach is frankly limited both in presenting the "problem" and offering its solutions.[1]

We consider our analysis fitting broadly into the critical theoretical category and, at times, crossing the boundaries of Coxian categories in its attempt to offer our readers a fuller and more nuanced framework for examining female suicide bombings. We make the case for the utilization of a critical gender approach that provides a social relational explanation of female suicide bombings, enables the reader to see how and why they were constructed in a particular way, and in subsequent chapters engages in significant reassessment of the counterterror measures generally proposed by the problem-solving scholars.

Definitional Conundrum

One immediate limitation of the problem-solving approach to studying suicide terrorism that undermines the claims of objectivity is the lack of terminological and definitional consensus. Suicide bombings received considerable scrutiny, generating spirited debates and producing a broad range of often contradictory understandings. Conceptually, these acts of violence, variously framed as suicide terrorism, missions, attacks, or martyrdom, are an elusive term, lacking clear scope and analytical consistency. Treating female suicide bombings as conducive to rational choice analysis rests on the belief that it is possible to engage with these acts of violence in analytically neutral manner. Such engagement inevitably begins with an "objective" definition of terrorism and unbiased identification of terrorists – a possibility vehemently contested by critically oriented scholars who reject the idea of value-free theorizing. Problem-solving scholars recognize that their research on female suicide bombings faces persistent challenges in defining the concept, determining its relationship to other forms of violence, over-relying on secondary material, making different empirical data sets compatible, and, above all, building integrative theory and engaging in a genuine debate over accepted knowledge. Martha Crenshaw (2007, 134) succinctly summarizes the challenges confronting problem-solvers when it comes to suicide terrorism: "Explanations are still at an early and uneven stage. The concept remains imprecise, the facts are not well established, and neither explanations nor policy recommendations distinguish sufficiently between suicide and other terrorist or insurgent attacks or account for variations within the phenomenon. Specifications of what is to be explained vary by author. Findings are often based on incompatible datasets, and references to cases or examples do not always fit the stated definition of the concept. Contradiction, ambiguity, and error are particularly consequential … Inclusion or exclusion of a few events can … shape the conclusions that are drawn."

Critical theorists argue instead either for the need to recognize the heterogeneity of the general category of suicide terrorism and illuminate the multiplicity of more contextualized and culturally specific kinds of suicide terrorism (Euben 2007); reject the very possibility of objective definition altogether (Bhatia 2005); or reframe suicide bombings as a form of resistance within the broader social movement framework (Gunning 2009). This position seems to be validated by the fact that to this point mainstream terrorism studies scholars have failed to develop a comprehensive, generally accepted definition of terrorism[2] or even to agree on the use of the term *suicide terrorism*. While Bloom (2007, 2011), Pape and Feldman (2010), and Pedahzur (2005) refer explicitly to *suicide terrorism*, other authors avoid the use of the term *terrorism* or both *suicide* and *terrorism* replacing them instead with *suicide missions* (Gambetta 2006), *suicide bombings* (Berko 2012; Reuter 2004), or *militancy* (Ness 2008a). Still others propose a definition as a matter of formality, without meaningfully engaging in serious conceptual explorations. Such lack of consensus on definitional and terminological issues confirms that suicide terrorism is an "essentially contested concept" (Gallie 1956): it blends descriptive and normative accounts by ascribing value to what it attempts to describe (Connolly 1993, 22).

It is also an inherently gendered concept, for it excludes states,[3] gendered as masculine security providers, from the terrorist category and obscures the fact that states may and often do inculcate fear and terrorize. Definitions of terrorism, while containing certain common threads, such as the centrality of its coercive nature, intentional generation of massive fear, and political goals, tend to focus overwhelmingly on motivational issues. The need to weave motivational aspects into the definition of terrorism is necessitated by the fact that terrorism's coercive nature makes it strikingly similar to the disciplining, corrective, and deterrent functions vested in the state. The last, as Pape suggests, applies to suicide terrorism as well. In Pape's words (2005, 237), "The heart of the strategy of suicide terrorism is the same as the coercive logic used by states when they employ air power or economic sanctions to punish an adversary." Herein lies a dilemma. If terrorism comprises all acts of the deliberate targeting of civilians, regardless of whether those acts are committed by state or non-state actors, then in its destruction and ruthlessness state-sponsored coercion far exceeds other acts of terrorism, including suicide terrorism committed by (semi)-clandestine militant groups and individuals. The bombings of Dresden, Hiroshima, and Nagasaki, the Rwandan genocide, and the mass killings in Darfur, to name just a few, certainly testify to Nassar's assertion that non-state terrorist acts "pale in comparison to acts of state terror" (2004, 28).

While considerable debate revolves around the question of the right to coerce and which actors can legitimately exercise it, the motivational factors enable some problem-solving researchers to draw a line between coercion that is state-sanctioned/legitimate and terrorism/ illegitimate violence that challenges state claims on the monopoly of the legitimate use of violence. However, at the conceptual level, the inclusion of motives into the definition of terrorism makes it an inherently value-laden term, open to subjective interpretations. Claims to present such interpretations as objective scholarship only uncover the ideological bias of problem-solving theorizing. Indeed, from a positivist perspective embraced by terrorism studies scholarship, a meaningful research concept should be determined solely by the nature of the action itself, rather than by its motive(s) and/or purpose. As Cooper (2002, 4) wrote, "It ought not to matter who does what to whom."

Despite unresolved controversy around the highly politicized issue of designating terrorist acts, groups, and/or individuals, terrorism studies scholars insist on the possibility of purportedly objective identification and application of the term *terrorism*. Rationalist ontology that informs these analyses denies the formative function of its meta-narrative in categorizing and labelling the violent social practice of suicide bombings. Terrorism studies scholars conceive of language and specific terms as objective representations of reality, naturalizing and normalizing the vocabulary they employ, and downplaying the epistemological implications of their theorizing. Effectively, these scholars rationalize and legitimize state-endorsed violence, mobilize support for state counterterror policies, and communicate to the opponents that they will be treated similarly to other groups designated by the same term (Harb and Leenders 2005, 174). As Brown (2011, 213) observed, "If suicide terrorism is only approached through a [state] security lens that is focused on 'winning/losing' a war, then the symbolic is overshadowed by a concern for the instrumental and rational." Critically oriented scholars who challenge the name-giving authority of the terrorism studies scholarship or the utility of the terrorist label in understanding violent resistance of the weak (see Barkawi and Laffey 2006) are sometimes accused of justifying suicide bombings, or openly ridiculed, as demonstrated by Crenshaw's (2005, 88) reaction to a 2005 special issue of *Third World Quarterly* on the politics of naming. "The terrorist label may impede American understanding of Hezbollah," she wrote, "but it is unclear how much that understanding would improve if the term were not applied."

Mainstream authors further disagree on the role of coercion in suicide bombings. Schweitzer (2001), Gambetta (2006), Hassan (2008), and others insist that individual perpetrators should be driven by free will and personal choice – a requirement that is difficult, if not impossible to verify. Such insistence on the consent of the perpetrator aligns with rational choice theory where agency is equated with and gendered as voluntary, independent, individual rational choice (this is discussed in more detail in chapter 3). No clear distinction is drawn between the acts in which both the perpetrator and victims die, the acts in which only the perpetrator dies without killing anyone, and the acts in which a would-be suicide bomber is apprehended, thus resulting in a failed attack due to the perpetrator's errors or some external intervention (Ricolfi 2006). Many authors cite premeditated death of a perpetrator as a criterion for acts of violence to be defined as suicide bombings. For Pape (2005, 10), for example, suicide terrorists are not expected to survive their missions. Along the same line, Bloom (2007, 76) defines suicide bombing as "a violent, politically motivated attack, carried out in a deliberate state of awareness by a person, who blows himself or herself up together with a chosen target." Pape (2005) is convinced that suicide bombings are undertaken as a strategic attempt at coercing opponents (9), compelling a target government to change policy (27), gaining control over a coveted territory (27), and advancing political, often nationalistic, goals (21). In Pape's own words, suicide terrorism is an "extreme strategy of national liberation" (23). Bloom (2007, x) concurs that "foreign occupation is a necessary although insufficient prerequisite for the evolution and spread of suicide terrorism" – a hypothesis for which Pape finds "strong confirmation" in his more recent work (Pape and Feldman 2010, 10). In light of these disagreements, Christopher Ankersen's (2007, 2) observation that "there is no one understanding of terrorism, but rather a plethora of differentiated meanings ... [that] vary across the spectrum of terrorist perpetrators, victims of terrorist violence, decision-makers aiming to respond to terrorism, and the 'rest of us'" certainly applies to female suicide bombings.

Terminology and the Symbolic

The embedded nature of knowledge and meanings about the violent practice of suicide bombings produced by different power-differentiated communities is inscribed in the very terminology employed. And gender can tell us a lot about the specific terms. *Suicide bombing* is the most common term for these acts of violence used in terrorism studies literature. The language of suicide bombings is primarily one of threat, death, and ruthless killing – all inextricably linked to masculinity.

It evokes popular association between masculinity, militarism, and power, effectively perpetuating patriarchal ways of understanding the world based on masculine domination and various forms of structural oppression. Coercion, control, and the political nature of suicide bombings point to naturalized male violence and imply a masculine essence of this practice. In this sense, Brunner is correct to observe that as the final phase of a long organizational sequence, female suicide bombings represent "a very masculine terrain" (Brunner 2005, 44) that does not allow for any meaningful notion of *female* suicide bombings, regardless of the number of women embarking on suicide missions. Therefore, female suicide bombings are not "a place of female or feminist business ... Even if the decision for participation in martyrdom is reached by a woman, the circumstances within which she can carry out her plan are very masculine ones" (45). Hence, a strong tendency to feminize female suicide bombers within terrorism studies literature through discourses of mothers/wives/brides or deviance that reduce female bombers to their biological sex and render them inferior to male bombers (we discuss this aspect in detail in chapter 3).

Significant empirical evidence suggests, however, that for numerous supporters the term *suicide bombings* does not reflect in any way their understanding and symbolic meaning of such violence (Haddad 2004). Even some mainstream authors recognize, albeit modestly, that their conceptions of suicide bombings differ from popular understandings among supporters of such violence. When discussing the terminology, Skaine (2006) notes that the label *suicide bomber* is a misnomer and agrees with Raphael Israeli, a former Israeli army intelligence officer and professor of Islamic and Middle Eastern history at Hebrew University in Jerusalem, that "an Islamic frame of reference and diagnosis is necessary to comprehend this 'unparalleled mode of self sacrifice'" (11). Drawing a distinction between altruistic (i.e., geared towards furthering the goal of the community) and egoistic (i.e., aimed at escaping intolerable life) suicide terrorism, Pape (2005, 22–3) mentions briefly that from the perspective of supporters, most suicide terrorists fit the paradigm of the altruistic type. "From everyone else's point of view, suicide attacks are murders" (23). Bloom, too, acknowledges complete dedication to the group and its cause by suicide operatives when she writes, "These people wilfully die spectacularly for one another and for what is perceived as the common good of alleviating the community's onerous political and social realities" (2007, 76). In other words, the practice of suicide bombings represents more than an element of strategic "outbidding" between multiple insurgent groups that compete for public support (79). In important respects, it signifies altruistic communitarianism. These brief remarks imply a possibility of alternative understandings of the violent practice of suicide bombings. Yet such alternative viewpoints are hastily discarded[4] as embedded, contingent, biased, and therefore not withstanding the test of objectivity.

Still, numerous supporters prefer to call this violent social practice "martyrdom," opting for the term that highlights self-negation, sacrifice, and honour. Many Arab publications on suicide bombings employ "poetic storytelling" that stands in sharp contrast with the language of instrumental rationality in the terrorism studies literature (Brunner 2005, 39). For example, an Egyptian newspaper compared Wafa Idris, the first Palestinian female suicide bomber, to the Mona Lisa, focusing on her "dreamy eyes and the mysterious smile on her lips." Others made references to Joan of Arc, or the Virgin Mary (Foden 2003). The language of martyrdom is, in many respects, one of femininity, as it connotes highly affective relations of love, care, and loyalty to the point of ultimate self-sacrifice for the collective. The act of martyrdom represents the fulfilment of femininity, as it alludes to women's reproductive functions and encapsulates a moment when a woman endures pain and sufferings to give birth to her newborn child. It is the language of feelings, kinship, home, and family. Its essence is self-denial and self-effacement symbolically representing life-giving to the collective (De Mel 2004, 77). As Hannah Arendt (1969, 67) observed, "Death, whether faced in actual dying or in the inner awareness of one's own mortality, is perhaps the most anti-political experience there is. We leave our fellow man – foundation of all politics. But faced collectively, death changes its countenance; now nothing seems more likely to intensify our vitality than its proximity. Our own death is accompanied by the potential immortality of the group we belong to."

From a critical gender perspective, the language of martyrdom speaks to the relational properties of gender. It carries strong overtones of femininity, but it is also fundamentally about power over life and death. It embodies deeply symbolic meanings of life and death, sacrifice and birth. On the one hand, life, birth, and sacrifice are all attributes of the feminine and female reproductive capacities. On the other, individuals embarking on the path of martyrdom are profoundly transformed. They enter spiritual immortality by physical death. In other words, the moment of their physical death is also the moment of existential rebirth in a new realm. Unlike their enemies, they are not killed, but sacrificed, and therefore born anew. Hence, the often-encountered signature "the living martyr" in their last testaments. In this move, the act of martyrdom signifies existential superiority and power over the adversary who is more powerful in conventional, material terms. Thus, an act of martyrdom fuses power and sacrifice, and effectively blends the masculine and the feminine. The moment of embracing one's death becomes a tipping point that shifts the balance of power, transforming the weak into the powerful. Death in this case proves existential/spiritual superiority over the adversaries (Reuter 2004, 15). The language of suicide bombings cannot capture or convey the symbolic affect of this violence.

This is not to suggest that the language of martyrdom is unproblematic. Admittedly, there is always a risk of romanticizing or appropriating the vision of the subjugated. One is certainly left to question the extent to which it represents the community on whose behalf such violence is purportedly carried out. Therefore, we do not wish to assign the notion of martyrdom a privileged epistemological status. Still, while not innocent or immune to critical scrutiny, the language of martyrdom often represents the perspective of the subjugated. Such perspectives, as feminist scholars persistently remind us, should be considered, perhaps even "preferred, because in principle they are least likely to allow denial of the critical and interpretative core of all knowledge" (Haraway 1988, 584). The *critical* aspect of the gender approach we employ lies then, in part, in unearthing and contesting the gendering effects of terrorism studies terminology. In this respect, we find the language of martyrdom particularly useful for dispelling the gendered and gendering effects of terrorism discourses. Perhaps counter-intuitively, in our analysis we have chosen to use the term *suicide bombings*, as it is most often employed in mainstream representations and is more familiar to Western audiences. We are, however, suspicious of this category and retain a critical stance to the process of categorization through which this term was produced. We use this term, while being conscious that it "inevitably leads to demarcation, and demarcation to exclusion, and exclusion to inequality" (McCall 2005, 1777).

Suicide Bombings as a Bodily Violent Practice Entangled with the Politics of Representation

Our critical gender approach to suicide bombings brings into focus two complex interrelated insights – one concerns the bodily dimension of this violence, and another one focuses on its multiple gendered and gendering effects. First, suicide bombings represent a bodily practice. Each act is predicated on the appropriation of the human body for political, military, and strategic purposes. It entails utter destruction and mutilation of the bombers' bodies, as well as of the bodies that happen to be nearby. As such, suicide bombings are a dramatic manifestation of the physical bodies serving not only as the frontlines and battlegrounds, but also as the actual weapons of political violence. In this sense, suicide bombers unsettle the boundary between biology and technology – their bodies are amalgamated with bombs and are no longer just biological and cultural, but become cyborg bodies (Rajan 2012; Ahall 2012; Wilcox 2013). Their abilities to act as a weapon are enhanced by the explosives becoming part of the material body. Suicide bombers, as Rajan (2012, 16) put it, "slip ideas of the bomb with that of the human body." As Reem Al Riyashi, a Palestinian female suicide bomber, put it in her video-recorded testament, "I have always dreamed of transforming myself into deadly shrapnel against the Zionists ... and my joy will be complete when the parts of my body will fly in all directions" (quoted in Wilcox 2013, 8). Effectively, the violence of suicide bombings dehumanizes human bodies and turns them, in Cavarrero's words, into the "heaps of meat" (quoted in Rajan 2012, 16).

This insight allows us to define suicide bombings as a form of social practice geared towards achieving political objectives through public acts of physical destruction of individual bodies as a violent expression of collective contestation and resistance within the context of unequal/gendered power relations.[5] Our definition warrants clarification. The constructivist notion of social practice, i.e., a relatively stable pattern of actions on the basis of intersubjective understandings that are constitutive of and constituted through these actions (see Wendt 1992; Mutimer 1998), provides a starting point for our conceptualization of suicide bombings. Defining female suicide bombings in terms of a social practice bridges social structures and agency within the process and allows for a more nuanced analysis of this violence through the lens of social relations. It avoids deterministic essentializing, typical in problem-solving works because they rely on static, clean-cut categories of structure-agency dichotomy. With this definition we consciously steer our analysis towards process-oriented understanding of political violence that makes and remakes social relations, while simultaneously being instigated by these relations. Such understanding is particularly important in studying individual and collective actors on the periphery of the structures of domination, for it "sensitizes us to the glitches left by structures, the positioning of certain actors within these glitches, and the strategies that they forge to deal with liminal life" (Neumann 2012, 476). In other words, conceiving of female suicide bombings in terms of processual understanding of political violence enables us to acknowledge perpetrators' agency in the acts of violent resistance against historically embedded oppressive structures, however constraining these structures may be.

As is clear from this definition, all suicide bombings involve a set of actions (i.e., individuals carrying explosives on, in, or close to their bodies, or driving bomb-laden vehicles, ready and willing to destroy their bodies in order to kill those whom they view as enemies, detonating themselves in unexpected, usually public places, etc.) that allow certain audiences to recognize these actions as suicide bombings. As a violent social practice, suicide bombings are not isolated from, but overlap with multiple violences (i.e., political, terrorist, insurrectionist, gender-based, nationalist, religiously inspired, community, structural, and discursive). We are not suggesting that there is anything neutral about these categories of violence or their substantive meanings, as all of the conceptualizations above are contingent on one's ideological perspective. Our reference to these violences is merely meant to highlight inherent complexity and embeddedness of suicide bombings along multiple axes of power, meaning, and identity. This means that various identities (i.e., bombers, martyrs, victims, enemies, perpetrators, innocent, etc.) and interests (i.e., liberation, independence, freedom, killing, revenge, security, prevention, etc.) of the actors involved in suicide bombings are, in part, constituted by and constitute the very actions (suicide bombings/martyrdom) they engage in. These identities and interests regulate and are regulated by numerous interactive and overlapping social practices and historically embedded norms. In other words, multiple social relations shape the political subjectivity of female suicide bombers and the meaning of their violent acts.

We wish to emphasize the social relational character of suicide bombings, while zeroing in on the individual body as a physical entity with agency[6] – that is, with the ability to act in a purposeful and conscious manner in order to unmake or remake social and political relations, as well as to unsettle the identities sustained by such relations. This definition recognizes that the violence of suicide bombings is not executed by some abstract entities – it is carried out by individuals, i.e., embodied and intersubjective beings who are socially embedded in and embody the collective. Such recognition highlights socially constructed and political circumstances of bodily existence and posits a dialectic relationship between the individual body and the collective. It instructs to inquire into the intersecting social relationships based on gender, race, religion, class, age, and ethnicity, and how they intertwine with instances and discourses of suicide bombings at every level, from personal to global. This definition, in other words, highlights the material-discursive character of female suicide bombings and calls for attention to intersectionality – an analytical category that endeavours to theorize the multiplicity of modalities and dimensions of social life with their attendant, often conflicting, identity-based forms of oppression and privilege. Intersectionality brings forward the onto-epistemological dimension of female suicide bombings, i.e., it underscores the ways in which socially constructed identities of gender, class, race, and ethnicity interrelate in female suicide bombings both as the form of violence and as an object of knowledge, allowing for a more complex and inclusive understanding of the politics of representation (McCall 2005).

By explicitly foregrounding the corporeal and social dimensions of human beings, this definition also posits the need to engage with the categories of sex and gender, as individuals performing the acts of suicide bombings are inevitably sexed and gendered. Feminist scholarship extensively discussed and theorized body, sex, and gender without reaching a definitive consensus on how they relate to each other or what a body is. Generally, feminists distinguish between sex as a biological body, often coding bodies as dichotomous, mutually exclusive male or female, and gender (masculine and feminine) as socially constructed symbolic meanings, practices, and norms assigned to biologically differentiated bodies. The ways in which material bodies relate to social norms of behaviour are informed by theories of gender broadly categorized as essentialist, constructivist, and post-structuralist (Shepherd 2013, 13–15). The first group accepts the naturalness of sex understood through "obvious" biological, reproductive, and psychosocial differences between male and female bodies and posits a direct relationship between sex and social behaviour. On this view, certain types of social behaviour are considered biologically predetermined and intrinsic to male or female bodies. For example, natural determinism a priori associates violence with men and masculinity and essentializes women as inherently peaceful, nurturing, maternal, and apolitical. Accordingly, gender differences are believed to be rooted in biological/sex differences. This essentialist approach conflates gender with sex as the categories of analysis and, as indicated earlier, informs terrorism stud-ies' explanations of female suicide bombings.

In contrast, post-structuralist theories of gender view sexual differ-ences as having no ontological standing prior or external to the dis-courses of gender. From this perspective, biological bodies acquire their meaning as a result of discourses of gender. Therefore, sex should not be viewed as a pre-discursive, politically neutral, and biological given, but rather as "constituted in the intersection of discourse, social insti-tutions and the corporeality of the body" (Sasson-Levy and Rapoport 2003, 381). As Butler (1990) masterfully argued, natural sex and dif-ferences attributed to the materiality of the body are not productive of gender, but rather derivative of it in that the discourses of gender infuse sex with specific meanings and institute the very possibility of sex differences. Therefore, ostensibly "natural" body and sex should be understood as a discursive ground "carrying the prime sites of ... identity and patriarchal control" (De Mel 2004, 80).

In between essentialist and post-structuralist views are constructivist theories of gender that deny any deterministic/essential link between sex and gender and allow for a more complex understanding of the relationship between them. That is, feminist constructivists believe that gender differences are only conventionally assumed to be linked to ostensibly biological male/female differences. At the critical construc-tivist end, feminists interrogate the biological male/female dichotomy, pointing to greater complexity and diversity of biological differences (i.e., asexual, intersexual, transsexual) (Sjoberg 2007, 83–4). They also question deeply and widely internalized sex differences and point to the co-constitutive relationship between essentialized sex binary and gendered power hierarchy (Peterson 2010, 20). That is to say, the very assumption of essential male/female differences is treated as one com-ponent of gender hierarchy.

Feminist constructivists theorize gender as a dynamic process of dis-cursively producing, modifying, and imposing meaning through which social hierarchies built around the privileging of masculinity and deni-gration of femininity are created and sustained (Sjoberg 2007, 83–4). In this view, gender is not a static concept with fixed content and uniform practices, but a continually unfolding systemic process of construction and deconstruction, negotiation and contestation over meanings and norms of behaviour. Central to individual and collective lives, gender is culturally and historically specific in that it is lived differently in various temporal and spatial locations. However, its attendant power dynamics is universally recognized and remains invariably a constant characteristic of all social life. The effects of gender are persistently codified and normalized in a way that "devalorizes *all* feminized statuses" (Peterson 2010, 18). Gender, as Prugl (1999, 13) observed, becomes "an institution that codifies power." Thus, we must remain attentive to the ongoing negotiations of power built upon and through gender in any given context.

Against the backdrop of unequal/gendered power relations, female suicide bombings can be conceived of as the forceful opening within historically embedded structures that carries the potential for social transformation and emancipatory change. Within the larger context of social resistance, the goal of female suicide bombings is to publicly redress collectively shared injustices and to generate a transformative effect in existing socio-political structures. Therefore, we view suicide bombings as a form of resistance against the power relational status quo, resistance geared towards contesting social injustices and potentially producing changes in culture, society, and politics that reorder gendered relations and reconstitute identities and structures at the base of those injustices. The destruction of an individual body entailed in the act of suicide bombing is instrumental to disrupting or destabilizing modalities of power rooted in the matrix of gender. This may appear similar to but goes beyond the pure instrumentality of the terrorism studies approach (Gambetta 2006; Pape and Feldman 2010; Pape 2005; Bloom 2007, 2011; Berko 2012). An important distinction lies in how we conceive of suicide bombers. We argue against treating them as "brute facts" or a "strategic datum" (Barkawi and Brighton 2011, 136). In other words, we recognize female suicide bombers as *both* victims and agents, or to borrow from critical postcolonial theorists, as "the authors and outcomes of social, political, and economic processes" whose final acts mark "the disruption of ... wider order and the people and other entities which populate it, the unmaking and remaking of certainties, of meaning, of – potentially – the very coordinates of social and political life" (ibid.).

Gendering/Othering

The second related insight that a critical gender approach brings into focus is the gendered and gendering nature of female suicide bombings. The violence of female suicide bombings is gendered in both material and discursive terms. Its gendered materiality derives from what Cynthia Enloe (2007, 13) has called a "gender impact analysis" that prompts us to raise a series of questions: How do the instances of female suicide bombings affect men and women? Is this violence likely to affect some men and women more than others, depending on their sex, race, gender, class, ethnicity, and geopolitical location? Are there any differences in men's and women's experiences of female suicide bombings? How do female suicide bombings affect the relationship between men and women?

In weighing the material impacts of this violent social practice on male and female bodies, it is important to note that women represent a disproportionately high number of victims of suicide bombings, making up 79 per cent of all fatalities (Chicago Project on Security and Terrorism). There is an element of surprise on which suicide bombings depend for their success. They usually strike in crowded public places at the time when they are least expected. Hence, civilian men, women, and children represent a large proportion of those immediately affected by female suicide bombings, given the time and location of these attacks (Sjoberg 2009, 70). Furthermore, at different times, both civilian and military men and women in Iraq, Afghanistan, Pakistan, Nigeria, Syria, Russia, Israel, Palestine, or Sri Lanka have been more likely to become the victims of these attacks because there is greater probability of experiencing them first-hand than women and men elsewhere. The Global Terrorism Index (Institute for Economics and Peace 2014, 26) shows that over 82 per cent killed in terrorist attacks in 2013 were people in only five countries: Iraq, Pakistan, Syria, Nigeria, and Afghanistan. In Iraq alone, nearly 4,000 people died from terrorist violence, which represented a 164 per cent increase from 2012. Another, less immediate aspect of gendered materiality of female suicide bombings is increased vulnerability and insecurity of Muslims living permanently in Western states, yet often perceived as "not belonging" and "'bare' – neither worth sacrificing nor saving" (Brown 2011, 202).

Gendered materiality of female suicide bombings is intertwined in complex and subtle ways with the discourses that terrorism studies scholars construct about these acts and their perpetrators. As we demonstrated earlier, these discourses are inherently gendered in that they are centrally guided by the logic and workings of masculinity and femininity, i.e., they build their explanations around normative expectations of proper behaviour for men and women and perpetuate gendered power inequality. Discursive violence by terrorism scholars who speak for the states produces a triple effect. First, it feminizes female suicide bombers as irrational, emotional, impulsive, and weak, "through the gendered characterizations of these women's violence by gendered states in gendered conflicts" (Sjoberg and Gentry 2007, 216).

Second, since the representations of female perpetrators are directly linked to the constitution of their political communities, discursive violence also feminizes the collective actors on whose behalf female suicide bombers carry out their violence. Terrorism studies literature produces the analogy between political community / body politic and the bodies of female suicide bombers. For example, Berko (2012, 1) begins her book with the story of a Palestinian would-be suicide bomber held in the Israeli prison by detailed description of her being highly sensitive, crying, and screaming all the time, not being able to dress herself because "her entire body" was scarred and burned, "even her fingers," during a gas pipe explosion in her house when she was young. Berko adds that the court transcript contains record of two instances of this woman's rape – first at the age of eleven and second at sixteen. The image of the would-be bomber's body serves as a symbolic and visual reification of the stateless status of Palestinian nation. In contrast to sovereign states, typically represented as a healthy, rational, able-bodied male, stateless nations are feminized as disabled, emotional, traumatized, and violated. Such an analogy is not a new one. In the *Leviathan*, a now classic text justifying the existence of the state, Hobbes constructed the sovereign state as an artificial man. This artificial man is more than a simple metaphor, for the "constitution of the state and constitution of the body are mutually entailed" (Wilcox 2013, 4).

Third, discursive violence materializes in the physical violence of female suicide bombings, as well as in the coercive counterterrorism that terrorism studies discourses support and justify. Thus, in its quest for order and security, discursive violence perpetuates the physical violence it seeks to counter. In this respect, deconstructing the gendered nature of terrorism studies discourses on female suicide bombings carries the potential for a positive social change, as the deconstruction of discursive violence is an indispensable first step to deconstructing material violence itself.

Female suicide bombings are also gendering in that they reproduce through the interplay of material and discursive violence some fundamental understandings of global politics and the role of power and violence in it – all centred on the privileging of hegemonic masculinity associated with Western states and cultures. Discursive violence is inextricably linked to productive power exercised by terrorism studies scholarship, i.e., the power to shape social processes, identities, rights, responsibilities, and capacities via "the systems of knowledge through which meaning is produced, fixed, lived, experienced, and transformed" (Barnett and Duvall 2005, 20). Productive power concerns discourse, especially the discursive (re)production of subjects, of the terms and direction(s) of action, and of the possible, desirable, and permissible practices through changing intersubjective understandings and meanings (22). Productive power translates into the ability to frame the violence of female suicide bombings in a way that elevates one's own epistemic constructions to the status of uncontested "truth" while feminizing (read: dismissing and denigrating) alternative viewpoints. Such a strategic use of discourse for political purposes or framing (see Johnston 2008; Gentry and Whitworth 2011) resonates with deeper cultural notions in the West and allows terrorism studies scholars to conceal both the embedded nature of their own discursive representations and the gendered power relations through which some collectivities and their ways of knowing/explaining the world become and remain subordinated. Thus, scrutinizing framing can tell us a lot about our own societies and the role we play in reproducing power inequality.

Discursive framing of female suicide bombings within terrorism studies is rife with gendered implications. Not only does it perpetuate troubling assumptions about individual perpetrators, but equally important such framing essentializes their communities and societies in terms of orientalized patriarchy. Occidentalism, or the concerns, images, and conceptions of the West underwriting representations of the Orient (Coronil 1996), provides a unifying theme within such framing. Occidentalist practices of representation portray non-Western communities as the feminized Other of the Western Self. They organize myriad complex, multiple, and intersecting social relations into a recognizable register of binary oppositions and create a seemingly distinct external reality they describe (the issue of occidentalist discursive practices is addressed in detail in chapter 5).

Gender and the Symbolic Meaning of Suicide Bombings

A critical gender approach emphasizes the salience of gender in understanding the symbolic dimension of suicide bombings. This violent social practice reminds us of the complementarity of gender in that social categories of femininity and masculinity do not exist as isolated, self-sufficient, and fixed, but are mutually dependent on one another and continually (re)produced in a complex interrelationship. Viewed through the gender lens, the violence of suicide bombings is inherently complex, ambiguous, and elusive. It disrupts, defies, and disturbs fundamental constructions of gender, while simultaneously reinforcing them. It testifies to the dialectical synergy of the feminine and masculine.

Female suicide bombers exhibit elements of masculinity in exercising a degree of power and control over matters of life and death – in some cases fairly substantial, in others minimal – determining when and where to detonate their explosives, whom to spare, and whom to kill. They kill and die in the public sphere, as part of the collective violent resistance. And they often do so on the terms that defy the laws of war established by masculine states. That is, female suicide bombers breach conventionally recognized limits devised by the states to manage organized collective violence and to discipline those engaging in it. Intended to limit the practices of interstate war, these laws were driven by the moral liberal concern to preserve human life. In practice, they have clearly compromised the liberal ideal regarding the value of human life, aiming to protect some lives, but not the others. The laws of war stipulate the range of justifiable criteria for the resort to force by states (*jus ad bellum*), and circumscribe the moral and legal basis governing the conduct of war (*jus in bello*). Through the principle of noncombatant immunity, these laws distinguish between two categories of individuals – the legitimate perpetrators and targets of the direct attacks (combatants) and individuals who should be protected from such attacks (civilians/non-combatants). The difference between combatants and civilians is not simply reflected in the laws of war. Rather, the laws of war "produce that which they seek to regulate ... for neither of those categories exists outside the law and practices that make them possible" (Kinsella 2005, 250).

Gender, or more precisely sex, is implicitly present in this categorization by way of men being positioned as combatants and protectors, and women, together with children and the elderly, relegated to the category of civilian/non-combatant. Whereas old men and children remain in this category temporarily and may grow in and out of it, women "belong" in it permanently. Subsequently, the laws of war not only recognize, but reinforce, conventional understandings of women as paradigmatic victims, rather than perpetrators of armed conflicts. This, in part, explains why female suicide bombers continue to evoke enormous shock almost thirty years after they first appeared in modern times. They challenge some fundamental laws that undergird interstate relations and cause, through their acts of violence, epistemic confusion in the normative space cultivated by masculine states. That is, they frustrate gender stereotypes about peaceful, passive women confined to the realm of the private and always in need of protection by the warrior men. Female suicide bombers confuse established legal and moral categories, blur the line between combatants and civilians, "erase the barriers between ... terrorists and innocent civilians" (Bloom 2011, 23), and transgress the entrenched boundary of gender and violence.[7] Stepping outside conventional gender norms makes violent women vulnerable to disapprobation (Sjoberg and Gentry 2007, 7). They are condemned and denounced for transgressing their inherited gender boundary. Ironically, "it is they who are rendered suspect, not that boundary itself" (Kinsella 2005 262).

At the same time, female suicide bombings represent uncontrollable femininity, dangerous, deceitful, and threatening sovereign states (Brunner 2005; Wilcox 2013). Since this violence entails the use of *female* bodies as weapons, it necessarily reproduces gendered constructions of women's bodies as threatening and, by default, strengthens stereotypical understandings of femininity (Wilcox 2013). Female suicide bombers disguise explosives on their bodies and display everyday normalcy to evade detection and strike where they deem appropriate, disrupting physical order and spreading deep fear and intense anxiety. When successful, they upset state ability to act as a warrior man – to rationally assess and then deter or eliminate the physical security threat female suicide bombers pose to state territory, governance structure, and/or people. Female suicide bombers demonstrate that their violence is "no longer a fringe phenomenon and the insurgents are all around you" (Bloom 2011, 24). They physically threaten state bodies: they carry out acts of violence on state territory, destabilize sovereign control over security, and undermine sovereign responsibility to provide security by protecting its citizens. They commit violence "for which there is no complete, effective, and appropriate response" (Rajan 2012, 16).

As mentioned before, suicide bombings simultaneously represent ruthless violence and the ultimate sacrifice, a deadly weapon of killing and an infinite love for one's community, a steadfast refusal to accept defeat and a profound surrender of one's will to live. Being carried out in the public realm, suicide bombings are *political* acts of social resistance and subversiveness. Even though each act is carried out by an individual, it "emerges out of the collective" and is "undertaken on behalf of a society as a whole" (Banner 2006, 218). At the same time, it is deeply intimate in that it blends in death the bodies of bombers and their victims, making it difficult if not impossible to identify and separate the body parts of different individuals and, by extension, permeating the boundaries between distinct bodies and identities (Rajan 2012; Bloom 2011; Wilcox 2013). As Spivak (2004, 95) put it, "[Suicidal resistance] is both execution and mourning, for both self and other. For you die with me for the same cause, no matter which side you are on" (quoted in Wilcox 2013, 7). It brings about intentional destruction and chaos, but aims to produce order and stability. It reveals despair and oppression, yet speaks of hope and empowerment. It connotes freedom, but its success is dependent upon a tight organizational grip. Suicide bombing exposes the artificiality and permeability of the boundary between the feminine and the masculine. Female suicide bombers suspend, unsettle, and destabilize gender dichotomy in the midst of the violent acts they carry out and call for a more complex conceptualization of political subjectivity in social relational terms, the issue we discuss in chapter 3.

Conclusion

In this chapter we drew on Robert Cox's categorization of theories to demonstrate that terrorism studies literature on female suicide bombings broadly falls under the category of the problem-solving theory. This approach is no doubt important in that it can reveal weaknesses in state counterterrorist tactics and strategies and explore the possibilities of improving and adapting those tactics and strategies to particular changing circumstances. This approach, however, is not without problems. Driven by contradictory commitments to analytical neutrality and policy relevance, the terrorism studies approach faces the challenges of defining its object of enquiry, distinguishing between suicide bombings and other forms of terrorism, addressing the questions of causation, etc.

Engaging with female suicide bombings from what Cox broadly framed as a critical theoretical approach allows for an explicit acknowledgment that suicide terrorism is an "essentially contested" and gendered concept in terms of both whose violence is considered legitimate and which actors count as terrorists. This gender bias is also projected in the very language used to describe this violence. While suicide bombings connote the symbolism of militarized masculinity, martyrdom – being simultaneously about sacrifice and power, i.e., sacrifice in power and power of sacrifice – highlights relational properties of gender. Drawing on a critical gender approach, we reconceptualize female suicide bombings in social relational terms as a bodily violent social practice of contestation and resistance to redress collective injustices and destabilize or potentially transform relations of domination. This reconceptualization shifts the analytical lens from the rational to the symbolic dimensions of female suicide bombings, emphasizes relational synergy of the feminine and masculine within this form of violence, acknowledges agency of the perpetrators amidst structural constraints, and highlights the gendered nature and multiple gendering effects of this violent social practice.

Chapter Two

The History of Modern Female Suicide Bombings: Contextualizing Acts of Violence

Introduction

Female suicide bombings have caught the attention of Western audiences fairly recently, when the practice erupted in 2002 in the context of the Palestinian-Israeli conflict. Widespread popular association between the Palestinian case and female suicide bombings sometimes generated claims about the "Palestinization"[1] of other conflicts. Palestinian women, however, do not hold the badge of distinction for being the first, as female suicide perpetrators have been active in political struggles elsewhere prior to the occurrence of this practice in the Palestinian-Israeli context. In the 1950s, male and female suicide bombers in Vietnam detonated explosives while riding their bicycles, as part of the resistance against the brutal French occupation (Speckhard 2008, 996). The first, most commonly cited instance of modern female suicide bombing took place in Lebanon in 1985. Since then, the number of female suicide bombings grew, with over 300 women challenging male monopoly on the suicide bombings in Lebanon, Sri Lanka, Turkey, Russia, Palestine, Israel, Uzbekistan, Pakistan, Afghanistan, Iraq, Somalia, Syria, Nigeria, and Cameroon. Many taboos were broken, shattering a typical profile of a suicide bomber. Over the years we have seen the first girl suicide bombers as young as seven years old, the first young mother of two small children sacrificing herself in this way, the first grandmother, and the first female bomber from Europe.[2] They drove bomb-laden vehicles, strapped heavy explosive belts to their bodies, wore explosive vests, carried grenades, and hid bombs in their purses. Female suicide bombers became unanticipated deadly agents who changed the political fate of several militant groups, disrupted military and humanitarian efforts, wrought havoc among civilian populations, ignited speculations about changing gender power imbalance, became short-lived media celebrities, and garnered world attention for their respective causes.[3]

This chapter contains empirical information about female suicide bombings in different contexts. It provides a historical and chronological survey of major attacks, background information to the conflicts in which women have been involved as suicide bombers, a brief description of the circumstances (whenever information is available) preceding these acts of violence, as well as the highlights of the collective reaction to and the ideological make-up of the militant groups behind the attacks. Admittedly, the origins and nature of the conflicts, as well as the character of the organizations employing female suicide bombers, are highly contested. Our central objective here is to restore the contexts of known female suicide bombings by providing an empirical overview of the background social and political conditions in which female suicide bombings occurred. This is a necessary step before unpacking the complex implications of their representations in problem-solving and critical analyses in subsequent chapters.

Female Suicide Bombings in Lebanon

The history of modern female suicide bombings is commonly claimed to have begun in 1985 in South Lebanon as a tactic in the campaign against the Israeli invasion. This campaign marked a recurrent pattern of violence and insurgency linked to Lebanon's colonial past and its quest for national self-determination. It reflected the complexities of Middle Eastern geopolitics, especially of Syrian and Israeli involvement in Lebanon, and demonstrated the trail of failures in the Middle Eastern peace process. Politically disadvantaged, economically deprived, and hard-hit by the 1975 civil war, South Lebanon is known as the heartland of Lebanese Shiism and the Hezbollah-land. The Lebanese Shia community traditionally maintained strong ties with Iran and Syria. Many of the Lebanese militants were inspired by the 1979 Iranian revolution and supported by Syria. In 1982, they formed Hezbollah (The Party of God) with the assistance of a contingent of Pasdaran (the Iranian revolutionary guards). Hence, the most common explanation for suicide bombings in Lebanon, both female and male, is Shia Islamic fundamentalism. However, the evidence we collected demonstrates that the majority of female suicide bombers in Lebanon were not linked specifically to religious extremism, but rather represented a wide range of ideological commitments – communist, socialist, nationalist, Christian, and Islamist.

On 9 April 1985, sixteen-year-old Sana'a Mehaidli, dubbed by her supporters as "the bride of the South" (Skaine 2006, 77), drove a truck laden with explosives into an Israeli military post, killing two soldiers and herself and wounding two other soldiers (Beyler 2003a; Zedalis 2004; Ness 2008a). Even though Mehaidli was of Shiite origin, she acted on behalf of the Syrian Social Nationalist Party / Parti Populaire Syrien (SSNP/PPS) – a secular pro-Syrian group with no commitment to religious extremism. Rather, SSNP/PPS embraced Marxist-communist ideology and employed suicide bombings across several countries in the Middle East in pursuit of nationalist objectives (Pedahzur 2005). Indeed, Mehaidli left behind a video-recorded final testament[4] explaining that her attack was a political act of revenge against the Israeli occupation. While mentioning her hope to go to paradise, she emphasized the need to free her community from foreign invaders, suggesting that she had embarked on her mission as a fervent nationalist: "I have witnessed the calamity of my people under occupation. With total calmness I shall carry out an attack of my choice hoping to kill the largest number of the Israeli army. I hope my soul will join the souls of the other martyrs ... I am now planted in the earth of the South irrigating and quenching her with my blood and my love for her" (quoted in Pape 2005, 134).

Mehaidli's attack was the first female suicide bombing in the Lebanese campaign against massive and asymmetrically more powerful Israeli occupation forces, which invaded the country on 6 June 1982 and were supported by Western multinational forces, mostly U.S. and French. Israel's initial goal was to expel the Palestine Liberation Organization (PLO) from Lebanon. South Lebanon is home to many Palestinians who initially fled there during the 1948 Arab-Israeli war. In the mid-1980s South Lebanon was also a sanctuary of the PLO's leadership (headquartered near Beirut) and of its troops. They controlled Palestinian refugee camps dispersed throughout the region, creating a de facto "state within a state" in South Lebanon (Dobbs 2002).

Having solidified public support and a secure sanctuary, the PLO launched the Palestinian insurgency against Israel in 1968, provoking two Israeli invasions of Lebanon in 1978 and 1982. As mentioned earlier, Israel's initial objective in 1982 was to eradicate the PLO – a goal that was at first welcomed by the Lebanese Shia (Ranstrop 1997, 30). Yet after the PLO were ousted to Tunisia, this goal was fundamentally reversed by Israel's decision to remain in South Lebanon as an occupying force.

This translated into increasingly tight control over the Shia community, including arrests of local leaders, which threatened the hopes for self-determination among the Shia and resulted in the Shia-led resistance against Israeli invasion (Pape 2005, 133). The campaign against foreign occupiers was waged mainly by Hezbollah, with the help of smaller organizations like the SSNP, Amal (pro-Syrian Shiites), the Lebanese Communist Party (LCP), and the Lebanese Baath Party (the Baath-Leb) (Pape 2003; Pedahzur 2005; Ricolfi 2006). Foreign occupation provided a necessary condition and unifying goal for the groups that otherwise shared little, if any, ideological affinity and political objectives. The practice of violent resistance in the form of suicide bombings, including female suicide bombings, was a particularly effective way of attracting international attention and demoralizing the occupiers.

The second female suicide bombing in the anti-occupation campaign occurred on 20 April 1985, when Loula Abboud shot at Israeli soldiers to allow her companions to escape arrest, and then detonated her explosive device (Ness 2008a; Davis 2003). Abboud, of Christian background, was the first non-Muslim female suicide bomber, who, in the words of her brother, was "fighting for the liberation of her own homeland" (Ali 2005). She was also the leader of a small resistance group associated with the Lebanese Communist Party, which actively opposed the Israeli occupation of South Lebanon's Bekaa Valley (Davis 2003, 68). Five of her cousins and brothers have also fought in Lebanon's political struggles since the 1970s.

The campaign to end Israeli occupation of Lebanon partially reached its goal, as Israel was compelled to withdraw its forces in June 1985 and to limit its presence to a six-mile security zone near the Lebanese-Israeli border. Although the frequency of suicide attacks (male and female) in Lebanon decreased significantly with the expulsion of foreign armed forces, female suicide bombings did not cease. The ongoing bombings inside the security zone against Israel and the Southern Lebanese army (SLA) – an army financially sustained and armed by Israel – manifested the determination among the Shia not to give up even an inch of the Lebanese territory to Israeli invaders. They also reflected a strong resolve to continue active resistance. On 9 July 1985, a SSNP female activist, Kharib Ibtisam, detonated an explosive device at the SLA checkpoint (Beyler 2003a; Zedalis 2004).

Like Mehaidli, Ibtisam left behind a video testimonial describing the political motivations of her action and stating that her wish was to kill as many Jews and their assistants as she could (Beyler 2003a). In fact, it became typical for Lebanese martyrs to send a final message to their community, indicating the enormous significance attached to the collective understanding and memory of their acts. Indeed, many of the statements were widely publicized within the Shia community following the suicide bombings. The role of the organizations in producing these testimonials cannot be underestimated and neither can the impact, since all of the testimonials were prepared for the community at large. All female martyrs claimed to have volunteered for their missions and none surrendered to Israeli forces (Pape 2005, 133–5). In a society where women are often forced into the background and are largely absent from the public sphere, these farewell messages provided a highly public demonstration of the political nature of the female suicide bombings perceived as martyrdom. Significantly, these violent acts of resistance through self-sacrifice resonated positively within the collectivity. Pape (2005) points out the strong public support for martyrdom visible in the city streets named after the martyrs and in the public commemorations that continue to this day.

After the barrage of female suicide bombings in 1985, Lebanon witnessed only one female suicide bombing in the following year. A twenty-six-year-old high school teacher, Norma Abu Hassan, detonated an explosive device in Jezzin (Beyler 2003a). Like Loula Abboud, she was a Christian. Two attacks during November 1987 concluded a series of female suicide bombings in Lebanon, with one of the perpetrators being Sunni. In both cases, the bombers belonged to the SSNP/PPS and the bombs were detonated via remote control, raising questions about the perpetrators' agency and their willingness to execute the attacks (Zedalis 2004; Ness 2008b).[5] In all, there were eight female suicide bombings in Lebanon, resulting in at least twenty-three deaths (including the eight bombers) and 106–110 wounded. Information about the attacks is summarized in table 2.1. Lebanon represents one of the spectacular cases in which conventionally weaker non-state actors emerged victorious over a much stronger state enemy. Forcing Israeli withdrawal contributed to the consolidation of Hezbollah, while the Lebanese strategy of suicide bombings subsequently "became a kind of model for the Palestinians and a sort of nightmare for the Israelis" (Ricolfi 2006, 87). The decisive success of Hezbollah played a significant role in the migration of the practice of suicide bombings to Palestinian territories, when Hezbollah-trained members of Hamas and Palestinian Islamic Jihad began to deploy the practice of self-sacrifice in the 1990s (Pape 2005, 129; Haddad 2004, 338).

Table 2.1. Female Suicide Bombings in Lebanon

Date	Features of the attack	Victims	Location
9 April 1985	Sana'a Mehaidli (16) of the SSNP drove an explosive-laden car into an IDF convoy.	3 killed, 2 injured	Jezzin, Lebanon
20 April 1985	Loula Abboud (19) of the Lebanese Communist Party shot at Israeli soldiers to allow her companions to escape. When the soldiers approached Abboud to arrest her, she detonated her explosive device.	1 killed	Aoun, Lebanon
9 July 1985	Kharib Ibtisam (28) of the SSNP detonated an explosive device at an SLA posting.	2 killed, 2–6 injured	Ras Al Bayda, Lebanon
11 September 1985	Khaierdin Miriam (18) of the SSNP detonated an explosive device at an SLA checkpoint.	1 killed, 2 injured	Hatzbaya, Lebanon
26 November 1985	Al Taher Hamidah (17) of the SSNP drove a car laden with an estimated 100 kg of explosive into an SLA checkpoint.	Unknown	Jezzin, Lebanon
17 July 1986	Norma Abu Hassan (26) detonated an explosive device after she saw soldiers looking for her. Responsibility was claimed by the SSNP and Hezbollah.	1 killed, 7 injured	Jezzin, Lebanon
11 November 1987	Sahyouni Soraya (20), a Sunni woman of the SSNP, killed herself when an explosive device concealed in a suitcase was detonated via remote control at an airport.	7 killed, 73 injured	Beirut, Lebanon
14 November 1987	Shagir Karima Mahmud (37), of the SSNP, detonated an explosive device concealed in a bag in a hospital. The bomb was detonated by a remote control. Some claim Hezbollah was behind the attack.	8 killed, 20 injured	Beirut, Lebanon

Female Suicide Bombings in Tamil–Sri Lankan Conflict

The Tamil–Sri Lankan conflict was the second to encounter documented instances of modern female suicide bombings. The roots of this violent conflict (primarily, but not exclusively between the Hindu Tamils and Buddhist Sinhalese)[6] are firmly embedded in both history and mythology. One foundational myth claims the Sinhalese originated from the union between an exiled Indian king and a Lioness in the fifth or sixth century BCE. Researchers have noted that the lioness is likely to stand for the Lion clan, which was influential around the time of the king's arrival (*sinha* means "lion" in Sanskrit) (Herath 2012, 30). While the lack of conclusive evidence and, therefore, consensus on the first settlers persists, Tamils insist they were the original inhabitants of the island. Historical evidence, however, points only to the existence of a Tamil monarchy during the arrival of Portuguese colonizers. Through policies that benefited certain groups and disadvantaged others, the colonial powers – the Portuguese, Dutch, and British – crystallized ethnic fault lines, exacerbated caste divisions, ignited religious intolerance, and increased socio-economic antagonisms. Under British rule, when administration and economy were centralized in an effort to build a modern Ceylon, ethnic distinctions became particularly pronounced (Davis 2008, 24). The colonial policies unequivocally favoured the Tamils over Sinhalese and prompted many more Tamils than Sinhalese to avail themselves of the educational opportunities offered by the missionaries and British authorities. This led to the greater proficiency in English among Tamils, which in turn opened up access to civil service and other well-paying jobs. The British also increased Ceylon's Tamil population by bringing Indian Tamils to work on the plantations (Bloom 2007, 48). Ceylon's independence from British colonial rule in 1948 and the creation of an independent Sri Lanka reversed the balance of power between these two groups. The Sinhalese majority determined the outcome of the first elections as well as the make-up of the government, and effectively embarked on the task of constructing a Sinhalese-Buddhist state. In their efforts to rectify perceived ethnic injustices caused by the British privileging of Tamils, the Sinhala people established a Sinhala ethnocracy and introduced a number of discriminatory measures against other minorities on the island. The implementation of the "Sinhala Only" policy entailed extensive job opportunities for the Sinhalese within the state-regulated economy and quickly disenfranchised the Tamil minority from positions of authority. The policy also enabled a series of constitutional changes that afforded Sinhala the status of the only official language in the country, limited educational opportunities for non-Sinhala speakers, and gave the Buddhist religion official primacy. Indeed, Buddhism, which was suppressed during colonial rule, was elevated to the status of a state religion in 1977, promoting national identity on the basis of religious affiliation (Herath 2012, 33).

The following decades of Sinhala domination effectively denied the multi-ethnic and multi-religious character of Sri Lanka through persistent efforts to build a Sinhalese state. Such ethno-centric policies ignited sharp ethnic polarization, intensified a sense of victimization among the Tamil minority, undermined trust in state institutions, and provoked riots by ethnically Tamil groups. These policies effectively erased centuries of peaceful coexistence and mutual tolerance between the Sinhala and Tamil groups (Herath 2012; Davis 2008; Stack-O'Connor 2007; Bloom 2007; Alison 2009). The consequence of a deeply embittered ethnic fault line was the essentializing of ethnicity. As Herring (2001, 161) put it, "*Tamils* and *Sinhalese* [were turned into] dangerous shorthand devices for politically complex communities." Steadily growing in intensity since the 1950s, ethnic violence climaxed in 1983 during "Black July," when the Sri Lankan government launched a major retaliatory campaign following the killing of thirteen of its soldiers in the Jaffna district by the Liberation Tigers of Tamil Eelam (LTTE), and anti-Tamil pogroms spread throughout the country. Since then, the war has claimed an estimated 90,000 lives (mostly civilians), and nearly one million people have been displaced as a result of it (Nadarajah and Sriskandarajah 2005, 89). De Mel (2004, 75) called it "the largest displacement of people in contemporary South Asia."

For several decades, until the recent self-declared "final" victory by Sri Lanka's government over the Tamil Tigers, the LTTE has been the largest Tamil militant group in Sri Lanka. Created in the early 1970s by a small group of fighters, it was initially one of several armed groups amidst the growing Tamil independence movement that mounted a violent challenge to the Sri Lankan state. These groups included the People's Liberation Organization of Tamil Eelam (PLOTE), Tamil Eelam Liberation Organization (TELO), Eelam Revolutionary Organization of Students (EROS), and Eelam People's Revolutionary Liberation Front (EPRLF). Under the leadership of Velupillai Prabhakaran, the LTTE eliminated Tamil rivals and political opposition and evolved into one of the most disciplined and organized military groups with substantive ground, navy, and basic air force. Following the anti-Tamil insurgency of 1983, the LTTE experienced rapid expansion, as many previously uncommitted Tamils joined the organization. The LTTE acted as a de facto state in Tamil areas under its control with its own "capital," civilian administrative infrastructure, significant financial and logistical resources, taxation system, and even customs regime on the "borders" (Nadarajah and Sriskandarajah 2005, 89). In its heyday, the LTTE controlled large parts of the North, including the central northern province of Vanni, and parts of the eastern province (Herath 2012, 1).

The organization also established a political presence, engaging in high-profile albeit failed peace negotiations initiated by the Sri Lankan government under strong international pressure. A political framework of the peace process, designed to preserve the territorial integrity and unity of Sri Lanka, foreclosed any chance of successful talks. At the same time, popular support for much-desired political independence, entrenched in deeply perceived ethnic discrimination and injustices, resulted in widespread backing of the LTTE and community support for martyrdom operations in Tamil areas.

The Tamil–Sri Lankan conflict earned a dubious distinction for institutionalizing the practice of female suicide bombings, thus providing a model for other groups. All female suicide bombers in the Tamil–Sri Lankan conflict came from the LTTE's commando elite wing, known as the Black Tigers (Gunawardena 2006). Women comprised 30 to 50 per cent of the Black Tigers (Gonzalez-Perez 2008a, 186). Cunningham (2003, 180) claims that the LTTE was the only group that permanently employed suicide bombings, although this practice became common only after the formation of the Black Tigers in 1990. Women were admitted to the Black Tigers in 1997 – seven years after men. According to some records, LTTE female suicide bombers have been responsible for carrying out over fifty suicide attacks (Eager 2008; Gunawardena 2006; Stack-O'Connor 2007; De Mel 2004).

The first and most notorious female suicide bomber in the Tamil–Sri Lanka conflict was Thenmuli "Dhanu" Rajaratnam (aka Gayatri) (Bloom 2007, 57), an LTTE suicide operative. On 21 May 1991 Dhanu presented Rajiv Gandhi, the former Indian prime minister at the time who was campaigning in the south Indian state of Tamil Nadu, with a flower garland, bending down to touch the feet of Gandhi as a sign of respect and then proceeding to detonate a bomb that killed both of them instantly, along with nineteen others (South Asia Terrorism Portal 2009). Fearful of the political backlash, for a long time the LTTE denied involvement in the attack, with the only admission made in private by Anton Balasingham, who called it a "historical blunder" (Pratap 2003, quoted in Herath 2012, 48). In 2006, the LTTE publicly apologized for the assassination of Gandhi, and the LTTE's chief negotiator, Anton Balasingham, referred to Dhanu's act as "a monumental historical tragedy which we deeply regret" (Huggler 2006). At the time it occurred, however, this high-profile suicide bombing sparked numerous allegations about the motivations of a perpetrator. These ranged from the claims that Dhanu was gang-raped at her home in Jaffna by an unscrupulous group of men, or her mother was raped by the Indian Peacekeeping Force (IPKF) (Bloom 2007, 160), to her brothers being killed by members of the IPKF sent to Sri Lanka by Gandhi. In order to distance itself from the attack, the LTTE claimed that Dhanu was raped by the IPKF, issuing a statement that she carried out the attack "to avenge her loss of sexual purity" (Herath 2012, 123).

Dhanu's act was followed by a series of ten other known female suicide bombings by the LTTE in the 1990s. Of these, five were targeted political assassinations of high-ranking army officials and Cabinet ministers. Sources indicate that out of the 241 suicide missions in the period between 1982 and 2002, 64 were carried out by women, the majority of whom were twentyone years of age or older (De Mel 2004; Herath 2012). Interestingly, the LTTE official website does not recognize Dhanu's suicide bombing. The first officially recognized Black Tiger woman was Captain Angaiyarkanni of the Sea Tiger squad specializing in suicide bombings at sea (Herath 2012, 158).

Between the signing of a ceasefire in 2002 and the end of 2005 there was only one suicide attack. This decline in suicide missions is due to the fact that the Sri Lanka Monitoring Mission (SLMM), which included Norvay, Finland, Sweden, Denmark, and Iceland, was involved in monitoring the ceasefire between the LTTE and Sri Lankan government. The Sinhalese viewed the SLMM as sympathetic towards the LTTE. Shortly before the official collapse of the peace talks, a female suicide bomber (identified as Thiyagaraja Jeyarani, reportedly on a mission to assassinate Cabinet Minister Douglas Devananda – a fierce critic of the LTTE) detonated an explosive device while being searched by an officer in a Colombo police station in July 2004. The LTTE clearly signalled its readiness to resume violence in 2006 when a female suicide bomber disguised as a pregnant woman detonated an explosive device at Sri Lanka's army headquarters. Lt-General Sarath Fonseka, head of the Sri Lankan army, was seriously injured in the attack. Female suicide attacks showed no signs of decrease until the 2009 declaration of victory over Tamil resistance by the Sri Lankan government. There are no current accurate data on the number of female suicide bombings between the unofficial end of the ceasefire and 2009. (Information about major recorded female suicide attacks by the LTTE is summarized in table 2.2.)

Female suicide bombings were pervasive in the Tamil–Sri Lankan conflict throughout the last two decades of the conflict. In May 2009, after a heavy offensive by the Sri Lankan army that included intense

Table 2.2. Major Female Suicide Bombings in the Tamil–Sri Lankan Conflict

Date	Features of the attack	Victims	Location
21 May 1991	Thenmuli "Dhanu" Rajaratnam (25) of the LTTE assassinated Rajiv Gandhi, the former Indian prime minister who was on the campaign trail. She was escorted by five other LTTE cadres, three of them women.	20 killed, unknown number injured	Sriperumbudur State of Tamil Nadu, India
24 October 1994	LTTE female suicide bomber detonated an explosive that killed herself along with the leader of the United National Party, Gamini Dissanayake, who was a presidential candidate, along with 58 other persons.	58 killed, unknown number injured	Thotalaga Junction in Colombo, Sri Lanka
11 November 1995	A female LTTE suicide bomber detonated an explosive near the Slave Island Railway Station, killing herself, 15 children, a policeman, and a soldier.	19 killed, unknown number injured	Colombo, Sri Lanka
24 November 1995	Two LTTE female suicide bombers targeting the headquarters of the Sri Lankan army detonated an explosive concealed in their vests.	18 killed, 52 injured	Colombo, Sri Lanka
4 July 1996	A female LTTE suicide bomber detonated explosives in an attempt to assassinate the housing and construction minister, Nimal Siripala de Silva, while his motorcade was stationary. The attack killed 20 military personnel and civilians, along with the Jaffna military commander Brig. Ananda Hamangoda, and wounded 59 others.	21 killed, 60 injured	Jaffna, Sri Lanka
6 February 1998	A female LTTE suicide bomber detonated an explosive device after being stopped and failing to penetrate a roadblock in a Slave Island suburb.	9 killed, unknown number injured	Colombo, Sri Lanka
14 March 1998	A female LTTE suicide bomber assassinated Brigadier Larry Wijeyaratne by detonating an abdominal belt bomb.	2 killed, 0 injured	Jaffna, Sri Lanka
18 March 1999	A female LTTE suicide bomber attempted to assassinate Chief Inspector Mohammed Nilabdeen of the Sri Lankan terrorist investigation unit. The attack killed only the bomber, but injured Nilabdeen and eight civilians.	1 killed, 9 injured	Colombo, Sri Lanka

(continued)

Table 2.2. Major Female Suicide Bombings in the Tamil–Sri Lankan Conflict (Continued)

Date	Features of the attack	Victims	Location
25 July 1999	A female LTTE suicide bomber detonated an explosive device targeting a ship docked in the Trincomalee harbour.	2 killed, 0 injured	Trincomalee harbour, Sri Lanka
4 August 1999	A female LTTE suicide bomber targeted a police truck, killing 9 police commandos and 1 civilian. Eighteen other commandos were injured.	11 killed, 18 injured	Vavuniya, Sri Lanka
18 December 1999	A female LTTE suicide bomber attempted to assassinate Sri Lankan President Chandrika Bandaranaike Kumaratunga of the People's Alliance party in an election campaign meeting. The president lost an eye but survived the bombing in which 26 people were killed and over 100 wounded. The attack killed Colombo's Deputy Inspector-General T.N. De Silva.	Over 20 killed, over 100 injured	Colombo, Sri Lanka
5 January 2000	A female LTTE suicide bomber blew herself up while being searched by police in front of the Prime Minister's Office.	17 killed, 27 injured	Colombo, Sri Lanka
2 March 2000	A female LTTE suicide bomber, targeting Col. Piyal Abeysekara, failed in the assassination attempt, killing only his driver and herself.	2 killed, 0 injured	Trincomalee, Sri Lanka
7 July 2004	A female LTTE suicide bomber, identified as Thiyagaraja Jeyarani, detonated an explosive device while in custody in the Kollupitiya Police Station next to the Sri Lankan prime minister's official residence.	5 killed, 9 injured	Colombo, Sri Lanka
25 April 2006	A female LTTE suicide bomber, disguised as a pregnant woman, detonated an explosive device at the military hospital within Sri Lanka's army headquarters. Lt General Sarath Fonseka, the head of the Sri Lankan army, was seriously injured in the attack.	9 killed, 27 injured	Colombo, Sri Lanka
6 January 2007	The bodies of two women, suspected of being LTTE suicide bombers, were recovered after an explosion on a private civilian transport bus from Colombo in Sinigima. The explosion killed 15 civilians and injured a further 50.	17 killed, 40 injured	Sri Lanka

(continued)

Table 2.2. Major Female Suicide Bombings in the Tamil–Sri Lankan Conflict (Continued)

Date	Features of the attack	Victims	Location
28 November 2007	A polio-inflicted female suicide bomber attempted to assassinate Social Services Minister Douglas Devananda near his office at Isipathana Road in the Narahenpita area. She detonated her explosive device during a security search.	2 killed, 2 injured	Colombo, Sri Lanka
3 February 2008	A female suicide bomber detonated an explosive device via a cellular phone in a Fort Railway Station. The bomber entered the station and avoided security checks via another train.	13 killed, 97 injured	Colombo, Sri Lanka
9 October 2008	A female suicide bomber carried out an attack on the motorcade of Minister Maithripala Sirisena in the Boralesgamuwa area of Colombo district.	2 killed, 5 injured	Colombo, Sri Lanka
4 February 2009	A 13-year-old suicide bomber detonated an explosive device, targeting military troops.	1 killed, 1 injured	Chalai, Sri Lanka
9 February 2009	A female suicide bomber detonated an explosive device at a checkpoint into an internally displaced persons' "safe zone" after arriving at the location with other displaced persons who were seeking protection.	25 killed, 45 injured	Mullaittivu, Sri Lanka
2 March 2009	A female suicide bomber detonated explosives when troops of the 55th Division attempted to approach her.	Unknown	Vannakulam area, east of Elephant Pass and south of Vettalaikerny, Sri Lanka
6 April 2009	A woman blew herself up at a checkpoint for Tamil civilians fleeing the war zones near Sundarapuram in Visuamadu.	28 killed, 45 injured	Ramanathapuram area of Mullaitivu, Sri Lanka

artillery shelling, the government declared victory over the LTTE, thus officially ending three decades of ethno-nationalist struggle in Sri Lanka. This victory, however, came at an enormous human cost, which may have the effect of radicalizing a new generation of Tamils. In addition, accounts of disappearance, rape, and torture of Tamils by Sri Lankan militaries and security forces, including within the official rehabilitation program for suspected former rebels, long after hostilities ended, continue to resurface and betray the systematic character of the ongoing abuses against Tamils (see *Report of the Secretary General's Internal Review Panel on UN Action in Sri Lanka*, 2012). Finally, although the LTTE has been defeated in the conventional military sense, it continues to enjoy significant financial and logistical support. Thus, it remains to be seen whether one of Asia's longest-running civil wars is actually over.

Kurdish Insurgency in Turkey

Chronologically, Turkey represents the third context in which female suicide bombings took place. As in the two earlier cases, the trail of the modern guerrilla violence in Turkey can be traced back to the colonial activities of the European imperial powers in the aftermath of the disintegration of the Ottoman Empire. The division of the region among the British Empire, France, and local rulers following the First World War resulted in arbitrary borders being drawn in violation of extant tribal, ethnic, and religious boundaries. As a consequence, the historic homeland of one of the largest ethnic groups in the Middle East, Kurdistan, was divided among four neighbouring countries – Turkey, Syria, Iran, and Iraq – with the largest population of Kurds ending up in Turkey. The division of Kurdistan laid the ground for the "Kurdish question" in each of the "host states." Often regarded as a "fifth column," the Kurds have been subjected to increased repression in all four states. They have been deprived of their culture, history, full citizenship rights, including the right to speak and be educated in the Kurdish language, giving their children Kurdish names, or flying the Kurdish flag. They have also been subjected to indiscriminate massacres and large-scale deportations (Eager 2008; Gonzalez-Perez 2008a). The apogee of anti-Kurdish discrimination was Saddam Hussein's 1988 genocidal gassing of the Kurds in the northern Iraqi city of Halabja. The Kurds reacted by consolidating powerful nationalist movements.

From the onset of Turkey's independence, Mustafa Kemal's (Atatürk) government embarked on a path of reforms geared towards solidifying Turkish nationalism and inventing the secular, Westernized, modern Turkish nation (Özcan 2006, 83). Atatürk's agenda left no room for the recognition of the distinctiveness or even existence of the Kurdish people, effectively denying their entitlement to minority rights. The official position of the Turkish government was that "we have no ethnic minorities" (Bloom 2007, 104). The Kurdistan Workers' Party or Partiya Karkeran Kurdistan (PKK) emerged between 1974 and 1978 out of the radical leftist student group called Ankara Democratic Patriotic Association of Higher Education. Its leader, Abdullah Öcalan, an ethnic Kurd and a political science student at the University of Ankara, steered the group's discussions and goals towards the interests of the Kurds in southeast Turkey (Eager 2008). The PKK's malleable ideological basis and socio-political goals represented a paradoxical blend of Marxism, nationalism, and Islam, aspiring to incite ethno-national uprising within a framework of proletarian revolution among the religious Muslim Kurdish community (174). Ideological eclecticism and adaptability allowed the PKK to gain popular support, distinguish itself from more traditional Iraqi-based Kurdish groups, and at the same time avail itself of the logistical support and training opportunities offered by Syria as well as acquire safe havens in Iran. Such eclecticism and adaptability allowed the PKK to shift away from its initial ideological emphasis on Marxism-Leninism, following the collapse of the Soviet Union, and to adopt the religious language and concept of jihad. The PKK's goals, too, ranged contradictorily from a maximalist objective of creating a larger Kurdistan that would include all Kurds in the Middle East to demanding part of the national territory in the form of Kurdish autonomy within Turkey.

Some observers have questioned whether the PKK's pan-Kurdish aspirations and the goal of independence were as non-negotiable as the organization often presented them to be, and whether the recovery of the homeland could be compatible with the federalist solution (Elster 2006, 247). To achieve its goals, the PKK used violence selectively against state officials in Turkey, as well as against Turkish diplomatic and commercial facilities throughout Western Europe. In an attempt to undermine the influence of the Turkish state, the group deployed conventional attacks and bombings, hunger strikes, self-immolations, and suicide bombings. Pedahzur (2005) claimed that it was Öcalan's decision to launch female suicide bombings. The Free Women's Union of Kurdistan served as the PKK's principal military arm for mounting female suicide bombings. The PKK carried out eleven female suicide bombings. They were launched against non-Kurdish Muslims and, according to Pape (2005, 163), represent the least aggressive or publicized suicide terrorist campaign, primarily because of the limited communal support the PKK received for suicide bombings. Following the arrest and incarceration of its leader, the organization briefly engaged in indiscriminate retaliatory violence. This was followed by a unilateral ceasefire declaration by the PKK in 1999, which was suspended in 2003 (Gambetta 2006, 301).

Zeynep Kinaci (Zilan) became the first PKK female suicide bomber. She carried out her attack in a way that immediately drew attention to her gender and highlighted the novelty of the attack. On 30 June 1996, Kinaci walked up to a group of Turkish soldiers during a flag ceremony in Tunceli, Turkey, as they were singing the Turkish national anthem and detonated her explosive belt, concealed as an advanced pregnancy (Beyler 2003a; Sakaoglu 1996; Pape 2003). Kinaci had a university degree and worked at the state clinic in Malatya. She became interested in the leftist Kurdish movement during her university years. Before embarking on her fateful mission, Kinaci allegedly wrote an open letter to the PKK leader, Abdullah Öcalan, in which she stated, "We are the children of a people that has had their country taken away and has been scattered to the four corners of the world. We want to live in freedom in our own land like human beings ... We do not want to cause war, to die or to kill. But there is no other way of gaining our freedom" (Özcan 2006, 176).

Two other female suicide bombings occurred in October 1996. Leyla Kaplan, disguised as a pregnant woman, detonated explosives at the entrance to the Adana Police Rapid Deployment Force Directorate. Prior to the attack, she allegedly witnessed the execution, by a PKK male operative, of another young woman who had refused to carry out the attack. In 1998 the PKK's second-in-command, Semdin Sakik, was arrested, and Turkey successfully pressured Syria to end support for the PKK and expel Öcalan from his safe haven in Damascus. Against this backdrop, three female suicide attacks took place in November and December in the southeastern region of Turkey (Beyler 2003a; Zedalis 2004).

Following Öcalan's arrest in February 1999, the PKK's female suicide bombings escalated. During his trial, two potential female suicide bombers (Bahar Ercik and Umut Gulya) were apprehended before they could execute their attacks (Eager 2008, 177), and a few Kurdish men and women, including an eleven-year-old girl, initiated self-immolations as an act of public protest against Öcalan's arrest. When Öcalan was given the sentence of capital punishment in June 1999 (later commuted to life imprisonment), another female suicide bomber blew herself up in Turkey. No group claimed the responsibility for the two female suicide bombings in 2003 and 2009, the latter of which failed. However, in both cases female bombers were involved in the Revolutionary People's Liberation Party-Front (DHKP-C). On 29 April 2009 Didem Akman (twenty-three) failed in her attempt to assassinate former Turkish minister of justice, Hikmet Sami Turk, during his lecture at Bilkent University in Ankara. A male suicide bomber, Onur Yilmaz, who was arrested trying to flee the scene, accompanied her. Akman was jailed a few times for previous involvement with the DHKP-C. The last known female suicide bombing in Turkey took place on 29 October 2011, the eighty-eighth anniversary of the Turkish Republic and ten days following the launch of a major military operation against Kurdish resistance in Southeast Turkey and Iraq (see table 2.3).

Table 2.3. Female Suicide Bombings in Turkey

Date	Features of the attack	Victims	Location
30 June 1996	Zeynep Kinaci (Zilan), a PKK operative (29), approached Turkish soldiers during a parade. The operative feigned pregnancy to disguise the explosive device.	10 killed, 30 injured	Tunceli
25 October 1996	Leyla Kaplan (17) detonated an explosive device concealed as a pregnancy. She attacked the police headquarters.	5 killed, 12 injured	Adana
29 October 1996	Otas Gular, also spelled Güler Otaç (29), of the PKK, carried out a suicide bombing at the Sivas police station after she was apprehended for questioning during the Republic Day parade. She concealed the bomb as a pregnancy and was veiled in the traditional black chador of devout Muslim women with only her eyes visible. She blew herself up in the police car en route to being searched by a policewoman of the anti-terrorist squad.	4 or 5 killed, 0 injured	Sivas
17 November 1998	Ozen Fatima of the PKK detonated an explosive device that she was wearing, in front of a police station. Her target was a military convoy.	1 killed, 6 injured	Yuksekova

(continued)

Table 2.3. Female Suicide Bombings in Turkey (Continued)

Date	Features of the attack	Victims	Location
1 December 1998	A female suicide bomber detonated an explosive device in a supermarket. The attack was linked to the PKK.	1 killed, 14 injured	Lice
24 December 1998	A female suicide bomber detonated an explosive device targeting a military vehicle in front of a military barracks.	2 killed, 22 injured	Eastern
4 March 1999	A female suicide bomber (25) detonated an explosive device within 10 metres of the central police station. Allegedly, the bomb went off prematurely, causing limited damage. The attack was attributed to the PKK.	1 killed, 4 injured	Batman
27 March 1999	Esma Yurdakul (21) detonated a grenade. The attack was attributed to the PKK.	1 killed, 10 injured	Istanbul
5 July 1999	Rusen Tabanci (19) flashed a V sign and detonated an explosive device strapped to her body near a security office that houses the Financial Department and the Wireless News Centre. The attack was attributed to the PKK.	1 killed, 17 injured	Adana
5 May 2003	Sengul Akkurt, from the province of Malatya, known as a member of the DHKP-C, who had previously been arrested for her involvement in the group's activities, detonated a bomb prematurely in the restroom of a cafe. No group officially claimed responsibility for the attack.	1 killed, 1 injured	Ankara
29 October 2011	A female suicide bomber detonated explosives at a teahouse near the Justice and Development Party (AKP).	3 killed, 20 injured	Bingol (predominantly Kurdish town)

The attacks killed about 30 people, of which 11 were female suicide bombers or their associates, and they wounded over 100 people. Since its onset in 1984, the protracted insurgency in Turkey has claimed the lives of approximately 30,000 people, mostly Kurdish civilians. In 2006, Öcalan declared another ceasefire and called on the PKK to seek peace with Turkey. But the militant wing of the PKK, the Kurdistan Freedom Falcons / Kurdistan Liberation Hawks, has continued to demand secession through violence. At the same time, the Turkish military command is determined to counter this group until the last rebel is killed.

Female Suicide Bombings in the Chechen-Russian Conflict

The long-standing Chechen resistance against Russian rule spans centuries and has featured massive exterminations and expulsions of the indigenous population. Chechens are a culturally and ethnically distinct people who settled in the mountainous areas of the North Caucasus thousands of years ago. Their social structure has been organized around self-contained clans and tribes, based on religious cohesion and tight family links. Chechens' first encounter with Russians took place in the early seventeenth century when Russian tsar troops attempted to invade Chechen-held territory, but were forced to retreat. In the eighteenth century Peter the Great attempted another unsuccessful bid to conquer the region. A Chechen rebellion led by Imam Shamil in 1859 temporarily put an end to Russia's imperialist ambitions. Following the Bolshevik revolution, Chechnya became part of the independent Republic of the North Caucasus, renamed in 1921 the Soviet Mountain Republic. Fifteen years later, Chechnya and neighbouring Ingushetia were granted the status of an autonomous republic with some territory populated by Russians added to this new political entity.

During the Second World War, the fear of a potential pro-independence uprising in the republic prompted Russia to accuse Chechens of collaboration with the Nazis. Chechens were forcefully deported to Central Asia and Siberia. Many of them died of disease, cold, and starvation in exile, as the result of severe food and housing shortages. Following Stalin's death, in 1957 the Chechen-Ingush autonomous republic was restored, thus allowing for Chechen repatriation. With the collapse of the Soviet Union in 1991, Dzhokhar Dudayev declared Chechnya's independence, but the robust movement for Chechen self-determination clashed with the Russian Federation's determination to defeat Chechen separatism, leading to the two "civil" wars (1994–6 and 1999–2009). In these wars, a pattern of horrendous human rights violations emerged, with both sides of the conflict bearing responsibility for crimes committed against civilians, including murders, kidnappings, abductions, and extrajudicial executions.

Prior to the outbreak of the first Chechen war in 1994, the republic was home to over one million inhabitants. Almost a decade of fighting forced hundreds of thousands to flee their homes in order to escape the violence, plunging the North Caucasus into a massive displacement crisis. With approximately 20 per cent of the population killed and 750,000 internally displaced, the Chechen-Russian wars have become "one of the deadliest conflicts in recent European history" (Khalilov 2003, 407). This protracted violence ruined the Chechen economy. Petroleum production used to be the foundation of the local economy, with oil refineries concentrated in and around Grozny. By the mid- to late 1990s, the refineries and most oil wells were destroyed by Russia, and Chechnya's major pipeline linking the Caspian oil fields to the Russian Black Sea port of Novorossiysk was closed for lack of security in the region. Chechnya has now deteriorated into a classic failed "state" with rampant lawlessness and numerous illicit activities prevalent on its territory.

A secular secessionist nationalist movement in its early stage, the Chechen struggle, according to some analysts, has been increasingly affected by "Islamization," or the ideological influence of Wahhabism (Bloom 2007, 127, 154). Jordanian-born Amir Khattab, also known as the "Black Arab," who fought against the Soviets in Afghanistan, reportedly exerted strong influence on Shamil Basayev, the powerful Chechen rebel leader (Eager 2008, 199). The influence of Soviet-Afghan jihadist veterans in Chechnya follows an established pattern witnessed in numerous regions, i.e., Algeria, Bosnia, and Egypt, as Qutbist/Wahhabist-influenced militants sought to expand Islamist authority throughout the Muslim world, especially in the regions that border on non-Muslim areas. Qutb/Wahhabi militants allegedly introduced suicide bombings in Chechnya and influenced Basayev to incorporate women into his suicide bombing squad, the Salakhin Riadus Shahidi group. These women are conventionally known as the "black widows," i.e., women willing to die for a cause, taking the lives of others, driven by the intimately personal motive of avenging their male relatives killed by Russian federal troops.[7]

The first Chechen female suicide bombing took place in 2000. Since then, nearly fifty known female suicide bombings in the Chechen-Russian conflict caused the most deaths in the modern history of these attacks: over 915 fatalities and over 1,500 wounded (information about known attacks and perpetrators is summarized in table 2.4).

Suicide bombings are not a Chechen tradition – the centuries-long resistance against Russian rule featured primarily male guerrilla warfare. The violent practice of female suicide bombings was introduced in the Russian-Chechen context only in 2000 and is generally considered

Table 2.4. Chronology of Women Suicide Bombings in Chechnya and Russia

Date	Terrorist act	Victims	Location
7 June 2000	Hawa Zhansurkayeva (22), aka Barayeva, and Kheda (aka Luiza) Magomadova (17) drove a car loaded with explosives into the OMON (Special Forces) headquarters.	29 dead (2 according to Russian sources), 5 injured	Alkhan-Yurt, Chechnya
11 June 2000	Suicide bombers, a woman among them, blew up a car at a checkpoint.	12 killed, 7 injured	Grozny, Chechnya
2 July 2000	Suicide bombers carried out five synchronized attacks against Russian federal troops in Chechnya. In one attack, a woman drove a truck loaded with explosives into a building housing Russian OMON (Special Forces).	45 killed, 0 injured	Argun, Chechnya
29 November 2001	Luisa Gazuyeva (17) blew herself up after approaching a military commander.	1 killed, 3 injured	Urus-Martan, Chechnya
23 October 2002	About 40 terrorists, 18 women among them, seized a Nord-Ost theatre and took about 800 hostages. Identified female terrorists were Zura Barayeva, Raisa Ahmadova, Fatima Ahmadova, Zareta Bayrakova (26), Larisa/Fatima Ganiyeva (23), Hadizhat Ganiyeva (16), Madina Ebiyeva, Aishat Bakuyeva (26), Amnat Isuyeva (26), Sekilat Aliyeva (25), Mariam Hadzhiyeva (24), Rayana Kurbanova (36), Aset Gishlurkayeva (29), Zura Bitsyeva (22), Madina Bisultanova (19), Zaira Biteva (24), Aset Gishlurkayeva (29), Madina Dugayeva (24).	After a three-day siege Russian forces stormed the building using gas and killing most of the rebels and 115 hostages.	Moscow
27 December 2002	Gelani Tumriyev (43), his son Ilyas (17), and daughter, Alina Tumriyeva (15), drove two trucks loaded with explosives into a government building.	72 killed, 210 injured	Grozny, Chechnya
12 May 2003	Two suicide bombers, one of them a woman, Zarina Alikhanova, drove a truck loaded with explosives into a government administration and security complex.	About 60 killed, over 300 injured	Znamenskoye, Chechnya

(continued)

Table 2.4. Chronology of Women Suicide Bombings in Chechnya and Russia (Continued)

Date	Terrorist act	Victims	Location
14 May 2003	Two of the three female suicide bombers – Shahidat Baymuradova (46), Zulaya Abdurzakova, and Shahidat Shahbulatova – detonated their explosive belts in an attempt to kill Chechnya's Moscow-appointed leader, Akhmad Kadyrov. A third woman terrorist was killed by the blast.	16–30 killed, 145 injured	Iliskhan-Yurt, Chechnya
5 June 2003	Lidiya Khaldykhoroyev (25) ambushed a bus carrying Russian air force pilots near Chechnya, blowing it up.	16 killed, 15 injured	Mozdok, North Ossetia
20 June 2003	A suicide truck bombing carried out by a man and a woman targeted a Russian government building.	8 killed, 25 injured	Grozny, Chechnya
23 June 2003	Luisa Osmaeva (23) was captured on her way to commit a terrorist act. She died in the hospital of gunshot wounds and general physical exhaustion exacerbated by incapacitating agents.		Grozny, Chechnya
5 July 2003	Two female suicide bombers, Marem Aliyeva and Zulihan Elihadzhiyeva (19) detonated their bombs at an open-air rock festival.	15 killed, 60 injured	Moscow's Tushino airfield
10 July 2003	A technical failure prevented a female suicide bomber from detonating her bomb in a cafe. The female bomber, Zarema Muzhikhoyeva (22), was arrested and sentenced to 20 years in prison on charges of terrorism and premeditated murder.	An expert killed in an attempt to diffuse a bomb	Moscow
27 July 2003	Iman Hachukayeva (26) detonated her explosive charge at a military base, as the son of Ramzan Kadyrov was reviewing troops. Security forces searched for another female bomber suspected to be on a mission to assassinate Kadyrov.	2 killed, 0 injured	Totsin-Yurt, Chechnya
5 December 2003	A female suicide bomber blew herself up in a commuter train. Two or three other women were involved in the attack.	42 killed, over 150 injured	Yessentuki train station, southern Russia

(continued)

Table 2.4. Chronology of Women Suicide Bombings in Chechnya and Russia (Continued)

Date	Terrorist act	Victims	Location
9 December 2003	Two female suicide bombers detonated their charges near the hotel "National." Police identified one as Hadishat Mangeriyeva (26), a second wife of Ruslan Mangeriyev, emir of Kurchaloyev district in Chechnya, killed in 2002.	6 killed, 14 injured	Moscow
6 February 2004	A female suicide bomber was suspected in a rush-hour metro train blast.	39 killed, 139 injured	Moscow
24 August 2004	Two Chechen women, Amnat Nagayeva (30) and Satsita Dzhebirkhanova (37), were suspected in the crash of two Russian passenger planes. Nagayeva and Dzhebirkhanova were suicide bombers, or their passports were used by other women. Islambouli Brigades claimed responsibility for the attacks.	89 killed	Russia
31 August 2004	A female suicide bomber detonated a bomb outside Rizhskaya subway station.	10 killed, 51 injured	Moscow
1–3 September 2004	Armed terrorists, among them allegedly 4 females, took hundreds of schoolchildren and adults hostage at a school. Two women allegedly blew themselves up inside the school. One was identified as the wife of Mayrbek Shaybekhanov, who participated in the siege. Another account suggests that rebel leader Ruslan Khuchbarov blew up one of the female bombers when she protested against holding children hostages. A recently formed organization, the North Caucasus Islamic Front, is suspected of organizing the attacks; it is reportedly a united front for the jihadi organizations of Chechnya, Dagestan, and Ingushetia that seek to establish an Islamic caliphate in the region.	344 killed, at least 172 of them children, hundreds more injured	Beslan, North Ossetia
6 May 2005	An unknown female suicide bomber tried to detonate an explosive belt near the police headquarters in the Staropromyslovsky district in Grozny, but was shot before reaching her target.	1 killed, 0 injured	Grozny, Chechnya

(continued)

Table 2.4. Chronology of Women Suicide Bombings in Chechnya and Russia (Continued)

Date	Terrorist act	Victims	Location
23 October 2007	An unknown female suicide bomber blew herself up in a minibus travelling from Khasavurt to Dylym. The bomb exploded as the bus neared a police checkpoint in Lenin-Aul.	1 killed, 8 injured	Between Khasavurt and Dylym, Dagestan
6 November 2008	An unknown female suicide bomber blew herself up next to a minibus at a central market.	12 killed, 41 injured	Vladikavkaz, North Ossetia
16 September 2009	An unknown woman detonated her explosives next to two police officers and their vehicle.	2 killed, 5 injured	Grozny, Chechnya
29 March 2010	Maryam Sharipova (28), a university student majoring in psychology, and Djennet Abdurakhmanova (17), who lost her militant husband only a few months after marrying him, detonated bombs in a coordinated attack in the Moscow subway at the busy Lubyanka interchange near the Federal Security Service headquarters. Chechen rebel leader Doku (Dokka) Umarov claimed responsibility.	40 killed, 120 injured	Moscow
9 April 2010	A female (26), allegedly the wife of a militant, opened fire on security forces during a counterterrorism operation, then detonated her explosives belt.	4 killed, 3 injured	Yekazhevo, Ingushetia
31 December 2010	An unknown woman, allegedly planning to blow herself up near Moscow's Red Square on New Year's Eve, accidentally blew herself up in a safe house. Her handler was Zeinat Suyunova (24) from Dagestan, who was believed to have been implicated in the Domodedovo Airport male suicide bombing on 24 January 2011 that claimed the lives of 40 and injured over 150 people.	1 killed	Moscow
14 February 2011	Maria Khorosheva blew herself up at a police station. Her husband, Vitaly Razdobudko, blew up his explosives-loaded vehicle at a police post a few hours later.	4 killed, 25 injured	Gubden village, near Makhachkala, Dagestan

(continued)

Table 2.4. Chronology of Women Suicide Bombings in Chechnya and Russia (Continued)

Date	Terrorist act	Victims	Location
6 March 2012	Two days after Russia's presidential election, Aminat Ibragimova (25), wife of Dagestani militant Zaur Zagirov killed in February 2012, detonated explosives at a checkpoint.	6 killed, 2 injured	Karabudakhkent village checkpoint, south of Makhachkala, Dagestan
3 May 2012	Two suicide bombers carried out a coordinated suicide car bomb attack at a police checkpoint. The remains of a male and female were found near the exploded vehicles and were believed to be the ones behind the attacks.	At least 13 killed, over 130 injured	Makhachkala, Dagestan
27 July 2012	During a counterterrorism operation, a female militant approached security forces, appearing to surrender, then detonated her explosives belt. Russia's Anti-Terrorism Committee identified her as Saidat Yusupova.	1 killed, 0 injured	Alburikent village, near Machachkala, Dagestan
28 August 2012	Aminat Kurbanova (née Saprykina), ethnic Russian (30), convert to Islam, married to an Islamic militant, was an actress in the Russian Drama Theatre in Makhachkala. She detonated her explosive belt in the home of Said Afandi (Atsayev), a Sufi sheikh in Dagestan with tens of thousands of followers, involved in lessening tensions between Salafists and Sufis.	7 killed, 0 injured	Chirkey, Buynakskiy region, Dagestan
25 May 2013	Madina Aliyeva (25), allegedly married twice to rebels Aliyev and Djapayev, blew herself up about 100 m from the Ministry of Internal Affairs.	3 killed, 17 injured	Makhachkala, Dagestan
21 October 2013	Naida Asiyalova (30), allegedly en route from Makhachkala (Dagestan) to Moscow, where she worked for seven years and, according to some accounts, studied at the university, got off in Volgograd and about an hour later blew herself up on a city bus. She was a sharia wife of Dmitri Sokolov, an ethnic Russian dubbed by the Russia media "Russian Wahhabi." Allegedly, Sokolov converted to Wahhabism under Asiyanova's influence.	7 killed, 47 injured	Volgograd, Russian Federation

in Russia a Middle Eastern import. In 2003, the reporters of *Komsomolskaya Pravda* discovered a 1985 KGB report predicting that "live" bombs would eventually be imported to the Soviet Union from Arab and West European countries (Lobanova and Selivanova 2003). At the time, KGB experts on terrorist psychology believed that women terrorists would be used more often than male terrorists, because female psychology is more receptive to the idea of sacrifice. Today, some experts even talk of the "Palestinization" of the conflict in Chechnya (Abdullayev 2003).

The conclusions about the "Palestinization" of the Chechen conflict do not seem substantiated, as far as female suicide bombings are concerned. This form of violent resistance was employed in Chechnya two years prior to the first Palestinian female blowing herself up. After the school siege in Beslan, some of the rebels have distanced themselves from Shamil Basayev, the former Chechen prime minister and leader of Chechen Wahhabi fighters at the time, who claimed responsibility for numerous terrorist acts in Russia. Akhmed Zakayev, a representative of the Chechen resistance movement in Europe, for example, deplored terrorist tactics as discrediting the whole Chechen resistance (Korchagina 2004). Unlike in Lebanon, Sri Lanka, or Palestine, female suicide bombings have not received widespread communal support, as most Chechens have not embraced the cult of martyrdom. Sulumbek Ganiyev, whose two daughters became *shakhidkas* (female martyrs), is quoted as saying, "If I knew what they were up to, I'd break their legs, so that they could not walk and stay home" (Rechkalov 2003). Thus, violent Islamism does not seem to have a strong grip on Chechen society. Perhaps more importantly, after the late 1990s and early 2000s, violence in Chechnya spilled beyond its borders to the entire region of the North Caucasus, including Ingushetia, North Ossetia, Kabardino-Balkaria, and Dagestan. The last found itself under a strong Wahhabi grip (National Strategy Institute 2013) and soon became the focal point of violence in the region (Center for Strategic & International Studies 2010). After Moscow-appointed Ramzan Kadyrov became president of the Republic of Chechnya in 2007, he quickly took control over violent resistance. So, in the last five years, most female suicide bombings in Russia have been linked to Dagestan, rather than Chechnya.

Female Martyrdom in the Palestinian-Israeli Conflict

The generally "overanalysed" Palestinian-Israeli conflict (Brunner 2005, 29) is too complex and multidimensional to do justice to its origins and dynamics within the limited confines of this chapter. Our account of the Palestinian-Israeli conflict will touch only upon those aspects that are important to understanding female suicide bombings within this particular context. In some respects, the origins of the Palestinian-Israeli conflict can be traced back to the end of British colonial control over Palestine and the creation of the state of Israel in 1948, shortly before the expiration of the British mandate. Israel's independence, accompanied by the large-scale displacement and dispossession of Palestinians, ushered in a protracted Palestinian-Israeli conflict that unfolded through major waves and noticeable turning points.

Some of the most important landmarks of this conflict were the 1967 Six-Day War, the first Intifada (1987–91), and the al-Aqsa Intifada that broke out on 28 September 2000. As a result of the Six-Day War, Israel tripled its territorial possessions by occupying the Gaza Strip, the Sinai Peninsula, the West Bank, and the Golan Heights. The aftermath of the humiliating Arab defeat also witnessed the emergence of the Palestine Liberation Organization (PLO) as a champion for carrying on the Palestinian struggle against the Israeli occupation (Eager 2008, 180). Formed in 1964 on secular nationalist principles, with Yasser Arafat's left-wing nationalist Fatah party as its largest faction, the PLO embarked on a mission to internationalize the Palestinian cause through increasing use of terror tactics, including spectacular airplane hijackings (e.g., 1968 El Al and 1972 Sabena Airlines hijackings) and hostage-taking operations (e.g., 1972 Munich Olympics massacre). Moreover, during the 1970s, the PLO, stationed in south Lebanon after its expulsion from Jordan, built up conventional military capabilities and launched artillery and missile campaigns against military and civilian targets in northern Israel. As discussed earlier, the PLO's growing infrastructure in southern Lebanon provoked two Israeli invasions of southern Lebanon.

Decades of economic deprivation under Israeli occupation and the absence of any tangible political and/or military solution resulted in the outbreak of a spontaneous popular uprising in December 1987. Known as the first Intifada, this "war of stones" was neither "foreseen, [nor] inspired" (Ricolfi 2006, 89) by the PLO, which was fraught with internal tensions and in exile. Yet it produced significant consequences. On the one hand, the Intifada brought the Palestinian issue into the international spotlight and shifted international public opinion in favour of Palestinians; on the other hand, it caused a deterioration of relations among Palestinian factions (Eager 2008, 181). Empirical studies of Palestinian suicide bombers have noted that roughly half of these individuals experienced some form of trauma during the first Intifada, leading to speculation that experiences of humiliation during this period contributed to later incidences of suicide bombing (Gentry 2009, 241). Whereas the PLO, faced with systemic corruption, financial difficulties, and serious challenges from other factions, signalled its willingness to enter peace negotiations with Israel in a concerted effort to revive its political stature, the radical Palestinian factions, mainly the ascending Islamic Resistance Movement, or Hamas (Harakat al-Muqawama al-Islamiyya), and the Palestinian Islamic Jihad (PIJ) opposed recognition of the Israeli state.

In the midst of the creeping civil war in Palestine, secret talks began between the PLO's leadership and Israel, which resulted in the signing of the 1993 Oslo Accords. The accords were viewed by its advocates as establishing a gradual process leading to a two-state solution, but denounced by its critics as the virtual "subcontracting of the Israeli occupation to the Palestinian Authority (PA)" (Scholey 2008, 134). They granted the PLO the right to govern in certain areas that were under Israeli occupation. In return, the PLO recognized the Israeli state. Crucial issues of the Palestinian right of return, Jewish settlements in the West Bank, Jerusalem, and the ongoing Israeli military violence against Palestinians remained unresolved. Radical factions on both Israeli and Palestinian sides opposed the Oslo Accords. In an effort to undermine the peace process, Hamas resorted to suicide bombings, carrying out thirteen such attacks in 1992 and ten in 1993 (three of which happened prior to the signing of the agreements). Subsequently, the 1994 Hebron massacre by Baruch Goldstein in the Ibrahimi mosque, the assassination of Israeli Prime Minister Rabin in 1995, the outburst of Hezbollah-style suicide attacks against Israeli civilians, and harsh Israeli measures against Palestinians effectively put an end to the Oslo process (Ricolfi 2006, 91).

The year 1999 witnessed strenuous diplomatic efforts to resume the peace process, leading to the top-level negotiations at Camp David in 2000. The promise to declare the state of Palestine by 13 September 2000 helped to revive Arafat's popularity among some Palestinians. However, in September 2000, a second uprising known as the al-Aqsa Intifada did much to solidify the popularity of Hamas and marginalize the increasingly corrupt, heavily bureaucratized, and discredited PLO. Ricolfi (2006, 93) makes an interesting observation that throughout 2000, until the outbreak of the second Intifada, there were no terrorist attacks, whether conventional or suicidal, in Israel and the Occupied

Territories, implying that the failure of the peace process was not due to terrorism. The outbreak of al-Aqsa Intifada is usually linked to the failed declaration of the state of Palestine, as well as to the controversial visit of Ariel Sharon, who was escorted by hundreds of police officers, to the Temple Mount complex in Jerusalem. The latter event was widely perceived by the Palestinians as an affront.

The al-Aqsa Intifada produced a powerful wave of suicide attacks and introduced a new perpetrator in the Israel/Palestine conflict – the woman martyr. On 27 January 2002, Wafa Idris, a 23-year-old paramedic working for the Palestinian Red Crescent Society, blew herself up in a West Jerusalem shopping mall, killing 1 Israeli man and wounding 131. This act prompted a range of speculations about her motives – from the claims that her death was an accident to suggestions that she may have been clinically depressed after witnessing the carnage and suffering of Palestinian people, to the assertions that her status as a divorced, barren woman caused her to become a martyr as a means of redemption of her family name. Interestingly, Idris carried out her mission on the same day that Yasser Arafat in his address to a crowd of more than 1,000 Palestinian women in Ramallah stressed the equal role of men and women in the Intifada. "'You are my army of roses that will crush Israeli tanks … *Shahida* all the way to Jerusalem,' he proclaimed, coining on the spot the feminized version of the Arab word for martyr, *shahide*, which previously existed only in the masculine form" (Victor 2003, 19). The responsibility for Idris's attack was claimed three days later by the nationalist al-Aqsa Martyrs Brigade – a military wing of Arafat's Fatah party that received its formal title following the outbreak of the second Intifada. The public reaction to the first act of female martyrdom by a Palestinian increased the popularity of the nationalist groups within Palestinian society and prompted intense discussions throughout the Arab world regarding the role of women in martyrdom operations.

Indeed, female suicide bombings in the context of the Palestinian-Israeli conflict is a relatively recent and rare phenomenon, with women appearing first on the suicide bombing scene in January 2002 during the height of the second Intifada and accounting for less than 7 per cent of all Palestinian suicide bombers (Sjoberg and Gentry 2007, 112). Even though it is estimated that nearly seventy Palestinian women have been involved in suicide bombing attempts (Schweitzer 2008, 131), only ten of them actually carried out the attacks (information about female suicide bombers in the context of Palestinian-Israeli conflict is summarized in table 2.5). The emergence of female suicide bombings in the Palestinian-Israeli conflict seems as much to do with the intensification of Israeli violence as with the intra-Palestinian factors, including competition between secular nationalist and Islamist groups for the hearts and minds of Palestinians, and the need to sustain Palestinian morale and stimulate the Intifada (Ricolfi 2006, 104–5). The first four successful female suicide bombings (all in 2002) occurred in a secular setting, as the Islamic leadership raised religious and social objections to women's participation in martyrdom operations. The second Palestinian female suicide bomber, Dareen Abu Aisheh, who acted on behalf of the al-Aqsa Martyrs Brigade, allegedly was rejected as a potential martyr by both Hamas and the Palestinian Islamic Jihad (Brunner 2005, 32).

Table 2.5. Female Suicide Bombings in the Palestinian-Israeli Conflict

Date	Features of the attack	Victims	Location
27 January 2002	Wafa Idris (28) detonated a 22-pound bomb in a backpack outside a shoe store on Jaffa Road. Responsibility for the attack was claimed by the al-Aqsa Martyrs Brigade.	2 killed, over 100 injured	Jerusalem
27 February 2002	Dareen Abu Aisheh (21) blew herself up at an Israeli checkpoint. The bomb went off as security guards tried to stop the bomber for a check-up. Responsibility for the attack was claimed by the al-Aqsa Martyrs Brigade.	1 killed, 5 injured	The West Bank, near Maccabim settlement
29 March 2002	Ayat al-Akhras (18) detonated explosives at the entrance to a supermarket. One mortar shell was left unexploded. Responsibility for the attack was claimed by the al-Aqsa Martyrs Brigade.	3 killed, at least 20 injured	Jerusalem
11 April 2002	Andaleeb Takafka (20) detonated an explosive belt, while being detained by a security guard at the entrance to the Mahneh Yehuda market. Responsibility for the attack was claimed by the al-Aqsa Martyrs Brigade.	7 killed, over 50 injured	Jerusalem
19 May 2003	Hiba Daraghmeh (19) detonated an explosive belt at the entrance to a shopping mall. Responsibility for the attack was claimed by the PIJ in cooperation with the al-Aqsa Martyrs Brigade.	4 killed, 48 injured	Afula, Israel

(continued)

Table 2.5. Female Suicide Bombings in the Palestinian-Israeli Conflict (Continued)

Date	Features of the attack	Victims	Location
4 October 2003	Hanadi Jaradat (27) blew herself up in a crowded Maxim restaurant – a popular Jewish-Arab gathering spot. Responsibility for the attack was claimed by the PIJ.	22 killed, 60 injured	Haifa, Israel
14 January 2004	Reem Al Riyashi (22) from Gaza detonated explosives at the Erez crossing. Hamas and the al-Aqsa Martyrs Brigade claimed responsibility for the attack.	5 killed, 8 injured	Erez border crossing checkpoint between Israel and Gaza
22 September 2004	Zeinab Abu Salem (18) detonated explosives at a checkpoint near a bus stop when policemen tried to stop her. The al-Aqsa Martyrs Brigade claimed responsibility.	3 killed, 12–17 injured	Checkpoint in French Hillel in Jerusalem
6 November 2006	Mervat Masaoud (18) blew herself up at an army checkpoint when approaching Israeli soldiers. The attack took place amidst extended Israel air bombings in the area. The PIJ claimed responsibility for the attack.	1 killed, 1 injured	Army checkpoint in Beit-Hanoun in Gaza
23 November 2006	Fatma Omar al-Najar (64), the oldest female suicide bomber on record, dubbed by the media as a "suicide granny," detonated explosives during a routine check-up when approached by the Israeli soldiers. Hamas claimed responsibility for the attack.	1 killed, 2 injured	Jabaliya refugee camp in Gaza

Days after Wafa Idris blew herself up, Sheik Ahmad Yassin, the wheelchair-bound spiritual leader of Hamas at the time, suggested that "a woman martyr is problematic for Muslim society. A man who recruits a woman is breaking Islamic law. He is taking the girl or woman without the permission of her father, brother, or husband, and therefore the family of the girl confronts an even greater problem since the man has the biggest power over her, choosing the day that she will give her life back to Allah" (Victor 2003, 30). The sheik's position, however, changed dramatically in just a couple of months, under increasing public pressure. In July 2002, when asked to explain his view on women suicide bombers, the sheik was quoted as saying, "We are men of principle, and according to our religion, a Muslim woman is permitted to wage Jihad and struggle against the enemy who invades holy land. The Prophet would draw lots among the women who wanted to go out with him to make Jihad. The Prophet always emphasized the woman's right to wage Jihad" (32–3). The religious sanctioning of female suicide bombings was then cemented with a fatwa that encouraged Muslim women to commit acts of martyrdom. Following this ideological shift, the PIJ, in cooperation with the al-Aqsa Martyrs Brigade, dispatched two female martyrs in 2003, and the next year Hamas (again, in cooperation with the al-Aqsa Martyrs Brigade) sent a twenty-two-year-old mother of two small children to sacrifice herself for the nationalist cause.

Many observers have struggled to uncover the reasons for female suicide bombings in Palestine and Israel. Dareen Abu Aisheh (21), an English literature student at Al-Najah University in Nablus, described as a career-oriented and independent feminist, is said to have suffered humiliation at an Israeli checkpoint when she tried to utilize her English skills to help a Palestinian woman with a sick baby pass through the checkpoint on the way to a hospital. Allegedly, Israeli soldiers told her to kiss her cousin as their condition for letting the woman with an infant through. As the cousins kissed, the baby stopped breathing. It is suggested that this humiliating episode brought public disgrace on Dareen Abu Aisheh, rendering her unmarriageable and leading her on the path of martyrdom (Eager 2008, 189). Ayat al-Akhras (18), who had planned to study journalism, is said to have personally experienced Israeli violence when her brother was wounded by Israeli troops and her three cousins, all members of Hamas, were killed in Israeli attacks. In addition, her father was pressured by the community to quit his well-paying job with an Israeli construction company, which he refused to do, despite the pleas of al-Akhras (190). Andaleeb Takafka was allegedly compromised by her relationship with a Fatah activist, by whom she became pregnant. Similarly, Reem Al Riyashi, in committing her act of martyrdom, was reportedly restoring her personal and familial honour and making amends for her unfaithfulness to her husband. Hiba Daraghmeh, according to some accounts, had been sexually assaulted by a mentally ill uncle.

The martyrdom messages left by these women reveal different reasons for their choices. These messages often point to the politics of violent resistance. For example, in her farewell video, Ayat al-Akhras reproached Arab leaders for "doing nothing, while Palestinian women are fighting to end Israeli occupation" (Victor 2003, 209). Andaleeb

Takafka in her martyrdom message also focused on the political dimension of the Israeli occupation, when she said, "When you want to carry out such an attack, whether you are a man or a woman, you don't think about the explosive belt ... We are suffering. We are dying while we are still alive" (Eager 2008, 191). Reem Al Riyashi disclosed her tightly knit religious and nationalist commitments, stating, "God gave me the ability to be a mother of two children who I love so. But my wish to meet God in paradise is greater, so I decided to be a martyr for the sake of my people" (Sjoberg and Gentry 2007, 121). Similarly, Hanadi Jaradat, a trainee attorney, pointed to the nationalist politics of her religiosity, declaring, "By the will of God I decided to be the sixth martyr who makes her body full of splinters in order to enter every Zionist heart who occupied our country. We are not the only ones who will taste death from their occupation. As they sow so will they reap" (123).

It appears, then, that the individual circumstances of Palestinian female suicide bombers reveal a cluster of motivations that include, to various degrees, a deep political commitment to the Palestinian cause, humiliation and the desire for revenge, and often the belief that they have been chosen by God to carry out this task on behalf of the downtrodden Palestinian people.

Global Jihadi Movement and Female Suicide Bombings in Iraq, Uzbekistan, Afghanistan, Pakistan, Somalia, Syria, Turkey, Nigeria, and Cameroon

Even though their number remains relatively low, since 2003 there has been a gradual increase in suicide bombings carried out by women associated with the Salafi global jihadi movement (GJM). Paradoxically, this movement is often perceived to be uniquely resistant, even hostile, towards women. Most of the women who are involved in the Salafi GJM carry out traditional roles as mothers of the future male jihadists or by providing support and safe havens. Yet there seems to be a growing number of women who have signalled their willingness to participate in violent jihad (Cunningham 2008, 94). The majority of female suicide bombings associated with GJM have been carried out in Iraq. The practice of female suicide bombings inspired by the radical religious interpretations of jihad, however, spread to Uzbekistan, Afghanistan, Pakistan, Syria, Somalia, Turkey, Nigeria, and, most recently, Cameroon.

Unlike other cases reviewed in this chapter, female suicide bombings sponsored or inspired by the jihadi Salafis are distinct in at least two ways. First, they are carried out through a tenuous, ad hoc arrangement of small, self-contained cells. These cells are ideologically/spiritually united under Al Qaeda's umbrella, but remain fairly independent. While they may act in cooperation, they do not necessarily have to establish any thick connections (Atran 2006a). Second, Al Qaeda–related female suicide bombings are meant to challenge perceived global domination and to reflect one's commitment to God through violent jihad. They occur in various geographic locations without necessarily sharing an affinity in national identity or culture.

Iraq

Before the U.S.-led invasion of Iraq in March 2003, the stated objectives of which were to rid the country of the weapons of mass destruction, to end Saddam Hussein's support for terrorism, and to free the Iraqi people, Iraq had not experienced any suicide bombings in its modern history (Skaine 2006 158; Hafez 2007). However, since 2003, the number of suicide bombings in that country increased exponentially. In the first three years of the insurgency, nearly 500 suicide attacks occurred in Iraq (Hafez 2007, 89). In 2004 alone, there were more suicide bombings in Iraq than in the entire world within any single year in modern history (Atran 2006b, 130). The suicide bombings campaign in Iraq unfolded amidst major internal crises marked by seemingly irreconcilable sectarian grievances, devastating economic collapse, large-scale social dislocation, and weak political and security structures. The suicide bombing campaign in Iraq differs from similar campaigns in other contexts, such as Lebanon, Sri Lanka, Palestine/Israel, Russia, and Turkey, in that many, if not most perpetrators are not Iraqis, but Muslim volunteers from other countries embracing a religious world view of jihadi Salafism (Hafez 2007, 89).

Strictly speaking, there have been two insurgencies in Iraq: one fought by Islamic nationalists and the other led by jihadi Salafis and ideological Baathists (Hafez 2007). Islamic nationalists pursue the twofold goal of ridding Iraq of the occupying coalition forces and reconfiguring political arrangements so that the power of Sunnis and nominal Baathists will be at least proportionate to that of the Shia and Kurds. The groups representing this category include the Islamic army in Iraq, Mujahidin army in Iraq, 1920 Revolution Brigades of the Islamic and

National Resistance Movement, and Salah al-Din al-Ayoubi Brigades of the Islamic Front of the Iraqi Resistance. They represent nominal Baathist and Sunnis, disgruntled by de-Baathification policies of the occupiers, which dismantled Saddam Hussein's armed forces without compensation and gave ascendancy to Shia and Kurdish groups at the expense of Sunnis. These groups adopted Islam "as the vocabulary of resistance against foreign occupation, not as a vehicle to wage a global jihad against the West" (36). Their emphasis is on strengthening pan-Arab credentials by drawing parallels among resistance struggles in the Arab world. Islamic nationalists direct violence against coalition forces, Iraqi security services, Shia militias, and foreign contractors. They try to avoid direct attacks on civilians, especially Shia civilians, because of their theological beliefs and they seldom employ or advocate suicide attacks.

The second insurgency has been led by the ideological Baathists, or Saddam Hussein's loyalists and jihadi Salafis. Keen on restoring the privileged status they enjoyed under the old regime, the former emphasize the similarities between British and French imperialism, which divided the Arab world arbitrarily without the consent of its people, and the current neo-imperialist occupation of Iraq. Two groups represent the Baathists – Baathists in the Leaders of the Resistance and Liberation, and Muhammad's Army. Their goal is to precipitate a complete state failure in Iraq, which would then afford them an opportunity to reclaim power and reinstall the old regime based on Sunni dominance. To achieve this strategic goal, ideological Baathists made a temporary alliance with jihadi Salafis. The latter are Sunni extremists who view Iraq as part of the Islamic *umma* (nation). Therefore, the U.S.-led invasion of Iraq has been perceived as an invasion against the entire Muslim "holy" land. Their struggle is framed in global terms, and establishing an Islamic state in Iraq is only the first step in their strategy of global jihad. While Baathists and jihadi Salafis are ideologically opposed and tend to pursue radically different long-term objectives, they do share the immediate goal of "overthrowing the new regime through a strategy of public insecurity, economic collapse, and a war of attrition" (Hafez 2007, 48). Ideological Baathists and jihadi Salafis direct violence against coalition forces, Iraqi government officials, security forces and Sunni collaborators, Shia and Kurdish civilians, economic infrastructure, and foreign contractors. The Baathists and jihadi Saalfis employ a range of tactics to achieve a systemic collapse, including the use of suicide bombings.

Generally, the Baathists have not used suicide bombings to the same extent as the jihadi Salafis. However, they formed two suicide brigades – the Fedayeen Saddam and the Faruq Brigades – and were the first ones to use this tactic by dispatching two female suicide perpetrators at the time when Iraq was still under the command of Saddam Hussein's security forces (BBC News 2003). The Arabic TV station Al Jazeera broadcasted videotaped messages from each woman. One of them, wearing a red-checkered keffiyeh, identified herself as "martyrdom-seeker Nour Qaddour Al-Shammari" and swore on the Qur'an "to defend Iraq ... and take revenge from the enemies of the (Islamic) nation, Americans, imperialists, Zionists." The second woman, who identified herself as Wadad Jamil Jassem, stated, "I have devoted myself for Jihad for the sake of God and against American, British and Israeli infidels and to defend the soil of our precious and dear country" (Von Knop 2007, 402). This first attack in Iraq signalled the advent of a growing spate of female suicide bombings that targeted and killed Iraqi and coalition soldiers and police officers, although some were also a manifestation of religious sectarian rivalry that targeted particular religious groups (mostly Shia). Many of these attacks coincided with major military and political developments in Iraq. However, most female suicide attacks in Iraq have taken place after 2004, or nearly two years following the fall of Saddam Hussein's regime, suggesting that the tactic was used primarily by the Salafis (information about major attacks in Iraq is documented in table 2.6). Overall, there has been more than sixty female suicide bombings in Iraq. They account for about 25 per cent of all female suicide bombings (Davis 2013, 281, 286).

Most female suicide bombers remain unidentified, with organizations rarely taking responsibility for the attacks. In 2003, Al Qaeda claimed to have established a female suicide squad. A woman allegedly in charge of the unit, self-identified as Umm Osama (mother of Osama) stated, in her 12 March 2003 interview to a London-based Arabic newspaper *A-Sharq Al Awsat*, that Al Qaeda, inspired by the successes of Chechen and Palestinian female martyrs, was setting up women-only training camps for female mujahedeens affiliated with Al Qaeda and the Taliban (Foden 2003). Nevertheless, observers agree that contemporary female suicide bombings are not typical of the entire Al Qaeda movement. In fact, Al Qaeda, which has been in existence since 1989 (Atran 2006b, 134), is known to have advised its male members to

Table 2.6. Female Suicide Bombings in Iraq

Date	Features of the attack	Victims	Location
15 April 2003	Two unidentified women, one allegedly pregnant, detonated a car bomb at a U.S. checkpoint. The attack occurred during the U.S.-led invasion of Iraq before the fall of Saddam Hussein's government.	3 coalition soldiers + 2 bombers killed, 0 injured	Checkpoint northwest of Baghdad
28 September 2005	An unidentified woman, disguised as a man, detonated an explosive belt filled with metal balls at the army and police recruitment centre. The Malik Suicidal Brigades, affiliated with Al Qaeda in Iraq, was reportedly behind the attack.	At least 5 killed, up to 57 injured	Tal Afar, Iraqi Army recruitment centre, northern Iraq
11 October 2005	A car bomb was detonated by a female suicide bomber at a U.S. military patrol site. Little information is available about this attack.	Unknown	Mosul, northern Iraq
9 November 2005	Muriel Degauque (38), recruited by the Moroccan Islamic Combatant Group, detonated a car bomb at a U.S. military patrol site.	1 bomber dead, 1 soldier injured	North of Baghdad
6 December 2005	Two unidentified women detonated strapped-on explosives at the police academy. The women were said to have been students at the academy. The first bomb exploded in the cafeteria, the second was detonated during the school's roll call.	29, including the bomber, killed, 32 injured	Baghdad
4 May 2006	A woman, who was denied entry into a courthouse, left her suicide vest in a bag outside the building.	10 killed, including the bomber, 46 injured	Baghdad
25 February 2007	An unidentified woman detonated an explosive vest studded with ball bearings at a mostly Shiite college of economy and administration, Mustansiriya University.	At least 41 killed, including the bomber, 55 injured	Baghdad
10 April 2007	An unidentified woman detonated an explosive vest at the gate of a police station in a crowd of 200 policemen. The town of Muqdadiyah is mostly Sunni.	17 killed, including the bomber, 33 injured	Muqdadiyah, Diyala province
23 July 2007	An unidentified woman detonated an explosive belt at a checkpoint. For more about her story, see Ghosh (2008).	3–8 killed, 10 injured	Ramadi, Al Anbar province
27 November 2007	A female bomber detonated an explosive belt, targeting a U.S. army foot patrol.	1 bomber killed, 12 injured	Baquba, Diyala province

(continued)

Table 2.6. Female Suicide Bombings in Iraq (Continued)

Date	Features of the attack	Victims	Location
7 December 2007	A female suicide bomber targeted a group of former Sunni insurgents, who had switched sides to join security forces helping the United States. The attack took place outside the Diyala assembly building used by the 1920 Revolutionary Brigades, on a crowded street before Friday prayers. The woman was reported to have been a member of Saddam Hussein's Baath Party. Reportedly, she was targeting one of the so-called Awakening Councils – militia that supported U.S. forces and the new Iraqi government in fighting Al Qaeda.	17 killed, 18–27 injured	Muqdadiya, Diyala province
31 December 2007	A female suicide bomber blew herself up at a checkpoint.	1 bomber killed, 5–9 injured	Baquba, Diyala province
2 January 2008	A woman exploded a suicide vest at a checkpoint, killing tribal chief Abu Sajad, a leader of the local Awakening Council.	2 killed, including a bomber	Baquba, Diayala province
16 January 2008	A woman detonated an explosive belt near a Shiite mosque and a market in a small town of Khan Bani Saad (Al-Qaeda in Iraq was suspected of planning the attack). The attack occurred during preparations for a religious holiday.	9–12 killed, 7–18 wounded	Diyala province
29 January 2008	A female suicide bombing occurred in a line at a checkpoint. The U.S. army denied that there was an attack.	3 killed, at least 5 injured	Baghdad
1 February 2008	Two unidentified women blew themselves up at a popular al-Ghazl animal market; the United States attributed the attacks to Al-Qaeda in Iraq. Explosives were set off by remote control. Iraqi authorities and American representatives stated that the suicide bombers were mentally handicapped, but this was debated later.	At least 100 killed, 200 injured	Baghdad
17 February 2008	A female suicide bombing in an electrical shop at a mostly Shia area in Baghdad.	4 killed, 10–12 injured	Baghdad
10 March 2008	A female suicide bomber targeted a prominent Sunni chief, Thaer Saggban al-Karkhi, the head of a local brigade working with U.S. forces. He was killed along with his 5-year-old niece and bodyguards.	5 killed, 2 injured	Kanaan, southeast of Baquba, Diyala province

(continued)

Table 2.6. Female Suicide Bombings in Iraq (Continued)

Date	Features of the attack	Victims	Location
17 March 2008	Accounts ranged from explosives strapped to a female suicide bomber to a bomb planted in the area. The attack targeted Shiite worshippers in the Imam Hussein shrine. The area was tightly secured. U.S. Vice-President Dick Cheney was visiting Baghdad at the time.	At least 43 killed, 58 injured	Karbala, south of Baghdad
19 March 2008	A woman detonated an explosive vest loaded with ball bearings at a bus terminal. The attack occurred near an organization that arranges religious pilgrimages and close to a police patrol.	5 killed, 12 injured	Balad Ruz, Diyala province
21 April 2008	A female suicide bomber blew herself up at the entrance of the office of Sons of Iraq, targeting a local brigade that was working with U.S. forces.	5 killed, 4 injured	Baquba, Diyala province
22 April 2008	A female suicide bombing occurred at the entrance to the police station in Jalawla, east of Baquba.	7 killed, 12 injured	Diyala province
27 April 2008	A female suicide attack occurred at a checkpoint close to a mostly Shiite area.	4 killed, 14 injured	Baghdad
29 April 2008	A female suicide bombing took place at a bus stop.	2 killed, 5 injured	Muqdadiyah, Diyala province
29 April 2008	A female suicide bomber targeted a local anti-Al-Qaeda group.	3 killed, 5–10 injured	Mukhisa, Diyala province
1 May 2008	Two attackers – a man, and a woman feigning pregnancy – detonated explosives in the midst of a wedding procession, targeting members of the Sunni Awakening Council, which was working with U.S. forces.	At least 36 killed, 65 injured	Balad Ruz
15 May 2008	A female suicide bomber targeted Sunni members of an anti-Al-Qaida brigade at an army position. The explosives were said to have been detonated remotely. Al-Qaeda in Mesopotamia was suspected of ordering the attack.	2 killed, 7 injured	Yusufiya
17 May 2008	A female suicide bomber targeted the house of an anti-al-Qaida brigade, the Sons of Iraq, which was working with U.S. forces.	2 killed, 16 injured	Diyala province
17 May 2008	A female suicide bomber targeted Iraqi security sorces.	1 bomber killed, 7 injured	Diyala province

(continued)

Table 2.6. Female Suicide Bombings in Iraq (Continued)

Date	Features of the attack	Victims	Location
20 May 2008	A female suicide bomber targeted a neighbourhood police station that sided with U.S. forces.	2 killed, 7 injured	Rutba
20 May 2008	A female suicide bomber targeted the house of a police chief, Sheikh Mutlib al-Nidawi, the head of the U.S.-backed neighbourhood police of Mandili. The chief survived the attack.	2 killed, 3 injured	Mandili
7 June 2008	A female suicide bombing occurred at the Al Bobali police station.	2 killed, 6 injured	Khalidiyah
14 June 2008	A female suicide attack in a marketplace targeted sports fans as they left a cafe where they were watching a soccer game between the Iraqi national team and China. The area comprises mainly Kurds and Shiite Turkomen.	1 bomber killed, 29–34 injured	Qara Tappa, Diyala province
22 June 2008	A female suicide bomber blew herself up at the entrance of a local government and law courts complex. Sunni insurgents with links to Al-Qaeda in Mesopotamia were suspected of planning this attack.	16 killed, at least 39 injured	Baquba, Diyala province
29 June 2008	A female suicide bomber was shot on the road near a town council building in Wajihiya before she was able to detonate her bomb, but the shot triggered the explosion.	1 bomber killed, 1 injured	Diyala province
7 July 2008	A female detonated her explosive belt in a marketplace. Officials suspected that Al-Qaeda directed the attack.	10 killed, 12 injured	Baquba, Diyala province
24 July 2008	A woman detonated an explosive belt at a checkpoint, targeting members of the Awakening Council brigade, which was working with U.S. forces.	9 killed, 24 injured	Baquba, Diyala province
27 July 2008	A female suicide bomber detonated an explosive vest studded with nails at a provincial headquarters building. The blast targeted Kurds who were protesting a new election law. The U.S. army denied that the attack was carried out by a woman.	At least 25 killed, 185 injured	Kirkuk
27 July 2008	Three women, led by Umm Ahmed, detonated two explosive vests and a bomb in a bag (the bomb was left in the women's tent) in three different locations: near the National Theatre; a tent for female marchers; and between two traffic checkpoints. The attackers targeted Shiite Muslim pilgrims heading for the Kadhimiya shrine.	27–31 killed, at least 62–90 injured	Karrada neighbour-hood of central Baghdad

(continued)

Table 2.6. Female Suicide Bombings in Iraq (Continued)

Date	Features of the attack	Victims	Location
11 August 2008	A woman detonated an explosive belt near a police station in a marketplace.	2 killed, 13–17 injured	Baquba, Diyala province
12 August 2008	A woman detonated her explosive vest, targeting an Iraq army convoy. The attack narrowly missed the provincial governor of Diyala, Raad Rashid al-Tamimi. The Islamic State of Iraq, a group linked to Al-Qaeda in Iraq, was suspected of directing the attack.	3 killed, 7 injured	Baquba, Diyala province
14 August 2008	A woman detonated an explosive belt loaded with metal ball bearings at a Shiite pilgrimage site. The attack took place in a resting tent.	19 killed, 68–75 injured	Iskandariya
15 September 2008	A female suicide attack occurred while police officers were holding Iftar, the meal that breaks Ramadan fasting.	At least 21 killed, 30 injured	Balad Ruz, Diyala province
8 October 2008	The female attack near a courthouse was intended as a double suicide bombing, but a man failed to detonate his explosives. Iraq army vehicles were targeted. Al-Qaeda in Mesopotamia was suspected of planning this attack.	12 killed, 19 injured	Baquba, Diyala province
17 October 2008	A would-be female suicide bomber was shot at a checkpoint before she was able to detonate the bomb she was carrying, but the shot activated the explosion.	1 bomber killed, 5 injured	Dhuluiya
9 November 2008	A female suicide bomber detonated explosives in an emergency room in the Amiriat Al-Falluja hospital. Falluja is a mainly Sunni town and a former symbol of the Sunni insurgency.	4 killed, 7 injured	Falluja, Anbar province
10 November 2008	A female suicide bomber targeted Sunni members of the Awakening Council Brigade, which was working with U.S. forces. A local brigade leader was killed.	5 killed, 15–18 injured	
24 November 2008	A female suicide bombing occurred at the entrance of the U.S.-protected Green Zone days before a vote was to be taken in the Green Zone on whether or not American forces would stay in Iraq until 2011. It was one of 3 attacks in Baghdad on the same day.	6 killed, 12 injured	Baghdad
15 December 2008	A female suicide bomber targeted the leader of a local patrol group cooperating with U.S. forces. The leader was killed, and the leader's son was wounded.	2 killed, 1 injured	Unknown
4 January 2009	A woman detonated her explosive vest, targeting Iranian pilgrims in a Shiite neighbourhood.	39 killed, 65 injured	Baghdad

(continued)

Table 2.6. Female Suicide Bombings in Iraq (Continued)

Date	Features of the attack	Victims	Location
13 February 2009	Al-Qaeda in Iraq was suspected of being behind the female suicide attack in a women's tent on a pilgrimage route in Iskandariya. The attack targeted Shiite worshippers.	41 killed, up to 84 injured	Iskandariya
23 April 2009	Baathist and jihadi militants were suspected of orchestrating a female suicide bombing at a food distribution site for war-affected Iraqis. The bomber was waiting in line while holding the hand of an unidentified 5-year-old girl.	29 killed, 50 injured	Baghdad
24 April 2009	A coordinated attack by two female suicide bombers targeted Shia pilgrims on the way to the Moussa al-Kadhim shrine. The women are believed to have used side streets to avoid security checks and entered the shrine from two different gates. No group claimed responsibility.	At least 75 killed	Baghdad
1 February 2010	A woman detonated an explosive belt amidst Shia pilgrims on the way to Karbala for the religious rite of Arbaeen.	At least 54 killed, over 100 injured	Baghdad
12 February 2010	A female suicide bomber detonated explosives amidst pilgrims on the way to Najaf. The attack was possibly linked to the parliamentary elections a month later.	4 killed, 10 injured	Kufa
4 July 2010	A female suicide bomber detonated explosives inside the provincial government building after leaving the deputy governor's office. U.S. Vice-President Joe Biden was visiting Iraq at the time.	4 killed, over 20 injured	Ramadi

exclude women from its membership and even condemned women's active participation in violent jihadist struggles (Sjoberg and Gentry 2007, 124). Since the 9/11 attacks, however, some of the Al Qaeda–affiliated organizations have changed their position regarding women for strategic reasons, developed the intellectual basis for removing religious obstacles to inclusion of female jihadis, and have begun to recruit, train, and operationalize female militants (Cunningham 2008, 92).

Female suicide bombings were reportedly a strategy specific to Abu Mus'ab Al-Zarqawi (until his death in June 2006) and his Al Qaeda in the Land of the Two Rivers (or Al Qaeda in Iraq) or allied Ansar al-Sunna. Since October 2006 Al-Zarqawi's group, also known after Zarqawi's death and merger with several smaller groups as the Islamic State of Iraq (ISI), has been allegedly responsible for most of the known female suicide attacks in Iraq, and has officially taken responsibility for several incidents.

In 2008, U.S. forces confirmed the death of two members of the Al Qaeda in Iraq group who orchestrated several female suicide bombings in the Diyala River Valley and Baghdad. Arkan Khalaf Khudayyir, a senior intelligence officer of Al Qaeda in Iraq, and Abu Ghazwan, the leader of Al Qaeda in Iraq's network in the regions north of Baghdad, were reported killed during raids by the U.S. and Iraqi forces. Moreover, in January 2009, Iraqi security forces detained Samira Jassim, who admitted to recruiting, indoctrinating, and training eighty women, of whom twenty-eight actually carried out suicide bombings for Ansar Al Sunnah (Roggio 2009). Salafis' preferential mobilization strategies rely heavily on the utilization of the web, especially message boards and the online magazine *Al-Khansaa*, and are geared towards recruiting female jihadis. The magazine assumes the position that women and men are equally obligated by jihad, suggesting that a woman does not have to ask permission of her husband or father to carry out an act of martyrdom (Cunningham 2008, 93).

In 2005, Al Qaeda in Iraq's female operatives were involved in a series of four suicide bombings. The first of these attacks coincided with American counter-insurgency in northern Iraq. In August 2005 the 3rd Armoured Cavalry Regiment and Iraqi forces began to make major gains in destroying the insurgency in and around the city of Tal Afar. In response, Al Qaeda in Iraq unleashed a spate of suicide bombings, six of which occurred on 14 September. Concurrently, Zarqawi issued a declaration of war against the Shia, indicating among other things that "the battles for revenge started all over the land of the two rivers. The raid for avenging the Sunni in Tal Afar has started" (quoted in Hafez 2007, 99). On 28 September a female suicide bomber disguised as a man detonated explosives at the US military recruitment centre in Tal Afar (Associated Press 2005). This specific target was chosen because it was a meeting place for converted volunteers. The Al Qaeda–affiliated Malik Suicidal Brigades claimed responsibility for the attack: "A blessed sister ... carried out a heroic act defending her faith. May God accept our sister among the martyrs" (Von Knop 2007, 402). Little is known about the 11 October attack in Mosul, including the number of casualties. However, it occurred almost in synchronicity with a major political event in Iraq in 2005 – a referendum on ratification of the proposed constitution.

The 9 November 2005 female suicide bombing was the first known female suicide attack by a European convert in Iraq. A thirty-eight-year-old Belgian woman, Muriel Degauque, allegedly recruited into the Moroccan Islamic Combatant Group, killed only herself and wounded one soldier (BBC News 2007a). Degauque, who was raised as a Roman Catholic in a Charleroi suburb near Brussels, converted to Islam after marrying a Moroccan Muslim, Issam Goris, in Belgium. Allegedly she was drawn to the cause after her husband was killed by U.S. soldiers in a separate incident (CNN 2005). That same day, three Iraqi male suicide bombers carried out coordinated attacks in Amman, Jordan. The Jordanian authorities arrested a fourth would-be suicide bomber, identified as Sajida Mubarak Atrous al-Rishawi, who was married to one of the bombers and claimed to be a sister of Al-Zarqawi's close aide (Von Knop 2007, 403).

The year 2007 saw a sharp increase in suicide bombings in Iraq, many of which targeted members of U.S.-backed local groups, police, and army patrols. Three of these attacks took place in the province of Diyala, which has special significance for Iraqi insurgents, having been designated by Al-Zarqawi as the capital of the future Islamic caliphate in the country (Associated Press 2007; India eNews.com 2007; Reuters 2007b; CNN 2007). Iraq's experience with female suicide bombings deepened in 2008, when thirty-nine female suicide bombers killed at least 363 people and wounded 974 in thirty-six attacks – the largest number of female suicide bombings in a single year. Most of these attacks targeted U.S. and Iraqi army personnel and police and their associates, as well as large religious gatherings of either Shiite or Sunni Iraqi Muslims. One of these attacks was clearly intended as a political assassination, targeting the provincial governor of Diyala, Raad Rashid al-Tamimi (Reuters 2008; Multi-National Corps – Iraq 2008). The Islamic State of Iraq was suspected of performing the assassination attempt on al-Tamimi. Two attacks that did not fit this pattern occurred in June and July 2008 and were linked to the Kurdish struggle. The first attack in June targeted largely civilian sport fans watching a soccer game between the Iraqi national team and China (CNN 2008). The attack took place at a crowded marketplace in Qara Tappa in Diyala province, when the fans were leaving a cafe after watching the historic game. The background to this attack is considered to be sectarian, as Qara Tappa is home to largely Kurdish and Shiite Turkmen (ibid.). An attack on July 27 targeted Kurds protesting a new election law in Kirkuk in northern Iraq. It was the second female suicide bombing against the largely Kurdish population in two months. At least 25 people and the bomber died in this attack, while 185 were wounded (Associated Press 2008).

No organization took direct responsibility for the attacks in 2009, but U.S. authorities voiced concerns that Baathist and jihadi militants were attempting to reassert themselves before the U.S. withdrawal from Iraq (Williams 2009). It is also speculated that another reason for these attacks was to reignite sectarian warfare on the eve of the U.S. withdrawal from that country (*USA Today* 2009).

The trajectory of female suicide bombings in Iraq conforms to the general patterns of suicide bombings in this country: the instances of female suicide bombings are timed with major counter-insurgent campaigns and/or political developments. They cause an increasing death toll among the targeted groups and are employed mostly by the jihadi Salafis as an instrument of igniting sectarian violence and undermining the state. In 2009, Iraq was listed sixth on the Failed States Index: a daunting finding amidst Iraq's deepening civil strife. The instances of female suicide attacks continued in Iraq in 2010.

Uzbekistan

The geographical location of female suicide bombings linked to jihadi groups was not confined solely to Iraq. In March 2004 several female operatives, who were veiled and spoke a language unknown to the locals, carried out a series of suicide bombings in Uzbekistan that claimed at least fifty lives. Among the perpetrators was nineteen-year-old Dilnoza Holmuradova, who detonated explosives at Tashkent's Chorsu market. Dilnoza was a computer programmer who enrolled at the Tashkent police academy in 2001. Besides her native Uzbek and Russian, Dilnoza also spoke English, Turkish, and Arabic. She was a devout Muslim who began her study of religious studies in 2002. Her elder sister, Shahnoza Holmuradova, is said to have gone missing the day of the suicide attacks. Another female suicide bomber, identified as twenty-six-year-old Zahro Turaeva, graduated from the University of Technology and was employed in a government office for architecture and construction (Ramachandran 2004). The prevailing assumption is that the Islamic Jihad Group, a radical offshoot of the Islamic Movement of Uzbekistan, and/or Hizb ut-Tahrir, which is seeking establishment of a caliphate in Central Asia, were involved in these attacks. Following the 11 September 2001 attacks on the United States, Uzbekistan provided an airbase for U.S. military operations in Afghanistan. The Uzbek government asserted that the female suicide bombings were meant to undermine Uzbekistan's support for the U.S.-led campaign in Afghanistan (Bloom 2007, 132) and accused religious extremists, including the Islamic Movement of Uzbekistan and Hizb ut-Tahrir, of masterminding the attacks. Without excluding the possibility of involvement by any of these organizations, some observers suggest that the attacks could have been linked directly to Al Qaeda (Knox and Kimmage 2004).

Pakistan

In 2007, the practice of female suicide bombings migrated to Pakistani territory. The first, little-known attack at the *Nation* newspaper office in Karachi, resulted in the deaths of at least five civilians and the female perpetrator (BBC News 2007b). The attack, commonly referenced in the Pakistani media as the first, however, took place on 4 December 2007, inciting suspicions about the existence of a female wing of Tehreeq-e-Taliban Pakistan. A day before the attack, pro-Taliban militants captured six Pakistani security officials and blew up their checkpoint. This led some observers to suggest that the target of the attack was possibly a military checkpoint. The woman was stopped by troops who suspected that she might have been an Afghan refugee. Rather than subjecting herself to interrogation, she detonated an explosive device that was strapped to her body, killing only herself and wounding none (ibid.). Interestingly, there was a different attack in October 2007 in Bannu by a man wearing a burqa, which initially led the authorities to believe that a woman carried out the bombing. Both attacks occurred during an upsurge of violence as the Pakistani militaries launched a fierce campaign against the sympathizers of the Taliban, operating from the border region of Pakistan and Afghanistan, mostly Khyber-Pakhtunkhwa province, and various militant groups, such as Tehreeq-e-Taliban Pakistan, unleashed violence in reprisal for Pakistan's support for the U.S. *munafiqeen* (infidel) actions in Afghanistan (see table 2.7).

Table 2.7. Female Suicide Bombings in Pakistan

Date	Features of the attack	Victims	Location
4 December 2007	An unidentified woman (30s–40s) in a burqa blew herself up near a Christian missionary school and a military checkpoint. Allegedly she was an Afghan woman and the detonation was triggered by remote control.	1 bomber killed	Peshawar
15 October 2009	At a military compound, three women were allegedly part of a militant suicide squad that launched an attack on the compound killing 37 people. The Taliban-aligned Amjad Farooqi group, a little-known organization named after a Punjabi militant linked with al-Qaeda, claimed responsibility. This is particularly significant because the Taliban operating in northwest Pakistan normally does not allow women to walk out of their homes unaccompanied by a male, much less train as suicide bombers.	37 killed	Lahore
17 October 2009	A woman joined two male militants in a suicide mission that targeted a police building used by the CIA. The Taliban claimed responsibility for that attack.	At least 11 killed	Peshawar
25 December 2010	A veiled female suicide bomber breached security and detonated explosives in a queue of people waiting to receive aid distributed by the World Food Program at a UN food station. She hurled a grenade before detonating the explosive-laden vest. The Taliban claimed responsibility, confirming the attack targeted members of the Salarzai tribe who support Pakistani military actions against the Taliban. The organization also stated that it had a large number of women bombers who would carry out more attacks.	46 killed, over 100 injured	Town of Khar, Bajaur region
10 May 2011	A female suicide bomber detonated explosives at the entrance to a court.	3 killed, 7 injured	Nowshera, east of Peshawar
25 June 2011	A woman and an Uzbek man, allegedly married, entered the police station, both dressed in burqas. Following a 5-hour standoff, when they took the policemen hostage, the couple blew themselves up. The Taliban claimed responsibility.	12 killed, unknown number injured	Kolachi, Dera Ismail Khan district, northwestern Pakistan

(continued)

Table 2.7. Female Suicide Bombings in Pakistan (Continued)

Date	Features of the attack	Victims	Location
11 August 2011	A female suicide bomber (about 17), dressed like a bride, targeted a police checkpoint in a coordinated double attack. Allegedly, she shouted, "God is great," threw a grenade, and pressed the trigger. Her vest failed to explode properly. The Taliban claimed responsibility.	2 killed, 17 injured	Peshawar
19 November 2012	An Uzbek female suicide bomber targeted Jamaat-e-Islami chief Qazi Hussain Ahmed. Ahmed was unhurt, but died on 6 January 2013 of cardiac arrest.	Unknown number of casualties	Mohmand
20 April 2013	An female bomber (18) detonated explosives at the main entrance of a government-run hospital. Allegedly she targeted security personnel. No group claimed responsibility. The Taliban were suspected to be behind the attack.	4 killed, 4 injured	Town of Khar, Bajaur region
15 June 2013	A burqa-clad woman detonated explosives while on board a Sardar Bahadur Khan Women's University bus. Lashkar-e-Jhangvi claimed responsibility.	At least 15 killed	Quetta

Afghanistan

After 2001, Afghanistan experienced a barrage of suicide bombings, by some accounts as many as 500. Until later that decade, none was carried out by a woman, although it was common for male suicide bombers dispatched by the Taliban to disguise themselves in burqas. Shortly after female suicide bombings were introduced in Pakistan, this violent practice spilled to Afghanistan. Indeed, Afghanistan's first encounter with female suicide bombers may have happened in 2007, when an elderly woman was arrested on 24 December 2007 carrying a waistcoat filled with explosives under her burqa, and detained for questioning (Reuters 2007a). It was unclear whether she intended to carry out an attack or was simply delivering the bomb. Hence, there is some hesitancy to declare her Afghanistan's first female suicide bomber. In 2008 there was a confirmed case of the first instance of female suicide bombing in Afghanistan, thus proving earlier allegations that females were beginning to play a direct violent role in Taliban insurgency in Afghanistan (see table 2.8). In 2007, twelve-year-old Ma Gul communicated to Afghan authorities about the girl suicide bombing squad training camp on the Afghan-Pakistan border. At the time, her story was dismissed, but four years later Taliban insurgents gave a bag packed with explosives to an eight-year old girl. The bomb detonated prematurely, killing the girl (Jalal 2013). Since that incident, two other Afghan female suicide bombers were apprehended before setting off on their missions. In July 2008, a would-be female suicide bomber was arrested by U.S. troops in central Afghanistan before she had the chance to detonate her explosives. Allegedly, during interrogation she admitted that she was actually from Multan, Pakistan, and entered Afghanistan along with three associates with the intention to carry out a suicide attack (Thaindian News 2008).

There are many reasons why female suicide bombings became part of the insurgency in Iraq, Pakistan, and Afghanistan, despite cultural and historical norms that prevent women's activism in the public sphere, let alone political violence. Some have to do with the tactical advantages and ideological adaptations. Others have been conditioned by the culture of martyrdom fuelled by a plethora of socio-economic and political grievances within the violent context of insurgency and foreign occupation.

Table 2.8. Female Suicide Bombings in Afghanistan

Date	Features of the attack	Victims	Location
15 May 2008	An unknown woman associated with the Taliban detonated a strapped-on explosive device in front of a police station in a market. The Taliban claimed responsibility for the attack, saying that a police commander was the main target.	At least 16 killed, 22 injured	Farah, Dilaram district
29 October 2009	A burqa-clad female suicide bomber (20s) detonated explosives at a female-only bus stop outside the National Directorate of Security.	7 injured	Asadabad, Kunar province
21 June 2010	Bibi Halima blew herself up at a checkpoint manned by American and Afghan forces. A senior Al Qaeda and Taliban commander, Qari Zia Rahman, claimed responsibility.	3 killed, 20 injured	Kunar province

(continued)

Table 2.8. Female Suicide Bombings in Afghanistan (Continued)

Date	Features of the attack	Victims	Location
4 June 2011	A woman detonated herself, targeting a convoy of foreign troops.	4 killed	Marawara district, Kunar province
26 June 2011	Taliban insurgents gave a bag of explosives to a girl (8). The explosives detonated before she reached the police outpost.	1 killed	Char Chino district, province of Uruzgan
29 October 2011	A female suicide bomber raised suspicion of the guards when attempting to enter the Afghan National Directorate for Security building. She blew herself up after the guards opened fire. Allegedly she was one of two female suicide bombers. The second managed to escape.	At least 1 killed, 7 injured	Asadabad, Kunar province
18 September 2012	A female suicide bomber, allegedly named Fatima (22), drove an explosive-laden vehicle into a minibus with mostly foreign airport workers, allegedly in retaliation for a film mocking the Prophet Mohammad. Hizb-e-Islami (Islamic Party) claimed responsibility.	13 killed, 11 injured	Kabul

Somalia

There were only two reported instances of female suicide bombings in Somalia. On 4 April 2012 Somalia's Al Qaeda–linked jihadi group Harakat Al Shabaab al-Mujahideen, commonly known as Al-Shabaab, staged the first female suicide bombing at a public ceremony in Mogadishu (Pflanz 2012). The group's deployment of an actual female perpetrator came nearly three years after it experimented with disguising male suicide bombers as women to increase the effectiveness of the attacks (Mukasa 2009). In 2011, *Somalia Report* revealed that some seventy women in a coastal town of Marka, south of Mogadishu, trained to become suicide bombers at Al Shabaab military camp, locally known as Alhayaa (the Life) (Ahmed 2011). Formally, the 2012 ceremony was organized to celebrate the first anniversary of the launch of a national satellite television station. Government officials, including the prime minister and members of parliament, were in attendance. In a country ravaged by over two decades of civil war, this public celebration had a deeper symbolic meaning. It signalled a return to normal life after the expulsion of al-Shabaab from Mogadishu in 2011. The explosion occurred in a newly reopened National Theatre at the moment when Prime Minister Abdiweli Mohamed Ali took the podium. At least ten people, including the head of Somalia's Olympic Committee and Football Federation, and a well-known female playwright, were killed in an attack. Nearly three years later, Al Shabaab claimed responsibility for the twin male and female suicide bombing at Mogadishu's luxury Central Hotel, near the presidential palace and frequented by government ministers and politicians. According to different sources, six to twenty-five people died in this attack carried out by Dutch-Somali citizens. The Somali National Intelligence and Security Agency identified the woman perpetrator as Lula Ahmed Dahir. She worked part-time in the hotel for a few months prior to setting off an explosives vest inside the hotel's prayer room.

Syria

The only female suicide bombing in Syria is not part of a global jihadi movement, but rather an act of violence against it. The bombing was carried out by a Kurdish female fighter in the context of Syria's fight against Islamic State, a jihadi militant group that through mergers and shifting affiliations metamorphosed over the years from Jama'at al-Tawhid wal-Jihad into Al Qaeda in Iraq to become the Islamic State of Iraq and the Levant (ISIL) and the Islamic State of Iraq and Syria (ISIS). The group declared itself a worldwide caliphate in 2014. IS actively participated in the Syrian civil war, which began in March 2011 when pro-democracy demonstrations were brutally crushed by government forces. As early as January 2012, IS established the affiliate in Syria called al-Nusra Front. The Front enjoys a reputation of one of the best-trained and most effective militant groups in Syria and has been instrumental in establishing extremist groups' territorial control, especially the seizure of the provincial capital of Idlib in northwestern Syria. In the north near the Turkish border, a Kurdish group called the Kurdish Popular Protection Units, or People's Defence Units (YPG), has been fighting IS. At stake for the Kurds is the fate of the autonomous region they established in 2013 after the Syrian government lost control of the territory. On 5 October 2014, as fierce battles raged between the Kurds and IS over the town of Kobane and the strategic Mistenur hilltop east of Kobane, a Kurdish female fighter carried out a suicide attack, killing an unknown number of IS fighters. The fighter was identified as Arin Mirkan, who was allegedly a commander of the YPG. Her act is the only known female suicide bombing in Syria.

Turkey

Istanbul was hit by a female suicide bomber on 6 January 2015. The woman entered a police station in the historic Sultanahmet Square, purportedly to report a lost wallet, and then she set the bomb off. One police officer was killed and another one injured in the attack. Turkish media reported the bomber's identity as Diana Ramazova, a Russian citizen from the Republic of Dagestan. Ramazova was the widow of Abu Edelbijev, a Norwegian citizen of Chechen origin, who died in Syria in December 2014 fighting for ISIS/ISIL. In 2014, the couple spent a few months in Istanbul before travelling to Syria. Ramazova returned to Turkey on 26 December 2014, less than two weeks before blowing herself up in Istanbul's popular tourist district (Atilla 2015).

Nigeria and Cameroon

In 2014 and 2015 female suicide bombings, unprecedented in frequency, became the feature of violent insurgency waged by a Nigeria-based jihadist group, Islamic State's West African Province (ISWAP), formerly Jama'atu Ahlis Sunna Lidda'awati wal-Jihad (People committed to the propagation of the Prophet's teachings and jihad), more commonly known as Boko Haram. In the Hausa language, Boko Haram means "Western education is forbidden." Founded in 2002, this radical Islamist group promotes an interpretation of Islam that forbids Muslims to participate in any socio-political activities associated with the West. This includes voting in elections or receiving secular education. In 2009, Boko Haram launched an insurgency in northeastern Nigeria to create an Islamist state. In August 2014, the group's leader, Abubakar Shekau, announced the creation of a caliphate, and in March 2015 the group swore allegiance to IS/ISIS, which declared the creation of a caliphate in parts of Iraq and Syria, changing its name to ISWAP. The insurgency has had far-reaching security and humanitarian consequences. It affected some three million people in Nigeria, causing about 15,000 deaths, and became a regional crisis when Boko Haram increased cross-border raids in neighbouring Cameroon and Chad. The escalation and expansion of

Boko Haram's violence prompted the African Union to dispatch in early 2015 a Multinational Joint Task Force with troops contributed by Cameroon, Chad, Niger, Nigeria, and Benin. Boko Haram has also influenced important political events in Nigeria. A presidential election, scheduled to be held in mid-February 2015, was postponed for six weeks in response to increased violence by Boko Haram. The group's declared goal was to create conditions to remove the previous Nigerian president, Goodluck Jonathan, a Christian from the South, from office. The newly elected president, Mohammadu Buhari, vowed to end the rebellion during his election campaign. One of his first measures as a president was to move a military command centre from the capital, Abuja, to Maiduguri in Borno State, which is a birthplace of Boko Haram. In response, Boko Haram increased the spate of violence, including suicide bombings.

While religion appears to be a strong motivator for Boko Haram recruits, some security analysts, such as Nigeria-based Bawa Abdullahi Wase and South Africa–based Martin Ewi, point to the socio-economic conditions and monetary incentives. In a country where job opportunities are scarce and poverty is on the rise, many Nigerians with university degrees join the group to fight the government (Clothia 2014). Boko Haram is credited with introducing suicide bombings in sub-Saharan Africa. The first female suicide attack occurred on 8 June 2014. A month later, a spokesperson for the Nigerian military announced that Boko Haram created a women's wing to collect intelligence and recruite wives for the fighters. Yet four female suicide bombings between 27 and 30 July clearly indicated the expanding range of responsibilities for female recruits of Boko Haram. On 30 July 2014 Nigerian police stopped a car at a roadblock in Funtua, Katsina state, west of Kano, and found a ten-year-old girl with explosives strapped to her body, accompanied by her eighteen-year-old sister and an older man. The following day, the media reported that Boko Haram trained some 177 girls under the age of fifteen to become suicide bombers, with 75 already in Nigeria (Pearson 2014). In August 2014, the Nigerian government confirmed the arrest of a man identified as Ibrahim Ibrahim alleged to be a trainer of female suicide bombers for Boko Haram. In December, a vigilante group apprehended a suspected female suicide bomber at the entrance of the University of Maiduguri, who revealed that Boko Haram deployed more than fifty female suicide attackers throughout Maiduguri (Magdaleno 2014). On 25 December 2014 journalists received a rare opportunity to interview Zahharau Babangida, a failed thirteen-year-old girl suicide bomber, who, along along with her mother, was handed to Boko Haram jihadists by her father (Ahmad 2014).

The identities and exact age of the Nigerian female suicide bombers are unknown; however, eyewitnesses claim that in about a dozen cases the attackers were between seven and seventeen years old. Some of these girls were believed to be abandoned children begging on the streets, others were thought to be the children of Boko Haram members, still others might have been children kidnapped by Boko Haram militants. Notably, in April 2014 about 200 female students were abducted from a school in Chibok, Borno state. Some of the girls escaped, but others are believed to have been trained as suicide bombers. In a May 2015 press release, UNICEF expressed concern about the alarming spike in the frequency and intensity of suicide bombings involving women and children (see table 2.9). The agency estimates that some 743,000 children have been left without homes by the conflict, with some 10,000 separated from their families (UNICEF 2015).

Table 2.9. Female Suicide Bombings in Nigeria and Cameroon

Date	Features of the attack	Victims	Location
8 June 2014	A middle-aged woman riding a motorcycle towards the 301 Battalion barracks of Nigerian Army was stopped at a checkpoint, where she detonated her explosives.	1 killed	Gombe, Gombe state, Nigeria
25 June 2014	A female suicide bomber parked a car next to a gasoline tanker in Apapa district of Lagos beside a fuel depot, then blew herself up.	Unknown	Lagos, Nigeria
27 July 2014	A teenage girl (about 15) blew herself up at a university campus.	1 bomber killed, 5 injured	Kano, Kano state, Nigeria
28 July 2014	A young woman detonated explosives while waiting in a kerosene line at a filling station.	3 killed, 16 injured	Kano, Kano state, Nigeria
28 July 2014	A teenage girl exploded her device at a shopping centre and trade fair complex.	6 injured	Kano, Kano state, Nigeria
30 July 2014	A teenager exploded herself in a crowd of students near the notice board at a college campus.	6 killed, unknown number injured	Kano, Kano state, Nigeria
7 November 2014	A female suicide bomber detonated explosive while waiting in a line to make cash withdrawals from a bank.	20 killed, over 37 injured	Azare town, Bauchi state, Nigeria
12 November 2014	A female suicide bomber blew herself up at the Federal College of Education outside a packed lecture hall.	At least 3 killed, 7 injured	Kontagora town, Niger state, Nigeria

(continued)

Table 2.9. Female Suicide Bombings in Nigeria and Cameroon (Continued)

Date	Features of the attack	Victims	Location
16 November 2014	A female suicide bomber, allegedly accompanied by two men, detonated explosives in a cell phone market. The attack came a day after the Nigerian army recaptured the town of Chibok, where Boko Haram kidnapped about 200 schoolgirls.	13 killed, 65 injured	Azare town, Bauchi state, Nigeria
25 November 2014	In a twin female suicide bombing at a crowded market, one teenage girl blew herself up and as people gathered to help the victims, the second girl detonated her explosives.	78 killed	Maiduguri, Borno state, Nigeria
1 December 2014	In another twin female suicide bombing at a market, the first female suicide bomber exploded when she refused to submit to a security check at the market entrance, while the second woman, with explosives tied to her back like a baby, ran into a shop and detonated her bomb when the owner pushed her out.	At least 16 killed, 25 injured	Maiduguri, Borno state, Nigeria
10 December 2014	In a double attack at a large Kantin Kwari textile market, two young female suicide bombers asked for directions to the public washrooms, where they detonated their explosives.	At least 6 killed, 7 injured	Kano, Kano state, Nigeria
31 December 2014	Soldiers opened fire on a woman who refused to be searched as she approached the barracks. She exploded as shots were fired.	Bomber killed	Bolari town, Gombe state, Nigeria
10 January 2015	A girl (about 10) exploded herself in the market.	At least 19 killed	Maiduguri, Borno state, Nigeria
11 January 2015	Two teenage female suicide bombers struck a crowded market amid an offensive by Boko Haram in the region.	At least 7 killed, 48 injured	Potiskum, Yobe state, Nigeria
13 January 2015	A female suicide bomber hit the office used by the military, during an evening Muslim prayer.	At least 3 killed, 21 injured	Gombe, Gombe state, Nigeria
2 February 2015	A female suicide bomber blew herself up near a stadium, minutes after President Goodluck Jonathan left a campaign rally.	At least 1 killed, 18 injured	Gombe, Gombe state, Nigeria
15 February 2015	A teenage female suicide bomber exploded at a crowded bus station. The attack coincided with the Boko Haram offensive to take over the capital of neighbouring Gombe state. This act of violence occurred at the time when Nigeria postponed national elections set for 14 February. Before this attack, Boko Haram warned people not to participate in elections.	At least 10 killed, 32 injured	Damaturu, Yobe state, Nigeria

(continued)

Table 2.9. Female Suicide Bombings in Nigeria and Cameroon (Continued)

Date	Features of the attack	Victims	Location
22 February 2015	A girl (7) detonated explosives as she was stopped by security guards at the entrance to a busy market.	At least 5 killed	Potiskum, Yobe state, Nigeria
28 February 2015	Two women exploded after they failed to get on a bus.	2 killed	Ngamdu village, Damaturu, Yobe state, Nigeria
7 March 2015	Four suicide bombers – three women and a man – detonated explosives in coordinated attacks at the main market, fish market, and a bus station.	At least 55 killed, 146 injured	Maiduguri, Borno state, Nigeria
10 March 2015	A woman detonated her explosives at a roundabout near the Monday Market, which had been attacked before.	At least 17 killed	Maiduguri, Borno state, Nigeria
16 May 2015	A female suicide bomber detonated an improvised explosive device at the entrance of the Central Motor Park.	At least 7 killed, 26 injured	Damaturu, Yobe state, Nigeria
4 June 2015	A female suicide bomber struck at a checkpoint near army barracks. This attack followed a spate of bombings in the city that killed around 80 people.	2 killed, 3 injured	Maiduguri, Borno state, Nigeria
6 June 2015	A female suicide bomber detonated an improvised explosive device along Baga/Monguno highway near Maiduguri.	2 killed, 4 injured	Borno state, Nigeria
10 June 2015	Three women wearing explosive vests accidentally blew up near the highway leading to Maiduguri.		Borno state, Nigeria
22 June 2015	Two teenage girls exploded at the fish market near a crowded mosque. One girl blew up as she approached the mosque during afternoon prayers during the holy month of Ramadan. The second teen appeared to be running away when she exploded.	At least 30 killed	Maiduguri, Borno state, Nigeria
23 June 2015	A small girl (12) detonated explosives in the middle of traders and customers at the grain section of the market.	At least 10 killed, 20 injured	Gujba, near Damaturu, Yobe state, Nigeria
2 July 2015	A woman and a girl strapped with explosives exploded near a mosque and a checkpoint. A girl (about 15) was seen around the mosque when worshippers were preparing for afternoon prayers. When asked to leave, she blew herself up.	13 killed, 7 injured	Malari village, outside Maiduguri, Borno state, Nigeria
3 July 2015	At least six female suicide bombers detonated explosives in the middle of a large crowd of people fleeing the village after an attack by Boko Haram.	At least 55 killed, 21 injured	Zabamari village near Maiduguri, Borno state, Nigeria

(continued)

Table 2.9. Female Suicide Bombings in Nigeria and Cameroon (Continued)

Date	Features of the attack	Victims	Location
5 July 2015	A female suicide bomber blew up in a crowded evangelical Christian church during service.	At least 5 killed	Potiskum, Yobe state, Nigeria
6 July 2015	A girl suicide bomber (13) was trying to enter the mosque after night prayers were concluded and detonated the bomb when she was stopped, killing only herself.	1 bomber killed	Kano, Kano state, Nigeria
7 July 2015	A teenage female suicide bomber detonated explosives amidst government workers lined up for routine screening.	25 killed	Zaria, Zaria state, Nigeria
12 July 2015	Two female suicide bombers dressed as devout Muslims detonated explosives. After the accident, the regional government banned women from wearing burkas.	13 killed	Fotokol, Cameroon
16 July 2015	Two simultaneous bombings took place at a market. One was caused by a female suicide bomber, the other by a bomb.	At least 48 killed, 58 injured	Gombe, Gombe state, Nigeria
16 July 2015	A young female suicide bomber blew herself up amidst a crowd of people gathered to mark a Muslim holiday, Eid al-Fitr.	At least 9 killed	Damaturu, Yobe state, Nigeria
17 July 2015	An elderly woman and a girl (10) detonated explosives at screening areas outside two sites where worshippers were gathering for prayers.	9 killed, 18 injured	Damaturu, Yobe state, Nigeria
22 July 2015	Two girl suicide bombers (under 15) disguised as beggars exploded at the entrance to the central market and the adjoining Hausa neighbourhood.	At least 13 killed, 32 injured	Maroua, Cameroon
25 July 2015	A girl suicide bomber (12) blew herself in a popular bar on Saturday night in the town of Maroua, which serves as a military base for Cameroon's elite force fighting Boko Haram.	20 killed, 79 injured	Maroua, Cameroon
26 July 2015	A girl suicide bomber (about 10) exploded in a crowd of people screened by security services at the entrance to the market.	19 killed, 47 injured	Damaturu, Yobe state, Nigeria
26 July 2015	A woman (40), described as mentally unstable, detonated explosives in a crowded market.	14 killed	Damaturu, Yobe state, Nigeria

Conclusion

The overwhelming majority of female suicide bombings to date (by some estimates as much as 95 per cent (O'Rourke 2008) have been carried out in the context of military campaigns against foreign occupying forces. Some attacks were aimed at creating or maintaining territorial sovereignty, some were defined significantly by religion, many others combined a nationalistic agenda with religious symbolism and rhetoric, and still other were carried out to reignite sectarian violence. A kaleidoscope of factors, including a colonial past, societal and sectarian tensions, mobilizing networks, legitimizing authorities, and general social conditions of mass disenfranchisement and dislocation play an important role in generating and sustaining the violence of female suicide bombings in modern times.

There is no single demographic profile of female suicide bombers, as their backgrounds reveal a broad range of personal experiences and ideologies. Thus, the commonly touted link between Islamic fundamentalism and female suicide bombers counters the facts. Many female suicide perpetrators came from Christian, Hindu, or other religious backgrounds or acted on behalf of secular organizations. Some came from fairly privileged families, others were born into poverty-stricken households in displacement. Some completed university studies and pursued promising careers, others were hardly literate. Some had their identities revealed in highly public commemorations, others remain unknown. Whether information about the perpetrators, attacks, organizations, and societies behind them is publicly accessible or not, discursive representations become powerful tools in producing generic explanations of why females engage in suicide bombings and crafting broader myths about peoples and cultures. We rarely think of female suicide bombers as written: they are as real to us as the images of carnage they inflict. It sometimes eludes us that what we make of this violence, the perpetrators, and their societies is often determined by the prevailing representations. Even if rooted only in stereotypes and misconceptions that are difficult to sustain empirically, these representations bear political and normative significance and can be used by particular actors in the pursuit of power.

In the following chapters we turn to the critical examination of the prevailing representations of female suicide bombings to uncover the political interests, gendered power dynamics, normative values, and context-specific perspectives behind them.

Chapter Three

Female Suicide Bombings: Between Agential Choice and Structural Determinism

Introduction

The violence of female suicide bombings raises myriad important and difficult questions for academic inquiry, not the least of which concerns the agency of female perpetrators. The notion of individual agency is central to academic efforts to explain female suicide bombings and to understand broader patterns of domination and oppression. It is not surprising, then, that it figures prominently in various analyses, even though its treatment diverges significantly. At the heart of scholarly disagreements are particular understandings and appropriations of gender that reflect the tendency of different perspectives to "foreground some things, and background others" (Peterson and Runyan 1999, 21). Terrorism studies scholars display a consistent pattern of viewing the agency of female suicide bombers with suspicion or openly repudiating it. They construct two images of female suicide perpetrators – a "romantic dupe" or a "feminist warrior" – while claiming to use purportedly gender-neutral language. Feminist scholars, on the other hand, focus mostly on problematizing the denial of agency in mainstream representations (Brunner 2005; Alison 2004; Sjoberg and Gentry 2007, 2011; Parashar 2009). While acknowledging that some scenarios do reflect the dupe/warrior images, feminist scholars, nonetheless, argue that such narratives misappropriate gender. Feminist scholars challenge the stereotype of women's intrinsic peacefulness, point to the tensions and ambiguities surrounding politically violent women, and discuss women's violence outside the victim/agency dichotomy.

The primary purpose of this chapter is to examine critically some prevailing representations of female suicide bombings focused on the personal/individual motives of their perpetrators so as to demonstrate how gender discourses shape explanations and understandings of female perpetrators' agency. Female suicide bombings offer fertile analytical ground for exploring the interconnectedness of gender, agency, violence, and oppressive structures in that all these issues converge around the images of female perpetrators. A critical gender approach reveals the ways in which terrorism studies scholarship draws on essentialist conceptions of gender to produce structuralist accounts that dismiss, by default, the agency of individual female suicide bombers. We then reconceptualize the notion of agency within a relational structure-agency framework and demonstrate agential capacity of female suicide bombers.

We begin this discussion with a general overview of the concepts of agency and structure, both of which appear frequently in the literature on female suicide bombings without sufficient or any discussion of ambiguities and contradictions in their usage. This overview is warranted because both concepts provide a foundation for the first step in our inquiry. Such a first step, as Ludwig Wittgenstein (1953, para. 308) once noted, "is the one that altogether escapes notice," while "commit[ting] us to a particular way of looking at things." Therefore, we consciously explore and unpack the concept of agency in its relationship with broader political, cultural, and social structures that both enable and constrain women's abilities to shape, control, and determine their own circumstances and actions. To do so, we revisit one of the most fundamental problems within the ontological and epistemological debates that has long structured the forms of social inquiry – the structure-agency problem.[1] We ask how the notions of structure and agency came to be understood in dichotomous terms, what gender can add to our understanding of agency and structure, and how a critical gender approach conceives of female suicide bombers' agency within the relational structure/agency framework.

Conceptualizing Agency and Structure

Discussions about agency and structure typically reach back to Max Weber and Émile Durkheim, the two sociological giants who developed influential ideal types – individualist and structuralist, respectively. Weber's individualist approach accorded primacy to agency and clearly pointed to the ability of individuals to act in accordance with their intentionality (1949). In other words, he equated agency with the capacity for self-conscious / intentional reasoning and volition. Weber, in all likelihood, would reject any notion of human agents as passive products of structural forces. While clearly accepting social collectives as distinct phenomena, Weber considers social wholes as lacking properties of their own. Structures, in his understanding, exist only through the subjective understandings of human agents and have no dispositions, beliefs, and/or intentions of their own. What Weber left unexplained is how the concepts of meaning and subjectivity relate to the notion of structure and constraint, for if culture refers to persistent schemas that pattern social relations and remain external to the individual, then culture itself constrains or facilitates agency.

Émile Durkheim turned this weakness of Weber's approach into the strength of his own perspective. Unlike Weber, he focused on the collective aspects of the beliefs and practices of a group. Durkheim (1982, 52) discerned a distinct category of ideational factors – social facts, defined as "ways of acting, thinking and feeling, external to the individual, endowed with the power of coercion, by reason of which they control him." For Durkheim, social facts express a certain state of "collective mind" (55), assume a shape distinct from their individual manifestations, and constitute a reality in their own right. Society, accordingly, cannot be reduced to individuals, but rather represents a specific collective individuality and consciousness, in which institutions embody "all the beliefs and modes of behaviour instituted by the collectivity" (45). In other words, individual ways of thinking, feeling, and acting are wholly shaped by society. Therefore, social outcomes cannot be explained in terms of individual beliefs, dispositions, intentions, and actions. Any explanations of social phenomena focusing on individual factors are not only reductive but also false.

Both Weber and Durkheim conceive of shared *intersubjective* beliefs, norms, and values as what holds societies together. Therefore, all social phenomena and processes ought to be studied as embodiments of cultural values, which lend meaning to certain acts, set standards for appropriate behaviour, and provide justification for actions. The crucial distinction between the two is that Weber accords ontological and analytical primacy to the individual (agency), whereas Durkheim attaches basic explanatory weight to the social collectivity (structure).

One attempt to transcend the individualist-structuralist dichotomy was made by Anthony Giddens (1986) in the form of structuration theory. Giddens reconceptualized the structure–agency relationship as a dialectic duality where agents continuously reproduce structures through social practices. Structures, by this account, are not static, monolithic referents, but rather malleable constructs whose meanings need to be constantly (re)negotiated and assessed among competing claims and actors within particular spatial and temporal contexts. As such, structures can never be defined once and for good. They need to be continuously reproduced through social practices. Thus, Giddens's solution to the structure-agency problem is relational in that agents and structures are best understood as part of a process. In other words, both agents and structures exist by virtue of the social practices that (re)create them. In the context of this book, Giddens's approach aligns with processual understanding of female suicide bombings as a violent social practice in that each act of female suicide bombing results from a unique synergy of the "self"/agent and multiple social structures conditioning it. That is to say, structures can be at the same time both constraining and enabling, but structural influence does not deflect agential responsibility. Structures, as Rupert (2005, 209) puts it, "have histories; they are (re)produced or transformed only through the mediation of historically concrete agency." The extent of influence that agents and structures exert should be determined on the basis of empirical evidence (Wight 2006, 119).

Structural Determinism in the Problem-Solving Literature on Female Suicide Bombings

Problem-solving literature on female suicide bombings leans heavily towards structural determinism, which bears profound implications for how the agency of female suicide bombers is understood, articulated, and produced. In line with essentialist understanding of gender, problem-solving works reinforce a long-standing tradition in social science literature of presenting women as *always/already* victims of their culture and/or biology. Noteworthy, no single structure "propels" women to become suicide bombers, but two in particular – orientalized patriarchy paired with natural/biological determinism – do.

Patriarchy represents the most common conceptual framework for explaining violence in global politics on the basis of natural determinism (Walby 1986). Violence, conventionally associated with men, is conceived as the product of unequal power relations within the hierarchical system of patriarchy and routinely presented as an inevitable, privileged, and immutable attribute of masculinity (Sjoberg and Gentry 2007, 3). Within this framework, women are consistently portrayed as powerless victims of male violence and domination or, as Segal (1994, 142) put it, "Violence is always … an act in the masculine position, by young men … and against women." Sustained through men's superior rights and authority, embedded in the patriarchal structures of society, and legitimized within family, violence against women is a systematic "universal phenomenon that cuts across all divisions of class, race, religion, age, ethnicity, and geographical region" (Pickup, with Williams and Sweetman 2001, 11). Masculine violence destroys women's lives, jeopardizes their freedoms, and aggravates their insecurities and vulnerabilities.

The customary definition of women as victims of violence (Elshtain 1987; Young 2003) and their consistent exclusion from the category of violent perpetrators are so potent that, as we argued in chapter 1, any recognition of violent women requires special mentioning and more often than not evokes open disapprobation (Kinsella 2005; Sjoberg and Gentry 2007). This is clearly reflected in the "need to continually establish that women can *also* be combatants and should *also* be allowed to be" (Kinsella 2005, 254). In those cases when actual or potential violence by females is acknowledged, explanations remain generally consistent with ideal-typical understandings of women and femininity. That is, even when engaging in the acts of terrorism or other forms of violence, females are destined to live events and situations in "the feminine way," caring for others, protecting them, and responding to their needs (De Cataldo Neuburger and Valentini 1996, 81). Indeed, some scholars have suggested that the only way to end all forms of violence – political, economic, and domestic – is to engrain "female values" of cooperation, harmony, and non-violence in men (Turpin and Kurtz 1997). Robin Morgan (1989, 24) articulated such a deterministic position noting, "The majority of terrorists … are men. The majority of women, caught in the middle, want no more of this newly intensified form of the old battle to the death between fathers and sons … Even when we collaborate – and we do, either in traditional roles of support or as tougher-than-thou token militants – we do so out of a disbelief, a suspended knowledge, a longing for acceptance, a tortured love we bear for the men we have birthed and sustain."

Alternatively, explanations of female violence align with the logic of deviance and denial through the conventional categorization of "bad" women (Sjoberg and Gentry 2007, 2) or "scandalous" subwomen (Marway 2011, 225). The theme of deviance has various manifestations. Having examined the recorded history of female terrorism, commencing

around the eighteenth century, Talbot (2000–1, 165) itemized five dominant representations of women terrorists, all circumscribed by the
boundaries of femininity: (1) extremist feminists; (2) women bound to
terrorism only because of a relationship with a man; (3) women who
performed only subservient roles; (4) women who were mentally inept;
or (5) women who appeared "unfeminine." Since women are perceived
to be non-violent, one way of explaining female violence is to assert that
women commit acts of violence when they take on masculine traits.
Cragin and Daly (2009, 103), for example, argue that politically violent
women "have given up their femininity, have been described as 'sex-
less' or 'witchy.'" This type of reasoning interprets violence as a sign of
emancipation and suggests that, with emancipation, women demand
equal opportunity both in the legitimate sphere and in illicit violent/
criminal endeavours (Barri Flowers 1987; Diaz-Cotto 1991).

In their nuanced analysis, Sjoberg and Gentry (2007) identified three
gender discourses of mothers, monsters, and whores about politically
violent women, each developing a different version of deviance. All
three discourses frame violent women in opposition to established
ideal-typical gender norms by accentuating their biological fate to
nurture, care, and belong (mother), portraying them as pathologically
insane and "more macho" (Alison 2004, 457) (monster), or driven by
sexual dependence or dysfunction (whore). These discourses employ
gendered terms to emphasize the failures of individual women to accept
their "natural"/biological and social roles, and effectively marginalize violent women "as not only aberrant, but aberrant because of their
flawed femininity" (Sjoberg and Gentry 2007, 13). That is, these discourses feminize and de-womanize female suicide bombers, i.e., deny
female suicide bombers' accountability for their acts of violence on the
grounds of "twisted" maternalism (Gentry 2009), flawed womanhood,
or sexuality. In all of these scenarios, violent women are portrayed as
deviant and exceptional, "less than women" (Eager 2008, 3), or even less
than human (Sjoberg and Gentry 2007, 13). Thus, both expert and lay
explanations that focus on patriarchy and essentialist theory of gender
inevitably conclude that "the essentially [violent] ... woman does not
exist" (De Cataldo Neuburger and Valentini 1996, 35).

We do not deny that male violence against women circumscribes
female lives from the most intimate aspects to the public ones. However, we strongly concur with Meintjes et. al. that the real world is much
more complex, as "[n]o woman lives in the single dimension of her sex"
(Meintjes, Turshen, and Pillay 2001, 13). Patriarchy-centred analyses

define individuals as the subjects and objects of violence primarily, if not exclusively, on the basis of their sex. Whether those locked into the positions of objects accept their status or not seems of little importance, since these designations are customarily determined without the voice, consent, or participation of the designated. More importantly, below the surface of such designations lies a larger issue of power, as the subject-object dichotomy operates in a discriminatory fashion by reiterating and reinforcing asymmetrical distributions of power between the two genders. Mohanty (1991, 57) underscores the salience of power dynamics within the object-subject duality and cautions that "defining women as archetypal victims freezes them into 'objects-who-defend-themselves,' men into 'subjects-who-perpetrate-violence,' and every society into powerless (read: women) and powerful (read: men) groups of people."

We contend that various forms of political violence, including suicide bombings, are linked to patriarchy one way or the other, but as Sjoberg and Gentry (2007, 19) observed, "All people ... have choices about their participation." Patriarchy-centred analyses, while accurate in describing the enduring social structures that determine women's positions and condition female capacities for social action, do not always allow for nuanced accounts of the dynamics of gender relationships in specific social settings. Such analyses are incomplete in that they fail to observe the agency of feminized subjects and examine the ways in which (re)production and transformation of gender relations and identities are mediated by class, race, ethnicity, and religion. Consequently, they produce three self-reinforcing effects: they dismiss violent behaviour by women as unthinkable, exaggerate difference in purportedly natural propensity towards violence between the two sexes (Hird 2002, 4), and reinforce prescribed gender norms that provide an evaluative framework for understanding violence and agency in world politics (Sjoberg and Gentry 2007).

Romantic Dupe Structuralist Account

Crucially, discursive representations of female suicide bombers in the problem-solving literature are intrinsically structuralist as a result of their embroilment with natural determinism and orientalized patriarchy (the latter is discussed in chapter 5). Natural determinism is mapped onto orientalized patriarchy in various ways. While some authors remain ambivalent on the issue (Eager 2008), others embrace natural determinism as a condition exploited by orientalized patriarchy, or see orientalized patriarchy as a cultural embodiment of biological determinism (Bloom 2007; Schweitzer 2008; Berko 2012) – an argument that feminizes female suicide bombers' societies. Barbara Victor (2003) is an early author who articulated the gendered, deterministic "romantic dupe" account that interpreted women's involvement in suicide bombings in sexualized terms. Victor "discovered" that all female suicide bombers she investigated were overburdened by personal "baggage" (Fighel 2003), i.e., personal problems and psychological predispositions that made them misfits or outcasts in their society and culture, ensuring that they could be easily manipulated or forced into participation in suicide missions. All females, Victor claimed, were recruited, trained, and sent on their missions (in Victor's language, "seduced" and "indoctrinated" [7]) by men, whether it was a trusted family member, a friend, an esteemed religious leader, or a teacher. Female suicide bombers, in other words, did not act intentionally, but were *duped* into violence.

Victor further stabilized the victimization of female suicide bombers by contrasting them with male suicide bombers. She referred to Shalfic Masalqa, a psychologist and professor at Hebrew University, and reiterated his claim that a "cult of death" (Victor 2003, 266) had permeated Palestinian society and made the idea of self-sacrifice widely acceptable within this specific social setting. Victor describes the "cult of death" as an "atmosphere" characterized by the absence of collective hope for the future (27, 266) and explicitly contrasted it with nationalism. The latter would make an uneasy fit within the "romantic dupe" account by seriously questioning the narrow socio-cultural niche the author carved for Palestinian female suicide bombers and women in general. Consideration of the structural influence of nationalism would require recognition that female suicide bombers are not simply desperate, powerless, confused, crazed, and oppressed victims of orientalized patriarchy. Rather, like their male counterparts, female suicide bombers are both the agents within and products of complex sociopolitical and cultural structures. As self-conscious, intentional agents, they possess a certain degree of autonomy, direction, and volition and advance political demands in pursuit of collective interests.

Victor's analysis represents a concrete and vivid example of structuralist denial of the agency of female suicide bombers – a denial firmly entrenched in the gendered constructions of sex. Victor conventionally represents female suicide bombers as victims of rigid cultural structures that predetermined their subordinate position within society, stripped them from their agential powers, and sidelined their contribution within collective political violence. She further relegates them to the position of insignificance within insurgent groups, reducing them to "cannon fodder" (Bloom 2011, 155) used by male leaders to increase the strategic and tactical advantages of hyper-masculine, militant groups. Female self-sacrifice through bombings is thus framed as something other than complete and active commitment to a political cause, "as less authentic" (Cunningham 2003, 175). Such gendered framing has serious ramifications in the long run, for membership in the nation (citizenship), as well as the benefits and rights deriving from such membership, are closely associated with armed masculinity. Denying the ideological commitment and contribution of female suicide bombers to a particular cause excludes women as a group from the rights and benefits associated with bearing arms and being prepared to kill and die for that cause. Since women are not deemed fully committed to the collective political goals, their expectations of social change may be marginalized or dismissed altogether, once the group's goals are achieved.

Other problem-solving authors have been even more explicit in their structuralist inclinations. Rosemarie Skaine (2006), for example, situates her analysis of female suicide bombings within a Durkheimian structural deterministic framework. She proceeds from an assumption that individual female suicide bombers are shaped entirely by social facts. That is, society precedes an individual and profoundly structures individual ways of thinking and acting. Therefore, individual conscience is predetermined and morally sustained by collective beliefs and practices. Skaine draws on Durkheim (1982) to argue that individual instances of female suicide bombings are best understood in "relation to the collective inclination, and this collective inclination is itself a determined reflection of the structure of the society in which the individual lives" (quoted in Skaine 2006, 1). Following Durkheim, Skaine sets out to explain female suicide bombings through the notion of anomie, i.e., the collapse of social norms and values that characterizes a society in crisis and manifests itself through suicide (2). The anomie in her work strikingly resembles Victor's notion of the "cult of death."

Without denying personal motives (a proposition that is difficult to sustain for someone overtly embracing the Durkheimian approach, since for Durkheim explanations focused on individuals are both reductive and false), Skaine argues that the individual motives of female suicide bombers are closely intertwined with social conditions. In her own words (2006, 2), "Suicide bombers seek harmony with the society in which they live and adopt the ways of thought and action around them. The bombers are so tightly integrated into their society that they commit suicide." In view of this statement, Skaine's conclusion that female suicide bombers are simply the products of omnipresent socio-historical structures, with no agency in and of themselves, comes as no surprise. Similarly to Victor (2003), Skaine reduces the plurality and complexity of socio-historical structures that shape the identities and capacities of female suicide bombers to orientalized patriarchy. For both Victor and Skaine, gender produces a distinction between male and female suicide bombers and reduces the agency of female suicide perpetrators to structural determination by the orientalized patriarchy.

Feminist Warrior Structuralist Account

A different structuralist account comes from the problem-solving authors who construct a "feminist warrior" image of female suicide bombers. In contrast to the "romantic dupe" account, these scholars accentuate the assumption that female suicide bombers are fighting for political equality, women's rights, including the right to fight, and the betterment of feminine gender within ostensibly patriarchal societies (Bloom 2007; Cragin and Daly 2009).[2] While acknowledging that many female terrorists in the Third World do not identify themselves with the inherently Western notion of feminism, these authors insist that, similarly to early Western feminists, women from developing societies carry out acts of terror because they are deeply committed to gender reform and public activism. These violent women should be seen as "new women" (Sixta 2008).

While the theme of victimization is present in "feminist warrior" accounts, it is given an additional dimension. Women active in political violence are generally seen as victims of "a triple bind of oppression" (Sixta 2008, 261) – i.e., societal masculine structural violence, gender inequality within terrorist groups, and Western imperialist domination of their nations. Female suicide bombers are thus presented as taking control over their destiny by struggling for their own emancipation, as well as the collective liberation of women in their societies. Since suicide bombings are carried out in the public domain from which women in patriarchal societies are usually excluded, this practice, according to "feminist warrior" accounts, allows female perpetrators to pursue opportunities forbidden for women in traditional societies. In other words, suicide bombings become an odd sort of equal opportunity employment, or in Bloom's words "equal opportunity martyrdom" (2011, 153).

The agency of female suicide bombers seems clearly recognized by the argument that when women choose to become "human bombs" their acts are self-conscious, intentional statements, "not only in the name of a country, a religion, a leader, but also in the name of their gender" (Beyler 2003b). Paradoxically, that same agency is also denied if the only way to overcome structural constraints of traditional patriarchal societies and to attain equality is through self-extinction. Naaman (2007, 934) hints at this point, noting that female martyrdom "enables people to bypass the loaded deviation from traditional gendered roles and as such mythicizes actions taken rather than engaging with their gender politics." In the "feminist warrior" accounts, the death of the subject that characterizes various structuralist philosophical positions means not only the death of a subject qua self, in terms of identity, but also a very real physical destruction of an individual.

The "feminist warrior" argument is also baffling in that it draws a highly problematic link between nationalist and feminist causes, while explicitly prioritizing patriarchal nationalist projects. Notions of gender permeate cultural and political constructions of the nation resulting in what Kuttab (1997, 95) calls an "unhappy alliance between nationalism and feminism." Nationalist discourses naturalize the nation as the building block of humanity so as to conceal the politics of its making. Both nations and nationalism are gendered in that they are constructed "on and through gender" (Pettman 1996, 45). Feminists have long argued for a need to interrogate nationalism so as to reveal multiple gender(ed) dimensions of nationalism and women's share in constructing and reproducing it (Ranchod-Nilsson and Tétreault 2000). On the one hand, nationalism uses seemingly inclusive feminine language of unity and belonging to create a collective nationalist "self" at the primordial intersection of territory and community. On the other hand, it relies on the masculine characteristic of exclusion and is bound up with modern capitalist development and social change instigated by the emergence of industrial society (Hurrell 2007, 123). Nationalist discourses create the "foreign other," the outsider, without whom a nation would inevitably cease to exist. Nations, as Parker et al. (1992, 5) argue, "are forever haunted by their various definitional others." Otherness is solidified through the construction of temporal and social distances, translating a rich diversity of people and communities into a recognizable register of differences and similarities. Any dissimilarity on the inside is purposefully disguised, while differences outside are overly accentuated. What is particularly significant is that the difference in nationalist discourses is not simply produced – it is also hierarchically organized, reinforcing masculine qualities of nationalism. Nationalism, in other words, both excludes and subordinates, and it does so by commanding extraordinary power to kill and sacrifice. This power is linked to armed masculinity all along – from the violent birth of the nation on the battlefields of nationalist struggle to the continued need for its active protection, defence, and control (Banerjee 2006).

Women, often depicted as the mothers of the nation, especially in mobilized or defeated nationalisms, play a significant role in inventing, imagining, and mythologizing the nation. Ahmetbeyzade (2007) has recorded how, in their narratives, exiled Kurdish women construct cultural and historical borders (both real and imagined) of their Mother Soil (*Ana Toprak*) and refer to PKK fighters as "our children." The author notes that the references to "us," "we," "our children" are much more than a simple metaphoric tool. These references serve as a means of authenticating the symbolism of blood as a source of belonging (69). The female body is thus discursively appropriated as a container of idealized symbols of the national honour and is used to demarcate the boundaries of national difference and power among men. The construction of women as mothers of the nation places female reproductive capacities at the service of their nation. As biological reproducers of national collectivities and social transmitters of national cultures, women and their bodies are claimed for the nation (Ranchod-Nilsson and Tétreault 2000; Hall 1993). The nation itself is feminized through its association with the female body and construed in affective, familial terms, such as home, motherland, blood, and kin. In this way, the life and destiny of the body politic are blended with the life and destiny of its women. Idealized images and real bodies of women serve as the markers of national boundaries, defining insiders and outsiders (Ranchod-Nilsson and Tétreault 2000, 5).

In a complex relationship between the nation and the state, the latter is framed as masculine. In this way, the search of a nation for status and recognition as a state is closely associated with the need for a woman to attain social standing through marriage. Such a construction implies that "women are the *symbol* of the nation, men its *agents*, regardless of the role women actually play in the nation" ("Editorial" 1993). It also reveals the special role ascribed to men as defenders and protectors of the nation within nationalist projects. The responsibility for defending and protecting the body politic, which is always at risk of violation and oppression by the threatening other(s), is squarely placed on its male citizens (Parker et al. 1992, 6). Women's roles in nationalism are circumscribed by their gendered domestic identity and reduced to those of "heroic mothers," "obedient daughters," and "chaste wives" of the male protectors. Within the limits of the gendered nationalist framework, foreign occupation is usually captured through the metaphor of "rape." Herath (2012), for example, observed that the rapes of women in Jaffna were perceived by Tamils as the violation of the Tamil national honour (127). This view is not surprising, for nationalism, as Cynthia Enloe (1990, 4) notes, "has sprung from masculinized memory, masculinized humiliation, and masculinized hope." The metaphor of rape signifies the scope of sexual violence during wars and highlights not only women's dreadful experience of rape as an instrument of war, but more importantly the intensity of humiliation experienced by the occupied/feminized nations and/or states. It entails "a complex move ... from actual women's bodies and the dangers they face, to nationalist discourse using images of women's bodies to mark national or communal boundaries" (Pettman 1996, 51).

Women's participation in nationalist movements and the extent to which they are capable of advancing feminist goals is contingent, in large part, on the particular nationalist projects. Those constructing the "feminist warrior" image of female suicide bombers acknowledge that the goal of women's emancipation and rights is generally subsumed by the goal of national liberation. Female suicide bombers rise above the gender divisions and political factions in their society to generate national unity (Rajan, quoted in Skaine 2006, 38). Certainly individual women suicide bombers who blow themselves up in the course of the collective struggle will not be able to enjoy the political rights and freedoms once the goal of national liberation is achieved. However, the involvement of female suicide bombers in nation-building is expected to bring extensive political rights to women as a group. This is a classic "later, not now" (Enloe 1990, 62) approach, whereby women put aside their group interests for the sake of the national cause.

Significant evidence proves, however, that causes "marginalized in the struggle are likely to be marginalized in its victories, and especially in the consolidation and institutionalization of victory in the state" (Pettman 1996, 61). Female participation in suicide bombings to achieve nationalist and feminist goals is caught in a self-defeating contradiction. Portrayed as mothers, virgins, and brides simultaneously birthing and defending their nation, female suicide bombers are trapped within the paradox of creating a new nation while reproducing the old one (Kinsella 2005). Even though these women unsettle older roles and carve out more space for themselves as agents, they are "still trapped in the symbolic use made of them as mothers of the nation" (Pettman 1996, 56). As such, they are both "actors in and hostage to nationalist projects" (56), which historically push them "back home" and their contributions into oblivion, once the nationalist goals are achieved. Indeed, the commitment or even willingness of secular or religious extremist groups employing female suicide bombers to institute gender equality is rather questionable. As Bloom (2007, 164) put it, "Fanaticism and death cults generally do not lead to liberation politics for women." In this context, a proposition of a twofold struggle against an inner enemy (patriarchy) and an outer enemy (the occupier) is difficult to sustain.

Overcoming Determinism?

Some problem-solving works on female suicide bombings demonstrate acute awareness of the risk of oversimplification and misrepresentation through victimization. Ness (2008a) is correct when she calls dupe/warrior structuralist frameworks reductive and expresses the need to move beyond the unidimensional representation of female suicide bombers within these accounts. Her proposed solution is to consider other "structuring conditions, like economics, war-zone realities – including the need to protect oneself – and the degree of popular support that female participation enjoys in a given society" (4). Indeed, there is no particular reason why gender oppression should be elevated above other types of structural violence. Recent research demonstrates that societal oppression is only one factor that affects individual women's decision to become suicide bombers. A likely set of direct and indirect causes include trauma, revenge, nationalism, alienation, marginalization, and negative self-identity (Speckhard 2008). Speckhard (2009, 36) also notes "anecdotal evidence" of economic motivations for Iraqi women (often widows) as "often completely financially dependent on the continued support from the groups their husbands had been affiliated with and, as a result, ... vulnerable to exploitation."

In the introduction to an edited collection, Ness (2008c) seems to understand structure both in material (economics) and ideational (culture) terms. In her own chapter, however, she attempts to explore the political agency of a "female terrorist/militant" and the growing sense of legitimacy for her actions by focusing on discourses and "structures of contention" employed by secular and religious groups to legitimize female martyrs. Both types of organizations are faced with the challenge of rhetorically packaging female martyrs as a way of obtaining societal sanctioning for political violence by women. Ness finds the discourses strikingly similar, despite the fact that secular and religious terrorism strives towards different social orders – one modern and one traditional. She also opens up room, at least initially, for feminine agency in transforming symbolic societal structures governing gender relations. In her own words, an act of female suicide bombing "constitutes a distinct expression of female militancy, in that females transgress gender norms, not only by taking life, but also by embracing their own death and, in the process, counter existing core symbolic structures delimiting gender while, at the same time, creating new ones" (2008b, 12).

This argument implies that by violating and transgressing gender norms, female suicide bombers challenge entrenched systems of meaning and signification. In effect, they exercise their agential power to negotiate and transform ideational/intersubjective structures. Yet in the end, Ness's structuralist inclination leads her to the deterministic conclusion that any gains associated with female involvement in nontraditional roles are only secondary and temporary: "Because females who commit violence flout ingrained gender roles and boundaries, they must in all other ways 'belong' to their social world, the organization of which is predicated on a host of structural arrangements and deeply felt moral beliefs; in the distal sense, because violent behaviour by females must be made to fit within a collectively shared past where it can draw its sustenance from symbols that transcend time" (Ness 2008b, 12).

It is clear that, for Ness, female suicide bombers at most irritate sex and gender norms in their societies, but they do not transgress their traditional roles or change their position substantively in the long run. Within such a framework, feminine agency becomes conditional/contingent. It may be exercised temporarily only when wartime tactical considerations warrant it. But even then, female participation in political violence must "be made to fit" within symbolic societal structures. It is suspended when it no longer serves the broader goals of political violence (nationalist, religious, or both). Ness's conclusion then is oddly in tune with the denial of feminine agency within the victim/warrior accounts, with which Ness herself finds fault. Despite her critique of the structurally deterministic framing of female suicide bombers as weak, emotional, and irrational, Ness nevertheless concludes her analysis in a very Durkheimian manner. The fact that she shares ontological affinity with the structuralist accounts she is critical of does not allow Ness to move beyond structural determinism and recognize permanent feminine agency.

Neither problem-solving nor critical authors find much evidence of gender reform being advanced either within the terrorist organizations or societies on whose behalf female suicide bombers blow themselves up (see Israeli 2004; Bloom 2007; Brunner 2005; Ness 2008b; Eager 2008; Cragin and Daly 2009; Qazi 2011). Brunner (2005) concludes her nuanced analysis of Palestinian female suicide bombers by suggesting that the image of a female martyr does not necessarily transform gender identities and relations in the long term. The violence of female suicide bombers and its gendered representations has not challenged gendered relations within Palestinian society or Israeli-Palestinian conflict (48). In other words, the transgression of gender boundaries by Palestinian female suicide bombers is only temporary.[3]

Both "victim" and "feminist warrior" images perpetuate the construction of enduring patriarchal structures. They strengthen occidentalist framing of female suicide bombers (discussed in chapter 5), cement their image as always/already victims, never the agents in and of themselves. Whether female suicide bombers are said to be motivated by personal misfortunes or feminist ideas, their agency is denied either by framing them as powerless victims of patriarchal structures, or by presenting them as rebels whose only way to liberate themselves from these structures is through death. Patriarchal structures thus become deterministic, immutable, and "natural."

Frequent appeal to feminine corporeality in both "romantic dupe" and "feminist warrior" accounts through references to looks and use of bodily metaphors, especially those of virginity, pregnancy, and motherhood, reveal the gendered structuralist character of the problem-solving representations of female suicide perpetrators. Female suicide bombers are often said to strap explosives to their "wombs," implying both the maternal role to which every woman is biologically destined and socially expected to perform and the potential motives for engaging in violence. In this way, physical and symbolic dimensions of the female body conflate. Women's only raison d'être is to be a mother, a giver of life. So the taking of life through the act that destroys the natural life-giving source is unthinkable (Gentry 2009).

Problem-solving literature employs womb symbolism, i.e., vacant womb or deviant womb, which permeates the meta-narrative of motherhood (Ahall 2012, 105) to present the sex of female suicide bombers as an ontological referent and repudiates their agency. The vacant womb discourse constructs female suicide bombers as maternal heroines within the boundaries of "normal" and "appropriate" femininity (110), whereas the deviant womb represents them as monsters who breached such boundaries (111). Either way, womb symbolism disciplines representations of female suicide bombers and at the same time obscures the integral role played by the discourses of gender in producing such representations and demarcating putatively self-evident, natural differences between male and female suicide perpetrators. Bloom's (in)famous observation about "a transition in women's roles in conflict from that of the *revolutionary womb* (giving birth to future fighters), to the *exploding womb* – using the IED (Improvised Explosive Device)" (2007, 130) epitomizes gendered language within problem-solving works. Despite ironic contradiction entailed in framing women who destroy their bodies in corporeal terms (Brunner 2005, 35), female suicide bombers in problem-solving works are mediated through their sexuality and their bodies. The issue of gender is thus reduced to the perpetrators' biological sex and a seemingly natural difference between men and women.

Female suicide bombers are canonically portrayed as "mothers," "daughters," "brides," and "widows." Their involvement in political acts of suicide bombings is explained in domestic and maternal language – through troubled relationships with men, inability to bear children, exposure to or experience of sexual abuse – all of which make female lives untenable under the conditions of orientalized patriarchy (Berko 2012; Bloom, 2011, 2007; Cragin and Daly 2009; Von Knop 2007; Eager 2008). Eager (2008, 171–211) offers what she calls "a standard set of reasons" for Kurdish, Palestinian, and Chechen women's involvement in suicide bombings. These include personal loss, severe trauma, emotional response to loss and trauma, failure to fulfil female roles, easier control over women, etc. Berko (2012, 3) refers to the "groom syndrome" to describe a sensation experienced by would-be female bombers, drawing "the link between the elation … before the attack and the supreme happiness of a bride on her wedding day." The act of bombing thus becomes a symbolic extension of social dictates regarding women's place in marriage and their motherhood, if "real" marriage and motherhood are denied (Cunningham 2003).

Victimization and concomitant denial of agency is often constructed specifically around the issue of rape, to the point where it becomes an inalienable symbol of female suicide perpetrators. In a chapter on female suicide bombings, titled "Feminism, Rape and War: Engendering Suicide Terror?," Bloom (2007) mentions "revenge for a personal loss, the desire to redeem the family name, to escape a life of sheltered monotony and achieve fame, and to level the patriarchal societies" (143). To dispel any possibility of political motivations at work, Bloom generalizes, without empirical substantiation, that "many of these women have been raped or sexually abused in the previous conflict either by the representatives of the state or by the insurgents themselves" (ibid.). Bloom seems to be aware of the gendered nature of her own analysis when she cautions the reader to get "past gender stereotypes" in her subsequent work (2011, ix). She concludes her analysis by discussing some of the challenges in understanding women's motivations to kill and makes a sweeping statement that victimizes all female suicide bombers by reducing their motives to "the four R's plus one": revenge for the death of family members, redemption for transgressions, relationship with a man, and respect of the community, as well as rape as a factor that completes female victimization (234–6). Female suicide bombers are "victims of the conflict, victims of their attackers, and victims of the situation in which they find themselves" (237). Similarly, Berko (2012) repeatedly emphasizes rape in her analysis of Palestinian female suicide bombers and conjecturally extends her arguments to women "active in the terrorist Tamil Tigers in Sri Lanka, the Kurdish PKK, and Chechnya" (4). These observations focus exclusively on female victims of rape in the context of war. They ignore the endemic, institutionalized nature of rape as a weapon of war directed against women and men and conceptualize conflict-related sexual violence as violence against women, rather than gender violence through which social hierarchies and power inequalities are sustained.

Alternatively, female suicide bombers' agency is dismissed through the narrative of a whore. This narrative reduces violent women to their sexuality and explains their violence in terms of female erotomania, in which case violence is presumed to be motivated by insatiable, uncontrollable perversion, or sexual dysfunction, when violence is explained by women's inability to please men sexually (Sjoberg and Gentry 2007, 46–7). Berko (2012, 6) provides an example of the sexualization of female suicide bombers when she details her interview with a supposedly liberal Palestinian journalist, Marwan, about general perceptions of female suicide perpetrators within Palestinian society:

You want to know what woman is a terrorist? I'll tell you. The woman who rebelled, crossed the lines, hung around with men, couldn't be controlled. Arab men don't like that kind of woman, they will call her a *shaheeda*, but subconsciously, they will call her a sharmouta [whore] ...

There's this joke you hear every time a woman carries out a terrorist attack: "She blew up masturbating ... She didn't get enough sex ... She wasn't satisfied."

All victimization accounts of female suicide bombers explicitly generate and reproduce the category of naturalized "hegemonic femininity" (West 2004–5) that relegates women to the realm of the familial, emotional, and sexual, and denies their intentionality, accountability, self-reflexivity, and autonomy. Such a binary framework reifies a naturalized men/women duality and the matching agents/victims dichotomy, accepts this distinction as given, and excludes women from an agential category. Assumed naturalness of patriarchal structures in problem-solving analyses derives from a particular epistemological, methodological, and ontological position. Such a position privileges structure and downplays the role of agency in (re)producing and transforming structures. This privileging is unnecessary, especially from the perspective of those who embrace relational understanding of structure-agency as a process in which agents and structures are mutually constitutive. That is to say, the process by which patriarchal structures are negotiated and (re)created is complex, contestable, and contested – it cannot be understood and explained without the feminine agency.

Recovering Feminine Agency

Is non-deterministic understanding of female suicide bombings possible, and if so, can a critical gender approach help us to formulate it? We argue that a relational understanding of structure and agency offers a richer, non-structuralist explanation of female suicide bombings. A critical gender approach brings into the spotlight two important insights: one concerns the need to contest and reconceptualize the gendered notion of agency entrenched in problem-solving analyses; and second entails the recognition of agential influence within and the effect of female suicide bombers on the gendered social structures at various levels.

On the first point, the concept of agency employed in terrorism studies analyses and earlier journalist accounts of female suicide bombings is understood in one particular way. This conceptualization of agency is associated normatively with masculinity and historically with men (see Mackenzie and Stoljar 2000). Central to this understanding is fundamentally atomistic, self-sufficient, and rational abstraction that deflects analytical focus from social dimensions of agency and postulates normative precedence of individualism and independence over social embeddedness, communal connections, and relational dependency. Despite its socially and culturally specific character associated with the West, this masculinist notion of agency manifests itself as a universal norm and functions, descriptively and prescriptively, to promote the realization of individualism. Such a gendered conceptualization of agency is problematic in that it arbitrarily arranges values in a hierarchical way, with feminine values of caring, friendship, loyalty, cooperation, etc. consistently depreciated. Those associated with feminine values are automatically denied agential capacity. In addition, this conceptualization oversimplifies agency, erases any difference within this notion, and reduces agents to "interchangeable sameness" (6). Finally, the masculinist conception of agency reinforces structures of domination by erasing those who are rendered incapable of agency (11).

A critical gender approach draws our attention to the need to reexamine ontologically and normatively problematic claims inherent in the masculinist notion of agency and to replace it with a fuller, relational account that offers a more nuanced understanding of agency, especially moral and political agency of the feminized individuals and groups. Such contestation begins with counter-individualism of sorts, i.e., the acknowledgment that social relationships of the family and broader community condition the development of persons, their capacities, values, and attitudes. Agency, in other words, is never fully independent, but rather developed within and influenced by social environments. Given the diversity of social contexts and the broad range of personal dispositions, experiences, characteristics, and capacities, the concept of agency should not be constructed exclusively on the basis of masculine values, in opposition to femininity. The contention that moral and political agency should not be equated with absolute freedom and rationality figures prominently in feminist analyses on relational autonomy (Sjoberg and Gentry 2007; Hirschmann 1989, 2003). In these analyses, agential capacity is conceived as "a complex relationship between 'internal' factors of will and desire ... and factors 'outside the self that may inhibit or enhance one's ability to pursue one's preferences'" (Hirschmann 2003, ix, quoted in Sjoberg and Gentry 2007, 193). Agential capacity, in other words, is inevitably constrained, albeit to various degrees, by the social positioning of individual agents and gendered power differentials entailed in such positions (Sjoberg and Gentry 2007, 193). Thus, agents should be recognized as relatively rational, partially autonomous, as well as embodied, emotional, feeling, caring, nurturing, imaginative, and interdependent (Mackenzie and Stoljar 2000, 21).

Reconceptualization of individual agency in relational terms bears serious implications for how the agency of female suicide bombers is understood. The dominant narratives about female suicide bombers in problem-solving literature vehemently deny that these women exercised their agential choice to embark on the path of violence, implying that if they were given a range of options, they would choose socially acceptable behaviour. These narratives reify gender-biased images and themes of mothers, monsters and whores and, effectively, repudiate female suicide bombers' agential capacities (Sjoberg and Gentry 2007, 190). Reconceptualizing agency in relational terms allows discovery of the capacity of feminized agents to act, despite structural limitations and power inequality.

Whether educated or illiterate, younger or older, devoutly religious or atheist, searching for personal escape or seeking liberation for other women, female suicide perpetrators do not share a single set of experiences, motives, or identities. Regardless of whether they blow themselves up as nationalists, feminists, rape victims, religious activists, and/or mothers, these women enter political violence neither as "free agents" nor as passive victims (Brown 2011, 199). Their violence is a sign of agential choice about what they consider the best means to demonstrate their discontent with political and personal circumstances and achieve certain political goals. For example, extensive fieldwork in the Tamil areas of Sri Lanka led Herath (2012) to acknowledge the role of gender violence and the socially prescribed norm of female sexual purity as a motive behind female suicide bombings. At the same time, she made it clear that "within the confines of the act there was a belief held by suicide bombers that they were saving the Tamil nation through suicide bombings" (127). In other words, Tamil female suicide bombers exercised their agency to make a choice and enter the realm of political activism through violence. This choice, as well as the responsibility and accountability for making it, should be acknowledged, regardless of the rationality of motives behind it, and even if female suicide bombers ended up reproducing or modifying, rather than dismantling their own oppression. Indeed, even if we accept the differences in the motivational imperatives driving male and female suicide bombers, despite their problems, the uncritical commitment of problem-solving authors to a fixed, masculinist notion of agency is simply insufficient to warrant the denial of female suicide bombers' agency. This leads us to the second insight.

Relational understanding of structure-agency calls for the need to denaturalize biological determinism and orientalized patriarchy by demonstrating the agential influence of female suicide perpetrators. In times of conflict, when the body politic is in stress, new spaces, including those of gender, open up for alterations and amendments of entrenched social identities and practices. Crucially, political violence introduces opportunities for challenging the status quo and creates room for change in gender identities, social relations and socio-political structures that shape them. This does not mean that change will inevitably be profoundly transformative and/or enduring. As mentioned above, gendered power inequalities within broader social and political structures differentially condition the capacities of individuals to (re) shape their socio-political structures. Generally speaking, power (im) balance favours hegemonic masculinity, constraining female capacity to engage in socially consequential actions. This, by no means, implies that there is no room for female agency. On the contrary, women, albeit positioned differentially from men, participate actively in social practices. The reason why female suicide bombers continue to exert such significant impact despite their small numbers is because, through their active participation in conflicts, they demonstrate agential capacity by challenging social structures and renegotiating social practices.

Female suicide bombers have challenged their societies and the world in many ways: they have violated male monopoly on suicide bombings, broken societal taboos, and transgressed, with varying degrees of success, established gendered boundaries. In many contexts, insurgent organizations had to overcome numerous social and ideological barriers to include females directly in the political violence. It is true that in most, if not all, cases women's access to suicide bombings has been controlled by men in the positions of secular and religious authority who employed discursive strategies of gender subordination to include women in political violence. That is, in order to justify the transgression of gender norms entailed in female suicide bombings, masculine authorities sanctioned these acts of violence by framing them as consistent with inherited traditions (Dunn 2010). Yet we need not dismiss the fact that these decisions came, in part, as a result of the pressures by women (Cunningham 2003; Alison 2009). For example, the decision by the LTTE leadership to create the Freedom Birds and the Black Tigresses was not least driven by women's demands for more active involvement in the Tamil nationalist struggle (Stack-O'Connor 2007). Indeed, Miranda Alison, who interviewed LTTE female combatants during fieldwork in Sri Lanka, observed that, despite ambiguity and tension attached to their violent role, these women acted "as agents making their own choices, though acting within multiple hierarchical structures" (2004, 449). Similarly, Cragin and Daly (2009, viii) recognized women's agency when describing the ways in which Al-Qaeda "struggled to contextualize the demand [for inclusion] placed upon it by Muslim women with its socially conservative worldview." Qazi (2011) pointed out that interviews with failed Palestinian female suicide bombers indicate that women were not easily manipulated into becoming suicide bombers. This is not to suggest that patriarchy in societies where female suicide bombers blew themselves up has vanished or that the general perception of political violence as a masculine domain has changed. Rather, the reproduction of gender relations in specific socio-historical settings has been affected by the violence of female suicide bombings. As a result, gendered structures, even in traditionally patriarchal societies, were forced to coexist, sometimes rather unhappily, with practices that allow the "second sex" to attain culturally and socially valued status.

The case of the Palestinian female suicide bombers exemplifies how symbolic societal structures have been adapted to legitimize female participation in suicide bombings / martyrdom operations. As noted in chapter 2, days after Wafa Idris became the first Palestinian woman to blow herself up, Sheik Ahmad Yassin, the wheelchair-bound spiritual leader of Hamas, suggested that "a woman martyr is problematic for Muslim society" and that recruiting a woman for such purposes was tantamount to breaking Islamic law (Victor 2003, 30). Yet the sheik's position changed within a matter of months (32–3).

Similar social adaptations have been observed in other contexts. For example, Tamara Herath (2012, 182) observed that while the elements of traditional feminine identity (modesty, chastity, shyness, respectful fear) persist in contemporary Tamil society, women's inclusion in the LTTE triggered major social changes for all Tamil women in their gender identity. Both combatant and civilian Tamil women participate in the process of social negotiation of a "new" kind of women – *puthumai pen* – characterized by independence, self-assurance, fearlessness, and assertiveness (183). This process originated within the organizational environment of the LTTE, which coined a new word *ah-lu-mai* to recognize resilience and the contribution of female combatants of the LTTE (there was no Tamil word for empowerment that would relate specifically to women). *Ah-lu-mai* is equivalent to the English word *empowerment* and captures "governance, authority, or leadership roles," and "authorize, give power, make able" (163). Women combatants, including suicide bombers, within the LTTE were successful in challenging some of the traditional social restrictions, especially arranged marriages, the dowry system, reverence for fertile married women, and exclusion of widows from the functioning society. Their achievements may not reflect Western feminist understandings of emancipation, but they do have broader social impact. Indeed, as Herath observes, within the Tamil social context, women embarking on the careers of motor mechanics or simply riding bicycles on the streets of Jaffna represent significant departure from traditional gender expectations and practices (2).

In other contexts, the emergence of female suicide bombers has led to the reconstitution of gender, nationalist, and religious identities (Parashar 2009). Francine Banner (2006), in her analysis of female suicide bombers in Chechnya, demonstrated how gender, religious, and national identities conflated in the persona of a Chechen "black widow." She drew on Ramphele's (1997) notion of "political widowhood" as the embodiment of the collective memory of struggle to argue that Chechen female suicide bombers serve as a catalyst for political mobilization, "giving voice to a collective mourning long silenced" (Banner 2006, 243).

Furthermore, female suicide bombers have exerted impact beyond their societies. The acts of suicide bombings involve what Friedman (2007) calls a symbolic political "testimony" in the name of the group and in support of the cause(s) for which they are carried out. Those who commit them also speak to the depth of their conviction, the intense nature of their reasons for sacrificing themselves, while personally gaining nothing earthly. Gender identity of an agent clearly matters, for it affects the extent to which testimony is or should be taken seriously by the audience. Whereas male suicide bombers do not derive additional credibility, gender identity of female suicide bombers adds an extra weight to their symbolic claims. Gender identity of female perpetrators, in other words, amplifies the gravity of their testimony. As

Friedman puts it, "Because women generally are, and are conceptualized to be, non-violent, women's symbolic claims of justified violence deserve even more serious consideration than similar acts or claims by men" (195).

Certainly, gender identity of female suicide bombers is not "a full-fledged epistemic warrant" (Friedman 2007, 196) of the legitimacy of the cause, even less so of the justification of the act of the bombing itself. However, the added credibility of the symbolic claims advanced by female suicide bombers regarding the seriousness of their reasons may have complex normative and political ramifications. Downplaying female commitment to the cause and explaining women's participation through coercion, manipulation, personal tragedy, or mental disorder undermines the strength of their symbolic claims and discredits altogether the cause on behalf of which the claim is made.

What is potentially of greater significance is the disruption female suicide bombers cause to the gendered boundary between masculine sovereign states, especially liberal ones, and feminized stateless nations. Female suicide bombers challenge the productive power of states exercised through exclusive authority to provide epistemic and normative determinacy by monopolizing "our understanding of how we organise ourselves politically, how political identity is constituted, and where the boundaries of political community are drawn" (Peterson 1992, 31). Female suicide bombers seem to abandon the limits "as we understand them with the democratic mind" (Rose 2004). They challenge one of the fundamental liberal rights – the right to life – threatening to disrupt both epistemic and ethical consensus based on the liberal idea of the desirability of physical preservation, as well as the identity of states as exclusive and effective security providers. In practice, the notion of the sacredness of human life is not absolute. It has been compromised by the extraordinary power of nationalism to command sacrifice, by the continued rationality and utility of war as an instrument of state policy, and by the acceptability of the use of coercive force in the relations among states. The challenge female suicide bombers pose to the states lies in their ability to contest the authority of states, particularly liberal states, to determine contested epistemic, ethical, and political claims. In each case of successful female suicide bombing, state failure to act as an effective security provider presents not so much a physical problem, as an ontological one that challenges the masculine state's identity as security provider.

Constructivists in IR argued persuasively that ontological security, understood as security of the self expressed in fairly stable identities and fundamental perceptions of self, is as important for the states as their physical security (see Lupovici 2012; Mitzen 2006). Ontological or identity security ensures subjective perception and experience of the state self as a whole actor and underwrites state actions and choices, in short state agency. It is predicated on and sustained through relationships with others and therefore requires certainty in and of these relationships. Uncertainty has destabilizing effects on state ontological security. One of the most fundamental state identities is its identity as security provider. It is based on the idea of masculinity and shapes the perception and practice of states in masculine terms as secure, unified, self-contained, and hierarchically ordered spaces. Women, described by Elshtain (1987) as beautiful souls who are pure and fragile and whose innocence and virginity have to be protected by men, are central to states' masculine identity as security providers. Symbolically, female suicide bombers endanger state's ontological security. They compromise states' ability to defend their identities against the danger and uncertainty of uncontrollable femininity. Effectively, female suicide bombers challenge not only the practice, but also the idea, of a masculine state and endanger the very sense of sovereign self that is constitutive of state ethos. At the same time, female suicide bombings generate the opposite symbolic effect on the collectivities they claim to represent. Here, the acts of female suicide bombings work to reinforce ontological security by bringing their collective political ends into a spotlight. These ends, as Mitzen (2006, 342) observed, "are constitutive of [collective] identity." Thus, through their acts of violence female suicide bombers sustain ontological security of the collective self they represent, which reinforces collective capacity for agency and unsettles gendered othering of their collectivities vis-à-vis masculine sovereign states.

In view of the inextricable link between epistemic and political claims, and especially considering that female suicide bombings represent the political act of contestation that emerges out of and is carried on behalf of the feminized nations, states cannot tolerate any challenges in definitional matters (Williams 2006, 258). In response, states employ a combination of discursive strategies to proscribe violent social practice of female suicide bombings as morally unacceptable (Sjoberg and Gentry 2007, 11) and to justify coercive counterterrorism. State propensity to engage in discursive and physical violence demonstrates an effort to reinstate state ontological security and gendered boundary between sovereign states and stateless nations. This explains state recourse to counterterrorism, even when state physical security against the threat of female suicide bombings cannot be fully achieved or has a counter-productive effect of provoking more acts of female suicide bombings and pushes the state into a protracted violent conflict. Coercive counter-terrorism and the conflict it perpetuates may be preferred because they erase the feminine challenge of deep uncertainty to state mascu-line identity and security. Coercive counterterrorism, in other words, fulfils the masculine state's need for ontological security, threatened by uncontrollable femininity.

Conclusion

In this chapter, we critically examined the ways in which gender per-meates different understandings and explanations of female suicide bombers' agency. An essentialist notion of gender in terrorism studies literature and journalist accounts posits a strong link between innate peacefulness and femininity. Such understanding of gender, combined with dichotomous framing of structure and agency, conditions a strong tendency towards structural determinism and concomitant denial of agency of female suicide bombers. Indeed, problem-solving literature represents female suicide bombers as always/already victims of their culture, i.e., orientalized patriarchy, and nature. Within this framework, politically violent females can be explained only through deviance, aberration, and exception to the ideal-typical norm of femininity, as women who failed to embrace and fulfil their natural and social roles.

Inspired by feminist security scholarship, we problematized the linkages between femininity and lack of female agency in political vio-lence. We challenged the dichotomous framing of structure and agency and argued for a more complex social relational approach that is key to understanding female suicide bombings as a violent social prac-tice that reflects the synergy of individual agency and socio-historical structures. Relational understanding of structure and agency as mutu-ally constitutive allowed us to reconceptualize the gendered notion of agency embedded in problem-solving accounts of female suicide bomb-ings and to recognize the agency of feminized subjects. Female suicide bombers exercize their agency to challenge socio-historical structures, social practices, and gender relations. In numerous cases, their move-ment to the forefront of political struggles has led to the negotiation of important societal compromises that accommodated deeper involve-ment and broader participation of women in the traditionally masculine domain of political violence. Perhaps, more importantly, female suicide bombers demonstrated their agential capacity in providing symbolic political "testimony" in the name of their collectivities, disrupting the entrenched gendered boundary between masculine sovereign states and feminized stateless nations, and effectively undermining the state's ontological security.

Building upon relational understanding of social structures and agents as a dynamic process of (re)production and contestation provides a necessary corrective to mainstream deterministic accounts of female suicide perpetrators. It allows us to see the multiplicity and fluidity of women's motives, identities, and commitments within the violence of suicide bombings, without reproducing them as victims, while simultaneously acknowledging the unspeakable victimization many women experience in times of conflict. Thus, a critical gender approach offers an analytical magnifying glass by demonstrating the potential of gender-sensitive analysis to dispel some of the stereotypes and misconceptions about the agency of female suicide bombers and the effects of their violence on gendered structures.

Gender, Power, and Violence: Exploring the Organizations behind Female Suicide Bombings

Introduction

Any account of female suicide bombings would be incomplete without the consideration of the organizations behind them. No matter how intriguing the story of an individual perpetrator, how important the individual choice behind the acts of violence, female suicide bombers do not act alone. Their violence is never spontaneous but epitomizes in most cases the culmination of a long, invisible organizational chain. Before a bomber performs a violent act, a series of well-orchestrated measures has to be envisioned, planned, and executed. Indeed, most observers come to the conclusion that a "successful" suicide bombing is rarely a lone act (see Pape 2005). It requires preparing suicide vests or belts, training potential bombers, and planning the missions. In some instances, it also means that the bomber is transported in proximity to the place where she will carry out the attack and, in some cases, a camera may be set up nearby to record the event. All of these steps highlight the importance of the organizational contexts. A recent trend in Iraq and Nigeria of carrying out sequential or simultaneous female suicide attacks clearly points to the presence of the organizations behind them.

This chapter shifts the focus of inquiry into female suicide bombings from individual women to the organizations behind their violence. The organizational aspects of female suicide bombings received considerable attention in both problem-solving and feminist security studies literatures. Mainstream terrorism studies scholarship produced important insights into the roles of terrorist groups in female suicide bombings, in-group gender dynamics between men and women terrorists, and the complexity of reasons why women join terrorist organizations in greater numbers than in the past. The argument and evidence in problem-solving works seek to demonstrate that the organizations employing female suicide perpetrators are rational actors and attempt to unearth the strategic logic of terrorist groups. Problem-solving literature also devotes considerable attention to examining gendered relations inside terrorist organizations. We share this scholarship's insight that terrorist groups mirror and reinforce gender subordination prevalent in the societies these groups claim to represent. Also, there exists a virtual consensus among numerous mainstream authors that female suicide bombings emerged from mutually reinforcing, coalescent processes that drove terrorist organizations to recruit women at the same time as women pressed for greater involvement in politically violent activities (see, for example, Cunningham 2003; Alison, 2009; Qazi 2011). Feminist security studies scholars, too, have been interested in the questions concerning women's precarious position inside terrorist organizations, the reasons why women become involved in terrorism, and the unique challenges they face as women terrorists (see Sjoberg and Gentry 2011). At the same time they emphasize that gender analysis is never exclusively about women and scrutinize complex connections between the broader categories of gender and terrorism. Feminist security studies scholars argue that terrorism itself is a gendered phenomenon (Sjoberg 2011).

When scrutinizing the bodies of literature on terrorist organizations produced by competing perspectives, we encounter striking parallels. These parallels indicate that there is some common ground already alongside divisive perspectivist and epistemic borders. Analysis of the organizational dimension of female suicide bombings therefore offers a real opportunity for dialogical engagement with contending knowl-edges, for loosening ideological boundaries and bringing forward commonalities. Drawing on the problem-solving and feminist security studies literatures, this chapter carefully explores gender dynam-ics among the members of terrorist groups, the ways in which gender roles are structured within these organizations and relate to the broader norms and behavioural expectations within the communities these organizations allege to represent. At the same time, we expand the lim-its of inquiry set in problem-solving literature and look into the aspects of terrorist groups left out in the mainstream analysis. More specifi-cally, we scrutinize the gendered character of the relationship between sovereign states and terrorist organizations, and demonstrate the role of the problem-solving scholarship in sustaining and perpetuating it.

We argue that terrorist organizations are caught up in an ironic gender paradox. On the one hand, as mentioned above, through their internal structures they uphold cultures and policies, gender biases, inequalities, and discriminations prevalent in the communities on whose behalf they allegedly act and engage in the politics of representing female militancy to their communities as congruent with traditional gender norms. On the other hand, they are locked in a highly gendered relationship with the sovereign states, in which they find themselves on the feminized end. In other words, terrorist organizations marginalize, sideline, and/or subjugate women and femininity at the same time as they are alienated, delegitimized, and disenfranchised within the system of relations that ascribes ontologically privileged status exclusively to the states. Their position, by default, is inferior to that of the sovereign states. This gendered relationship is sustained by the politics of representation in problem-solving analyses and has important implications for the gender identity of terrorist groups. While embodiments of masculinity themselves, speaking and fighting for larger communities, terrorist organizations are emasculated by the refusal of sovereign states to recognize their violence and political demands as legitimate. Their masculinity is further "damaged" by the feminized status of their communities whose claims, often legitimate, to self-determination are bluntly denied. This precarious position within different sets of social relations – vis-à-vis their own communities and vis-à-vis sovereign states – sets a deep tension into the gender identity of terrorist organizations, making the need for restoring feminized, "damaged" masculinity an imperative. Re-masculinization by the terrorist organizations is achieved by sustaining in-group gender subordination and by committing violence against sovereign states.

This chapter begins with a brief history of women's participation in political violence, highlights multiple and often overlapping factors behind their expanding involvement in various terrorist activities, and carefully examines the issue of increased deployment of female suicide bombers by the terrorist organizations as "today's weapon of choice." While exploring the issue of expanding female involvement in terrorism, we unearth the ways in which gender has shaped the internal structure and functioning of terrorist organizations, and demonstrate the centrality of gendered representations of female terrorists in general and female suicide bombers in particular in the interactions between terrorist organizations, the communities they claim to represent, and sovereign states.

Women's Involvement in Terrorist Organizations

Female involvement in terrorist organizations and activities is not new. Gentry and Sjoberg (2011, 58) observe that women participated in terrorism activities long before academics began to write about them. Their relationship with gender stratified terrorist organizations has always been problematic. More often than not, women terrorists were relegated to supportive activities performing subservient tasks, such as providing safe houses and cooking, smuggling weapons and ammunition through checkpoints and across enemy lines, serving as messengers, distributing propaganda, supplying medical aid and nursing the wounded, acting as liaisons to the community, and collecting intelligence. Gender stereotypes rendered traditional female roles in terrorism secondary, although one may question whether any terrorist group could be effective if most, let alone all, women withdrew their support (Enloe 1983). Still, the fact that women's activities differed little from their routine household responsibilities outside terrorism made women practically "invisible" within most organizations. Effectively, female terrorists were backstaged as the "homefront dweller" in political violence (Sylvester and Parashar 2009, 179). The failure to recognize women's roles as essential in terrorism had broader ramifications. It solidified stereotypical perceptions of female terrorists as peripheral actors with marginal influence and responsibilities. Ironically, it is precisely this gender-dictated invisibility and marginalization associated with the "second sex" that has rendered women tactically advantageous to terrorist organizations, allowing women to graduate from traditional roles and engage in militancy (Cunningham 2003; Weinberg and Eubank 2011).

In time, women's roles in terrorist organizations grew increasingly diverse. A noticeable trend in modern terrorism has been the expanded number, roles, and importance of women within terrorist organizations (Cunningham 2003; Sjoberg 2009). Women terrorists fulfil multiple and at times contradictory functions, often simultaneously, reflecting their ambiguous in-group status. Women became actively involved in traditional "male" activities, serving as combatants, operational leaders, ideologues, fundraisers, and recruiters. Empirical evidence abounds. Kesire Yildirim, a founding member of the PKK and the only female member of its central committee in 1978, was credited with infusing the PKK's strategic vision with feminist ideas (Cragin and Daly 2009, 93). Female recruiters, albeit relatively rare, were important in a number of organizational contexts, including the Sendero Luminoso (aka the Shining Path) in Peru, the Revolutionary Armed Forces of Colombia (FARC), the Provisional Irish Republican Army in Northern Ireland, and the al-Aqsa Martyrs Brigades in the West Bank and Gaza Strip (41). For example, Wafa al-Abis, a failed Palestinian female suicide bomber who was intercepted by Israeli security forces in June 2005 at the Erez checkpoint between Israel and the Gaza Strip, claimed to be a member of al-Aqsa Martyrs Brigades recruited for her mission by another woman and friend (43). Similarly, the Palestinian Islamic Jihad developed a network of well-trained female facilitators and propagandists responsible for identifying and recruiting potential candidates for suicide missions (Zedalis 2008, 53). A woman dubbed by the media as the "Black Fatima" was allegedly in charge of recruiting Chechen female suicide bombers (Parfitt, 2003). The families of Chechen female suicide bombers involved in the Nord-Ost theatre hostage in October 2002 and Russian security authorities repeatedly made references to the "Black Fatima," who allegedly also recruited Zarema Muzhikhoyeva for her suicide bombing mission in 2003 (Cragin and Daly 2009, 44).[1] More recently, in July 2014, the Nigerian military broke one of Boko Haram's cells and arrested Hafsat Usman Bako, who allegedly was a recruiting sergeant for the organization (Clothia 2014). The most high-profile female recruiter, however, has been Samantha Lewthwaite, a thirty-year-old British woman, wanted by the British, U.S., and Kenyan security services, reportedly in charge of recruiting and training female suicide bombers for ISIS in Syria. Also known as the "white widow," Lewthwaite took the name Sherafiyah after converting to Islam. The widow of 7/7 bomber Germaine Lindsay, and daughter of a former British soldier, Lewthwaite has been mythologized by the media as the most wanted female terrorist allegedly involved in a 2012 Mombasa grenade attack and the 2013 Westgate shopping centre massacre in Nairobi, Kenya (Williams 2014). It is also fairly well known that the members of the LTTE Women's Front in Sri Lanka had acted as propagandists since the early 1980s, preparing and disseminating materials about atrocities committed by the Sri Lankan government against Tamils that helped to recruit new members (46).

Some authors contend that high levels of female terrorist activity appear predominantly in leftist organizations because the ideological messages projected by these organizations resonate positively with women (Cunningham 2003). Others argue that anti-state or "liberatory" nationalist movements provide greater ideological and practical room for women than do pro-state nationalisms (Alison 2004, 2009). Still others insist that women tend to participate more in domestic, rather than in international terrorism (Gonzalez-Perez 2008b), or believe that secular, rather than religious groups are most open to the idea of accepting female membership (Ness 2008a). What emerges as a common point in terrorism studies and feminist security studies analyses is that women tend to be more active in secular left-wing nationalist terrorism than in religious, right-wing groups. Despite important distinctions in local and religious traditions, right-wing religious groups usually espouse highly conservative, scripture-oriented attitudes towards women and gender, manifesting support for a return to religious orthodoxy and orthopraxy. In response to political and socio-economic changes affecting gender and family relations, right-wing religious groups tend to underscore traditional gender roles much more than the scriptures themselves, which they invoke in order to restore conservative patriarchy (Keddie 1999). In contrast, leftist groups, at least in rhetoric, aspire towards progressive goals, including gender egalitarianism, contest existing socio-economic structures, and seek their radical transformation. Revolutionary organizations seem to exhibit more attention to women's interests, incorporate women's demands into their agenda, and develop an explicit position in support of women activists. As such, they are "ideologically more suited to justify and advocate women assuming combatant and other non-traditional roles" (Ness 2008b, 13).

One early example of a strong female presence in revolutionary terrorist groups was Narodnaya Volya.[2] It emerged in 1879 Russia as a group of young idealistic intellectuals rebelling against a repressive state and willing to test in practice the evolving anarchist dictum of "the propaganda by deed." The group's resort to violence began almost by accident, when one of its female members, Vera Zasulich, attempted, on her own initiative, to assassinate General Trepov. At the meeting with the general she fired several shots at him, wounded Trepov, and showed no resistance when his guards arrested her. Her sensational trial was used to "raise the consciousness of the masses" and popularize the revolutionary cause (Clutterbuck 2004, 158). Vera Figner, another female member of Narodnaya Volya, a noblewoman and a former medical student, became an iconic figure and a revolutionary legend. Not only did she play a pivotal role in the assassination of Tsar Alexander II but, more importantly, she was the only member of the Executive Committee left in the aftermath of the regicide who single-handedly attempted to resurrect the organization until her arrest and imprisonment two years later.

Almost a century later, women continued to be drawn into the leftist (this time New-Left) radical groups that shared the same revolutionary ethos and conceived of themselves as vanguards of the masses. Female terrorists like Ulrike Meinhoff, a co-founder of the Baader-Meinhoff Gang in Germany, Shigenobu Fusako, the founder and leader of the Japanese Red Army, Adriana Faranda of Italy's Red Brigade, and Bernardine Dohrn of the American Weather Underground became symbols of anti-imperialist resistance that often overlapped with the feminist struggles in their respective societies (Ness 2008b, 13). Where revolutionary goals blended with ethno-separatist aspirations, women have also played crucial roles in the nationalist liberation struggles. Women joined numerous nationalist groups throughout the world in comparatively large numbers. The Sendero Luminoso of Peru, the Puerto Rican Armed Forces of National Liberation, the Tupamaros in Uruguay, the Kurdistan Workers Party, the Revolutionary Armed Forces of Colombia, the Liberation Tigers of Tamil Eelam, the Euskadi Ta Askatasuna (Basque Homeland and Unity), and the Irish Republican Army were all strengthened by females who accounted for anywhere between 15 and 45 per cent of their fighting force (Ness 2008a; Cunningham 2003; Gonzalez-Perez 2008b).

Mainstream and feminist scholars agree that extending membership to women was driven in many cases by tactical and strategic imperatives of recruiting organizations (Bloom 2007; Davis 2003; Sixta 2008, Alison 2009). These include demographic trends, such as manpower shortages and dropping birthrates, intensification and increased effectiveness of government counter-insurgency measures, competition for public support with other local groups, and women's ability to use their sexuality to collect intelligence (e.g., Mata Hari) and evade detection. Nearly 70 per cent of identified suicide bombers from Chechnya were female (Banner 2006, 216). Eleven out of fiften suicide bombers dispatched by the PKK were women (Eager 2008, 176), and the estimates of the LTTE female combatants range from 15 to 33 per cent of the organization's combat forces (Alison 2004, 450).

Mainstream authors have pointed out the practice of coercive recruitment of female terrorists in general and suicide bombers in particular. Eager (2008, 176), for example, describes Leila Kaplan's path to becoming a PKK suicide bomber. She mentions specifically that Leila did not volunteer for the mission, but was allegedly coerced into it when another female PKK member was executed in front of her eyes for refusing to carry out the suicide mission. There is also some evidence that a formal policy of forced recruitment may be embraced by religious extremist groups that began to employ female operatives in the last decade or so (Ness 2008a). Rape is often emphasized, explicitly or otherwise, as a tool used in forcing women to join terrorist activities (Sixta 2008; Weinberg and Eubank 2011; Herath 2012). Bloom (2007, 143), for example, asserts that most LTTE and PKK female cadres were raped or sexually abused before becoming operatives in their respective organizations. Unlike men, Bloom (2007, 163) writes, "women are subjected to special treatment by recruiters such that women are abused in some fashion deliberately to coerce them into becoming bombers." Stack-O'Connor (2007) shares a similar observation and underscores the use of the fear of rape by the LTTE to recruit, motivate, and control Tamil women.

While we do not deny that coercive recruitment takes place, a strong and sometimes exclusive emphasis in mainstream analyses on rape and sexual violence as a way of recruiting female cadres reinforces women-as-victims construction that underscores gendered representations of female terrorists. Forced recruitment, as Jon Elster (2006, 239) noted, is at odds with the extent of dedication and self-discipline required of "successful" suicide attackers. Even some problem-solving authors questioned the validity of the general claims about forced recruitment. Speckhard and Akhmedova (2008, 118), for example, argue that most female recruits who join Chechen militant groups are not coerced. Jessica Davis (2008), while not ruling out coercive recruitment, contends that women joined the LTTE for a variety of reasons, including support for the cause and societal inequalities. She observes that the first women operatives of the LTTE came primarily from rural areas severely affected by war. Disrupted livelihoods, marginalization, and poverty may have had some impact on their decision to join the group (29). Some mainstream authors, in other words, recognize that coercion alone cannot explain relatively large numbers of female members in ethno-nationalist terrorist groups (Cunningham 2003; Ness 2008b).

Indeed, regardless of the rationale of the group's leadership for including women, it is plausible that many women make their own choice to join extremist groups and sometimes demand more active involvement (Alison 2009; Gentry 2011a). In the context of pervasive violence, women and girls often exhibit ingenuity, resourcefulness, and creativity instrumental to their physical survival and at the same time indicative of their agential capacity to resist (Brown 2011; Denov and Gervais 2007; Alison 2004; Pettman 1996). Violence saturates the social fabric so thoroughly that war itself becomes quotidian.

Violence becomes the maker and marker of social order, erasing differences between war and peace, and routinizing new social practices, networks, and processes, including shifts in gender norms and roles. Wartime social processes, including political mobilization, military socialization, polarization of social identities, militarization of local governing authority, transformation of gender roles, and fragmentation in the local political economy sometimes have enduring effects, reconfiguring pre-war social relations, fracturing and dissolving some and creating others (Wood 2008). Gender affects the extent and nature of risks and opportunities available to individuals in the context of war. Gender-specific insecurities often overlap with cultural, racial, political and economic insecurities of the larger ethno-national communities. While some females, like women terrorists, become agents of indiscriminate violence against other women and men, women are disproportionately direct and indirect casualties of the fighting, victims of torture and starvation, forced relocation and labour, disappearances, and sexual violence. At the same time, they are often the key agents solely responsible for generating and carrying out strategies of survival and resistance within the context of the "heightened masculinization of war zones" with their deepening patriarchal attitudes (Peterson 2008 15). Many contemporary irregular wars "privatize violence," erase the war/home boundary, with the combatants increasingly relying on the ongoing support of civilians and more women and children participating in combat (Alison 2004; Wood 2008).

Self-preservation and social reproduction of families and households can be achieved in a variety of ways: through high-risk sex work, looting, smuggling, theft, collaboration, or fighting. This includes a conscious decision to join the militant group. Membership in such organizations often decreases female chances of victimization, presents social opportunities and a degree of status, and offers both protection from violence and a way of ensuring the provision of basic needs. The last also points to the strong political economic logic of female activism in political violence, in which informal coping, combat, and criminal economies overlap and interact (Peterson 2008). The responsibilities of women and opportunities available to them in times of war and social instability multiply instantaneously. Some of the problems and challenges they face are material, but many others relate to the existential issues of social status, values, and aspirations. When conflict undermines formal economy and disrupts social stability and traditional livelihood, women suddenly become national political actors, soldiers, primary caregivers, and heads of households. This frees them from male control and allows them to transgress the boundaries of traditional social practices, even if only temporarily. Having assumed new roles in their households and communities, women in conflict zones are less inclined to accept conventional gender restrictions on their involvement in political violence (Pettman 1996, 133). There are gains for women in patriarchal societies who join terrorist groups, especially when their families approve of such decisions. Membership in such groups tends to loosen overt family control and, in some respects, offers increased opportunities for exercising female agency, albeit often within culturally accepted gender norms. Thus, at least some demand for increased participation in executing violence comes from women themselves. Against this brief backdrop of expanding women's engagement with modern terrorist activities, the introduction of female suicide bombings in the 1980s is not fully surprising. The emergence of this violent practice represents the next step in a logical trajectory of the widening female involvement in political violence, which coalesced with the increasing willingness of the terrorist organizations to employ women as suicide bombers.

Female Suicide Bombings as a "Tactical Adaptation"

Problem-solving authors make related arguments that can be briefly summarized as follows. Terrorist organizations are strategic, rational, power-seeking actors capable of learning goals, methods/tactics, financing, and organizational structures as they adapt to the changing environment (Cunningham 2003; Bloom 2007, 2011; Zedalis 2008). Such adaptations are crucial to the political survival of terrorist groups. As Bloom (2007, 85) puts it, "Those terrorist groups that are not rational, and do not adjust to circumstances, can lose support and may cease to exist." Within the context of this argument, female suicide bombings represent a "tactical adaptation" (144; see also Zedalis 2008) by terrorist organizations, both secular and religious. Non-state militant groups are said to use this tactical innovation alongside other violent means, typically against strategically more powerful opponents. Considering its highly controversial nature and risks of possible rebound effects, this tactic is rarely a first choice among militant groups. Rather, it is employed in circumstances when deeply entrenched power asymmetry renders other tactics, both violent and non-violent, of advancing political demands and affecting change futile or unavailable to the weaker side. The spread of this tactic is commonly associated with the learning process by insurgent organizations, or "social contagion" (Bloom 2007), i.e., a deliberate imitation of "successful" tactics by rational, calculating, self-interested, and competing militant groups in the context of the globalization of terror. Reference to the global dimension is not incidental. Rather, it plays strongly to the tendency of problem-solving literature to conceive of U.S. interests in universal terms. Even though the waves of female suicide bombings rose, broke, and subsided in different geopolitical settings, the use of this tactic is generally believed to be on the rise.

While not all terrorist organizations embrace this tactic, being constrained by normative preferences and/or the negative and counterproductive effects that this method may have had on other groups (Kalyvas and Sanchez-Cuenca 2006), there is a number of reasons why militant organizations can be motivated to use suicide bombings. Human bombs are a relatively inexpensive and effective way of intimidating, demoralizing, and coercing an enemy that has superior military capabilities, while at the same time gaining publicity and support from a sympathetic constituency and increasing the prestige of the sponsoring organization. Suicide bombings can signal infinite dedication to the cause and community in whose name they are carried out, inspire new recruits, and gain legitimacy for the organizations behind them (Bloom 2007; Crenshaw 2007). Suicide bombings are more likely to be positively accepted by supporters after other tactics have been tried and proved unsuccessful. Therefore, as mentioned above, they are rarely a tactic of first choice. Rather, they are often claimed to be the last resort and used in combination with other tactics. Bloom (2007, 78–9) explains the intensification of suicide bombings through the strategic "process of outbidding" among insurgent groups competing for support of a single constituency. She contends that when violence is perceived positively and even demanded by the local population, suicide terrorism gives a sponsoring organization an upper hand vis-à-vis its rivals in local power struggles. Other problem-solvers generally agree. Ami Pedahzur (2005, 159), for example, sees popular demand for radical violent tactics, such as female suicide bombings, as "a highly cultivated topdown phenomenon," fostered by local organizations in the context of prolonged conflicts.

Generally, reliance on radical tactics, including suicide bombings, is driven by the desire of sponsoring organizations to distinguish themselves from and outbid local political opponents, as well as garner greater popular support. By now, there is an established consensus that the benefits reaped by terrorist organizations are greater if female operatives carry out suicide attacks. They increase the pool of potential recruits not only by opening the door for other women to become suicide bombers but also by shaming and inducing men into participation (Bloom 2007, 144–5; Stack 2011, 89; Aslam 2012, 266). This advantage is well understood and exploited by those organizations that recruit women. One slogan in Chechnya reads, "Women's courage is a disgrace to that of modern men" (Bloom 2007, 145). Similarly, Stone and Pattillo (2011, 160) note that the rationale behind using female martyrs by al-Qaeda in Iraq may have been partially to shame Muslim men into enlisting. Terrorist organizations gain an additional benefit from women's involvement that adds moral high ground to their agendas and violence (Aslam 2012, 266). Female suicide bombers also attract media attention, provoke sensationalism, and exert psychological impact on a more powerful scale than do their male counterparts (Zedalis 2008, 50). These "benefits" explain the remark by Hamas leader Al-Rantisi that suicide attacks should not be monopolized by men (Aslam 2012, 265).

The Gendered Context of Terrorist Organizations

A point of convergence in terrorism studies and feminist security studies accounts is the gendered nature of terrorist groups. Despite the fact that women increasingly take on an expanded range of "male" responsibilities in logistics, recruiting, combat, ideological support, and even leadership, recognition of their contribution to the cause is significantly mitigated by their gender. Terrorist organizations – not only with leftist ideologies, but also militant Islamist groups – often masquerade as promoting gender equality and present themselves to women "under the guise of gender equality" (Aslam 2012, 265). Yet all terrorist organizations cultivate environments that are deeply gendered and hostile to women, providing little, if any, room for the pursuit of feminist aspirations. These organizations tend to replicate oppressive patriarchal practices and power structures prevalent in the communities, which they purport to represent – practices that benefit males rather than all members. Terrorist organizations offer men higher status, enable them to live up to gender expectations associated with hegemonic masculinity, and provide opportunities for self-actualization. In contrast, women terrorists almost always find themselves in an inferior status, facing intense in-group sexism and patriarchal control (Bloom 2007; Sixta 2008; Eager 2008). Even the organizations that claim to be gender inclusive, such as the PKK and the LTTE, tend to maintain and reproduce gender hierarchy through their internal cultures, structures, and leadership patterns. Examined through a gender lens, militant groups represent the "masculine ideal" (Aslam 2012, 266), the "enactments of masculinity," where the dominant organizational practices are "saturated with gendered meanings" (Ferber and Kimmel 2008, 870). As Deborah Galvin observed, "Female terrorism has no autonomy. It is part of a male engineered, male dominated activity and even the most ardent feminist must recognize both the fact and the remote likelihood of it changing. Terrorism is all about power. The male terrorist struggling for power is not about to share it with a female, though he welcomes her aid and actively seeks to co-opt it" (Galvin 1983, 3, quoted in Eager 2008, 193).

The ongoing shift in the number and responsibilities of female terrorists complicates gendered power relations between female and male terrorists. The fact that more and more women take on traditionally "masculine" roles makes any justifications for maintaining male authority (i.e., greater resilience, resourcefulness, capacity to act) demonstrably refutable, yet rarely challenged. Women's active participation in terrorist groups, especially in combat roles, threatens their male comrades' masculinity and creates gender confusion. While in need of protection, women fight alongside men; while they are comrades carrying an equal burden of responsibilities, women are not entitled to or even expected to achieve equal status (Riley 2008, 1202). This invariably pits women terrorists against their male comrades' effort to reify their masculine superiority. Such complicated gender dynamics led some researchers to suggest that female operatives "have to be more tough, ruthless and less-sympathetic – in a word, more macho – in order to compete for status and recognition in a traditionally patriarchal context" (De Silva 1995, 184). It is not surprising that sexism and traditional gender norms become convenient tools in the hands of the terrorist organizations that help them maintain gendered power imbalance and constantly force female terrorists to negotiate and assert their in-group status. An often repeated story about female members of Italy's Red Brigade who were given a list of things to do ending with "Oh, and don't forget to clean the fridge" epitomizes the persistence and centrality of gender in reifying terrorist organizations as the site of masculinity. Thus, we need to interrogate gendered group dynamics and the ways in which well-scripted sets of rules, practices, and discourses generate and reproduce gendered power asymmetry within and outside terrorist organizations.

Terrorist organizations are gendered in a number of ways. Most evidently, they are gendered in their composition, structure, symbolic images, and ideologies. Male cadres typically dominate terrorist organizations and, in an effort to guard the organizational domain of masculinity, rarely welcome females into their ranks other than in subservient roles. In her study of global female terrorism, Cunningham (2003, 179, 184) found that women who were incorporated into left-wing or nationalist terrorist cells, like the al-Aqsa Martyrs Brigade, were nonetheless barred from the top echelons of the organization. Even when women constituted a fairly significant percentage of an organization's membership and formed conventional combat units (as with the LTTE, which had a special well-organized and highly disciplined section for women, called Vituthalai Pulikal Munani [Women's Front of the Liberation Tigers]), few women reached leadership positions within such an organization (Bloom 2007, 164; Davis 2008, 22). The explanations are mixed, however. In her interview with Miranda Alison, "Thamilini" – the leader of the Women's Political Wing for the whole of Tamil Eelam – explained that men's longer involvement with the LTTE allowed them more opportunities to achieve high political position, yet gender representation in the highest echelons of the organization was changing. Of the twelve members of the LTTE's Central Committee before it suffered its most recent defeat, five were women (Alison 2004, 458–9). It is worth mentioning that the LTTE female unit had its own leadership structure. At the same time, the fact that male and female units within the LTTE were housed and trained separately both diluted gender tensions and conformed to cultural norms of appropriate behaviour prevalent in the broader Tamil community. In fact, both the PKK and the LTTE female and male cadres were separated into different units after fears of sexual liaisons plagued both organizations and incidents of rape and sexual harassment surfaced (Özcan 2007; Stack-O'Connor 2007, 50–2). Such separation was allegedly upheld by al-Qaeda in Iraq (Brown 2011, 211) and allowed to maintain the image of female members as modest and chaste purveyors of honour. After the separation of male and female members, many of the PKK and LTTE women were assigned less militarized duties, like intelligence gathering and communications, nursing and social work.

Unequal power relations are embedded within the gendered structure of insurgent groups. Although the degree of gender differentiation and inequality varies significantly among individual organizations, all terrorist organizations sustain patriarchal power relations and gender hierarchy. Their structure is based on a dichotomous gender order, which mirrors gender inequality within the societies these organizations claim to represent. It is typical for terrorist groups to prescribe specific roles to their male and female members, with female cadres often performing domestic duties of cleaning, cooking, and serving food. For example, both the PKK and the LTTE were modelled as traditional family units in which the male leader serves as the head of the clan, and women fulfil some of the most negligible support roles (Özcan 2007). Female members of the LTTE were expected to feed their "revolutionary sons" before giving food to their daughters or eating themselves (Sixta 2008, 272). Moreover, the privileging of men and masculinity over women and femininity is further reinforced by the "cult of personality" many terrorist organizations develop around the figure of a male leader. In her examination of the PKK and LTTE, Eager (2008, 175) discovered that neither of their respective leaders (Abdullah Öcalan and Velupillai Prabhakaran) tolerated resistance or disagreement that could potentially indicate the questioning of authority.

The hierarchical differentiation between male and female operatives sometimes affects their respective training and abilities to perform the same missions. Speckhard and Akhmedova (2006, 72) interviewed the families of twenty-six female suicide bombers in Chechnya. They found out that only three bombers had received any sort of military training before the execution of their mission. Generally, these women had little say in the group's operations. Many suicide bombings are planned and controlled by the male members of militant groups. For example, in the 2002 Dubrovka theatre siege, the female suicide bombers left behind to guard the hostages seemingly lacked the authority to detonate their explosive vests and were eventually overtaken by Russian forces (Speckhard and Akhmedova 2006, 73). Witness accounts of this sensational hostage crisis indicated that nineteen Chechen women participating in this operation "were almost hostages" themselves (Struckman 2006, 348). Even though they had bombs strapped to their bodies, they were to detonate them only on command from the men. Some of the hostages later recalled how one of the women reassured them, saying, "Don't worry. Without the order, I won't set off the bomb" (ibid.). Their femininity was further reinforced by their responsibility to care for the hostages (Stack 2011, 86).

Zarema Muzhikhoyeva, a failed Chechen female suicide bomber captured and brought to trial, had told her interrogators that she was "a virtual slave" to her Chechen rebels cell (Murphy 2004). Bloom

(2007) and Eager (2008) also note that Palestinian women are not the ideologues or decision-makers in the organizations behind their martyrdom operations. Berko and Erez (2007) interviewed several failed Palestinian female suicide bombers who spoke of the limited freedoms they had within their terrorist organizations, as well as their subservient roles in the planning and execution of missions. All the interviewed women were supervised and supported by men in their missions, even if these women performed only support functions. Most of the interviewed women, as well as most "successful" Palestinian female suicide bombers, did not become full members of nationalist organizations before the execution of their missions (510). Many of the Hamas and Fatah operatives interviewed by Yoram Schweitzer (2006, 30) attested that while they did not see a difference in principle between male and female terrorists, they opposed the recruitment of women as suicide bombers. Within the Iraqi insurgency movement, a female suicide bomber recruiter with the Ansar al-Sunnah group told how male cadres sought out and raped potential recruits, whom she would then have to convince to become suicide bombers (BBC News 2009).

Terrorist organizations also tend to assume highly militarized symbols and uniforms, which are meant to manifest ultimate manhood and masculinity embodied in militant groups and their activities, while preserving strong notions of femininity and womanhood. For example, even though the LTTE female operatives who were recruited into the military wings wore short hair and took on masculinized and militarized camouflage clothes (Gunawardena 2006; Stack-O'Connor 2007), the LTTE enforced a traditional dress code among non-LTTE Tamil women and girls (Wood 2008, 552). Many terrorist organizations utilize symbols and uniforms to further segregate gender and control female recruits. Some Chechen female suicide bombers took on intentionally conservative Muslim attire, which they never wore prior to their indoctrination (Speckhard and Akhmedova 2006, 72). Similarly, the LTTE instructed its retired cadres to dress in conservative and traditional clothing like the sari and wear head coverings (Bloom 2007, 102). These regulations clearly distinguish female members of terrorist organizations, including suicide bombers, from their male counterparts, and subordinate and control women terrorists. For the execution of their missions, some LTTE and Palestinian female suicide bombers wore Western clothing like short skirts (100), while Iraqi female suicide bombers were recruited particularly because they were able to conceal bombs under their flowing religious garments (BBC News 2009). These tactics help conceal the women in the general crowd, but also further distinguish them from male suicide bombers.

Finally, ideologies of all terrorist organizations involve gendered assumptions about femininity, masculinity, and gender roles. As mentioned earlier, some organizations, most notably left-wing secular and nationalist groups, rhetorically espouse the ideals of women's rights and equality. Yet they do so mainly for propaganda and fundraising. For example, in a speech on the International Women's Day, the LTTE's leader Prabhakaran allegedly stressed the need to eliminate male chauvinistic oppression, violence, as well as the dowry and caste system (Schalk 1994, 167). In practice, however, terrorist groups do not pursue egalitarian gender goals and rarely implement the principle of gender equality, even within their organization, let alone the society in general. Incorporating women into national liberation movements and groups may indicate symbolic equality of all members of the collectivity. No matter how sophisticated the blending of feminist ideals with Marxist-nationalist principles, nationalist aspirations always seem to take precedence over the feminist ones. Such precedence ensures a nearly universal pattern of post-war marginalization of women combatants and their return to traditional roles. Women's contributions to nationalist struggles generally do not get translated into women's inclusion as equal citizens. As Wilford (1998, 15) observed, "Even where women have been active warriors ... they invariably are left holding the wrong end of the citizenship stick."

Terrorist Organizations and Restoration of Feminized Masculinity

Examining terrorist organizations from a critical gender perspective brings into focus another gendered aspect of their existence that received no attention in problem-solving literature. Terrorist organizations operate within different sets of social relations. On the one hand, they position themselves as legitimate political representatives of the communities whose political demands for autonomy or self-determination are not fulfilled. In this role vis-à-vis their communities, as we have discussed in the previous section, they take on a highly masculinized identity, which is projected on their internal structures and practices. On the other hand, terrorist organizations are also embedded within the broader set of social relations with sovereign states against whom they direct their violence. In this relationship the identity and status of hegemonic masculinity shifts to the sovereign states, which successfully claim monopoly on the legitimate violence. Thus terrorist groups find themselves in an inverted gender status, on a feminized side, since their legitimacy to serve as political representatives of stateless groups is bluntly denied or vigorously questioned by the states. This contradictory position of terrorist organizations within different sets of social relations – hyper-masculine vis-à-vis their communities and feminized vis-à-vis sovereign states – represents an ironic gender paradox of terrorist organizations. Their inferior status in relation to states undermines their masculine identity and forces them to remasculinize by upholding gender inequality within the organizations and by engaging in violent confrontation with the states.

In a brilliant study of Muslim masculinities, Islamism, and terrorism, Maleeha Aslam (2012) notes that collective experience of marginalization through social isolation, economic deprivation, and life under oppressive governance, both domestic and global, challenges masculinities of postcolonial Muslim men, producing *aggressive masculinity* and *emasculated/subordinate masculinity* among indigenous men (75, 270, emphasis in the original). The former channels its political agency into militant resistance, commands authority, and provides ideological justification for militancy. The latter lacks confidence for engaging in aggressive behaviour, but being aggrieved by its marginalized position, becomes increasingly vulnerable to the influences of aggressive masculinity, which promises to restore dignity and honour for emasculated masculinity (33). Resentment and desire for vengeance against their feminized position within the existing world order and their societies erase social distance between rich and poor, erode the boundary between aggressive and emasculated masculinities, thus generating *protest masculinity*. Symbolically coded as feminine, emotions of hopelessness, powerlessness, humiliation, marginalization, shame, lost dignity and honour, etc., feed into politically motivated, strategic, power-seeking actions of terrorist groups.

To be sure, the role of humiliation and other grievances, whether real or perceived, is frequently mentioned in the problem-solving literature. Stern (2003), for example, emphasizes the role that deep humiliation plays in fuelling religious terrorism: "Holy wars take off when there is a large supply of young men who feel humiliated and deprived; when leaders emerge who know how to capitalize on those feelings" (32). Similarly, Bloom (2007, 84–5) explains ethno-separatist terrorism with reference to a combination of instrumental rationality (cost-benefit calculations with respect to goals) and value rationality (religious, ethical, and other beliefs). However, problem-solvers generally do not analyse emotive aspects of terrorism through a gender lens, even though some authors cursorily admit the role the perceptions of emasculation play in igniting violence. In the context of Iraq, for example, Bloom (172) notes, "Young Iraqi men feel emasculated by the presence of foreign troops, engaging in violence makes them feel manly and proactive that day."

Embracing a critical gender approach, however, allows us to emphasize two interrelated points. First, the problem-solving literature feminizes terrorist organizations by rendering them marginal, inferior, and devoid of historical agency and by delegitimizing their violence. Such feminization entails deliberate discursive subordination of terrorist organizations vis-à-vis sovereign states. The rivalry between hegemonic masculinity of sovereign states and more "backward," subordinated, fundamentalist masculinity of the terrorist groups (Runyan 2002) is expressed in the dialectical violence between terrorism and counterterrorism. Sjoberg (2007, 94), for example, observed how the war in Iraq was fraught with multiple genderings offering "a forum for the revitalization of manliness through competitive conquest." We contend that not only the war itself, but also the representations of the war in problem-solving literature were rife with genderings. This observation is true of all conflicts in which women acted as suicide bombers, i.e., Israeli-Palestinian, Russian-Chechen, Sri-Lankan–Tamil, etc. For example, Russian-Chechen wars produced discourses that juxtaposed "militarized, ordered, patriotic Russian masculinity" against "destabilizing, aggressive, criminal Chechen masculinity" (Eichler 2006). All these conflicts represent contests between the hegemonic masculinity of sovereign states that uphold their power and superior status by feminizing masculinity of the adversaries and keeping the latter in a subordinate, inferior position. The abuse of Iraqi (and we can add Chechen, Tamil, Palestinian, Kurdish, etc.) prisoners epitomizes the competition between masculinities and underscores hegemonic masculinity as "the standard that is to be met by or enforced on subordinated masculinities in Iraq [and elsewhere]" (Sjoberg 2007, 94).

Competition between hegemonic and feminized masculinities is framed in ethical and progressivist terms. Mainstream authors view the communities represented by terrorists "as at best the site of liberal good intentions or at worst a potential source of threats" (Barkawi and Laffey 2006, 332). Thus, Western (and Russian, Turkish, Sri Lankan, Israeli) warrior man engages in counterterror violence legitimated by sovereign states. He is presented in the problem-solving analyses as normatively superior because his violence is defended "on the basis of more humanitarian grounds" (Runyan 2002, 363), one of which is precisely the liberation of non-Western women from the clutches of feminized indigenous masculinity. Ironically, the success of Western hegemonic masculinty does not guarantee any favourable changes in the status of women, i.e., it does not signal any fundamental transformation of patriarchy and introduction of women's equality and participation. Rather, as the recent experience of Afghanistan demonstrates, such "success" may mean re-establishing the right form of patriarchy that supports Western hegemonic masculinity and shields it from threats of subordinated feminized masculinity (ibid.)

Our second point concerns the importance of *men* feeling emasculated through the experience of "feminine" emotions, like humiliation and hopelessness. A critical gender approach establishes the link between *feminized men*'s sense of victimhood and the restorative function of terrorism. We argue that terrorist violence performs an important restorative function to the gender identity and status of these organizations. Essentially, terrorist organizations seek to restore, through violence, their "damaged masculinity" (Ferber and Kimmel 2008, 874). Indeed, Ferber and Kimmel make the link between terrorism and the symbolic manifestation of damaged masculinity: "The terrorist feels emasculated, 'feminized,' and seeks through the application of rational, strategic political action, yoked to a sense of aggrieved entitlement to seek retaliatory revenge against one's perceived enemies, to restore that damaged masculinity. Both instrumentally (rational calculation) and expressively (displacing humiliation with socially approved masculine rage), terrorism is intended to be restorative" (ibid.).

Terrorist organizations manipulate gender in their discourses to recruit new members by deliberately using a strategy to effeminate men in order to make them feel that they need to recover their masculinity by joining the group. Furthermore, the experience of humiliation and the sense of other grievances are inseparable on the individual and collective levels. Thus, the perception of individual emasculation is projected onto the community/society, on whose behalf terrorist groups act. Terrorists often stress how they perceive of their societies as being exploited, marginalized, emasculated, thus confirming the victim (feminine) status of their often stateless communities. Terrorists feel that "their" feminized collectives have been degraded, threatened, colonized, and dishonored by the occupier. So they resort to physical violence (the way "real men" do it) to defend their communities, while at the same time reclaiming their patriarchal authority over society and manifesting their masculinity inside their organizations. A strong element of gender inversion is present in this ethos of the weak emasculated men turning into the strong warriors, defending their feminized communities against the enemy while reclaiming their entitlement and re-establishing their own control.

Within this context, the parallels between domestic violence and terrorism take on a heightened significance (Aslam 2012; Johnson and Leone 2005; Ferber and Kimmel 2008). Aslam, for example, called domestic violence in any form, be it psychological, emotional, or physical abuse of women by men, "inter-gender 'terrorism'" (Aslam 2012, 35), because it entails a permanent "possibility of being violated," combined with feelings of "fear, insecurity and worthlessness" (36). This type of violence is often the result of the erosion of patriarchal authority. Similarly to terrorism, it "is restorative, an act of retrieval, of reclamation of lost but rightful [masculine] authority" (Ferber and Kimmel 2008, 885). It is not surprising, then, that the growing trend to incorporate women into the ranks of terrorist organizations, regardless of their numbers, does not shake the inherently gendered nature of these groups. Inclusion of women into terrorist organizations is yet another means of maintaining control and defending masculinity.

Comparison of the roles played by Palestinian women in the First and Second Intifada underscores this argument. Women self-organized collectively during the First Intifada and sustained the national liberation struggle in multiple ways. The rapid development of the women's movement after 1987 also reflected the growing awareness of the collective power and conscious attempts by Palestinian women to ensure that they would not be marginalized. Palestinian female activists demanded, among other things, the creation of the Women's Affairs Technical Committee to equalize gender representation in the peace negotiations; engaged in legislative battles to end all forms of discrimination and inequality against women; drafted a Women's Bill of Rights; and advocated a proportional representation system with a 20 per cent quota for women (Musleh 2008). Nonetheless, as much as their civil activism promised to cement national unity, it also threatened the structural patriarchy within Palestinian society. This left Palestinian men ambivalent in their attitudes towards female activism (Brunner 2005, 43). In contrast, women's involvement in martyrdom operations during the Second Intifada seemed entirely a part of masculine undertaking. The practice of female suicide bombings gives individual women presence amidst their usual invisibility. However, there is little evidence that female suicide bombers effectively challenged the gender order within Palestinian society. Even though these particular women capture the spotlight, the presence of Palestinian women in general during the Second Intifada was not as visible as the participation of women in the collective struggle fifteen years earlier (ibid.).

It is clear that strict gender demarcation does not stem naturally from sex differentiation within the membership ranks of terrorist organizations but is socially inculcated and purposive. Terrorist organizations often reflect and actively reproduce gender patterns and identities, as well as social and cultural ideals and symbols of the larger society that uphold gender roles. Female members' transgression of established gender boundaries by joining combat or assuming other "male" responsibilities, including suicide bombings, posits a challenge to the groups themselves and to the larger society. Therefore, militant groups make every effort to ensure that even if their female members overstep the generally acceptable boundaries of femininity, the image of the group itself is not compromised or mitigated by "femininity."

Rhetorical Strategies of Legitimizing Female Suicide Bombers

Militant groups that sanction female suicide bombings, whether secular or religious, must engage in the politics of representation, i.e., they must explain themselves to themselves and to their societies in order to legitimize this tactical innovation that violates entrenched familial and societal codes (Ness 2008b, 12). This task is particularly problematic for religious militant organizations because their ideologies are highly conservative and religious extremism attaches heightened significance to women remaining in traditional roles. In Islam, only men of a certain age are under divine obligation to participate in combat jihad. Women are allowed to join in supporting roles only in exceptional and extraordinary circumstances, such as mass struggle against aggression or in self-defence (Aslam 2012, 264). This allowed contemporary Islamist movements to determine what constitutes such extraordinary circumstances, enabling women to participate in combat jihad, while preserving gender codes of behaviour (Brown 2011, 210–11). Women of al-Qaeda, for example, are expected first and foremost to follow a gender-specific interpretation of Islamism, the female jihad. The female jihad signifies and prescribes a number of traditional supporting feminine roles to be performed by women. The most important of these include raising children in the spirit of the "right" belief and supporting their male warrior relatives. Palestinian suicide bombers were initially allowed to carry out martyrdom operations only if chaperoned by men. This restriction was later replaced by the requirement that would-be female suicide bombers should obtain permission from their male relatives (Brown 2011, 211).

It is critical for militant groups that the new practices they introduce are rationalized "with reference to old values if they are not to appear anomalous" (Schalk 1994, 177). In other words, historical roots of the new practice should be "found" either within one's own past, or with reference to the experiences of other collectivities, preferably within the same culture. In an attempt to justify, encourage, and mobilize female involvement in political violence, and particularly women's participation in suicide bombings, secular and religious groups adopted many of the same gendered images and rhetorical strategies (Davis 2008; Ness 2008b; De Mel 2004). Female suicide bombers in various contexts became known by gendered names, such as the "Army of Roses" in Palestine alluding to the beauty of a flower, the "Black Widows" in Chechnya to connote an analogy with a deadly spider or widowhood, and the "Armed Virgins" in Tamil areas of Sri Lanka to symbolize respect for the social norm of female sexual purity (Herath 2012, 125). Militant groups are known to exploit ideas about femininity by using the imagery of a woman as a mother and nurturer of her children and by blending it with that of a warrior. They often picture a woman with a child and a weapon to signify that her militant role does not convey a rupture with tradition. This image shields terrorist groups from the criticism that they violate social guidelines for sex-appropriate behaviour. This image alludes that even as a warrior, a woman remains a mother whose motherhood extends from her own biological children to the entire community. As soon as the struggle is over, she will go "back home" (De Mel 2004; Davis 2008).

Indeed, a recurrent representation of female suicide bombers in the Palestinian-Israeli conflict is the idealized mother who sacrifices all for her family. Female suicide bombers are often portrayed symbolically as the mothers of the nation (Tzoreff 2006), and realistically as the mothers of children (i.e., Reem Al Riyashi). While this depiction allows women to stand at the forefront of the nationalist struggle, it also equates female suicide bombers with their ability to bear children, preferably male children, thus denying them legitimate agency as political actors. As discussed in chapter 3, female warriors, rebels, or even suicide bombers simply grant a new expression to a traditional feminine role. Their violence is explained within certain normative limits consistent with dominant patriarchal rules and understandings. Effectively, their violence is diluted to make women's militant behaviour more acceptable to the general society (Struckman 2006, 341).

Rhetorically, secular and religious militant groups employ strikingly similar strategies to justify female militancy. When introducing a break with the conventional feminine behaviour, both types of groups attempt to rationalize the role of women fighters by (re)inventing certain communal traditions and situating a new practice deeply in history and/or scriptures. This move ensures continuity in collective identity and reproduces gender norms (Schalk 1994; Ness 2008b; Cook 2008). Whereas secular groups tend to invoke a "glorious cultural past," "an imagined golden age" of their people (Ness 2008b, 21), religious groups are more inclined to justify female suicide bombings through references, often out of context, to the sacred. Herath (2012, 124) carefully documented the ways in which the LTTE constructed death of suicide bombers as a form of reverence. In the case of Islamist groups, the practice of female suicide bombings is cast as a form of jihad. Cook's (2008) examination of the classical Islamic literature demonstrates the reluctance of conservative Muslim legal scholars to accord women a role in "male" jihad. The impediments to women fighting on the battlefield were well recognized and sagely acknowledged in classical sources. However, the spreading practice of female suicide bombings required that this issue should be legitimized. Granting it historical depth was the easiest way to achieve legitimacy. This called for some examples of women fighting in jihad around the days of the Prophet Muhammad or his close companions.

To radicals committed to making a strong case for female martyrdom, the actual dearth of such examples was not an obstacle. Consequently, the first unsigned fatwa sanctioning female participation in martyrdom operations issued after the first Chechen female suicide perpetrator, Hawa Barayeva, blew herself up was decidedly ambiguous. Ironically, this fatwa made no mention of female participation in jihad. Nevertheless, radical Muslim scholars often refer to this fatwa as an authoritative legitimization of female martyrdom operations (Cook 2008, 43). The issue of a woman's right to wage jihad remains unresolved, but it certainly speaks to the daunting complexity of trying to (re)invent what some see as a tradition. Attempts to legitimize this practice reverberated throughout the Muslim world, demonstrating simultaneous malleability and stubbornness of historical memory, drawing deep fault lines, and igniting antagonisms between the more progressive and more conservative social circles in the Muslim world (ibid.). These attempts also revealed the importance of recasting "new" practices in terms of historical experiences, so that "what would otherwise be interpreted as aberrant behaviour becomes contextualized in a history of accepted ideas. The female martyr is constructed as embracing culturally accepted gender norms at the same time that she steps out of them" (Ness 2008b, 22).

Conclusion

In this chapter we demonstrated that there is a real possibility for dialogue and mutual learning between terrorism studies and feminist security studies analyses of the roles of the terrorist organizations in female suicide bombings. The two perspectives converge on a number of points: (1) women's participation in terrorism is not a recent development; (2) terrorist organizations are generally hostile to feminist and gender-egalitarian agendas; and (3) in their rhetoric and practice militant groups reproduce gender patterns and identities of the larger societies they claim to represent. A dialogue between alternative perspectives furthers our knowledge about the numerous challenges to women's involvement in terrorism. As Leila Khaled, an iconic figure in the world of female terrorism, confessed in her autobiography (1973), her major problem was that of being a woman. As a Palestinian female terrorist, she was repeatedly confronted with "four kinds of oppression: national, social (the weight of traditions and habits), class, and sexual" (Khaled 1973, 58). Indeed, traditionally, most female terrorists have been and continue to be relegated to the subservient positions within their organizations, performing routine household duties. In this sense, their responsibilities and status within militant groups do not differ much from those of other women in the broader society. At the same time, there is evidence to suggest that women's participation in terrorist activities has been expanding in numbers and responsibilities.

Problem-solving scholars emphasize strategic and tactical calculations by sponsoring organizations in their decisions to resort to female suicide bombings. They also point to the potential multiple benefits this violent practice generates so that even far-right religious terrorist organizations utilize it, despite significant difficulties of justifying female militancy. Having examined the doctrinal evolution of female suicide bombings in Islam, Gonzalez-Perez (2011) concluded that the reinterpretations of religious doctrine to legitimate female martyrdom have been dictated primarily by utilitarian and pragmatic considerations such as strategic and military tactics. Mainstream authors also devote considerable attention to the issue of female recruitment into terrorist organizations. Some authoritative voices, like Mia Bloom, tend to emphasize disproportionately coercive methods, especially sexual violence in recruiting women. Such emphasis reinforces gendered representation of women terrorists as always victims, stripped of agential capacity, deviant, and troubled. While acknowledging that there are instances of coercion, a critical gender approach reflects critically on the limitations and distortions that an emphasis on coercive recruitment entails. It offers a more nuanced understanding of the complex reasons for women's involvement in terrorism generally, and suicide bombings in particular. This approach shows that terrorist groups, despite their pronounced gender bias, offer possibilities for women in conservative societies to participate in politics / political violence without losing the protections traditionally attributed to family relations. This attracts some women who join militant groups, sometimes in large numbers, and not exclusively as followers, but sometimes in leadership roles, too. This approach also unearths a strong political-economic logic of female resilience, activism, and survival strategies in the context of pervasive and long-term violence.

In addition, a critical gender approach reveals an ironic gender paradox whereby terrorist organizations enjoy a hegemonic masculine status in relation to the communities they claim to represent, but find themselves feminized in relation to sovereign states. Competing sets of representations underpin both statuses and their concomitant gender identities. Terrorist organizations develop elaborate discursive strategies to bolster their masculine identity in the eyes of their communities and explain female involvement in militancy as conforming with communal gender norms. Mainstream academic works, on the other hand, develop counter-representations that delegitimize terrorist organizations, their violence and goals, and undermine their masculinity. Terrorist organizations pursue two strategies for restoring their "damaged" masculinity: through violence against sovereign states and the endorsement of strict gender norms in their in-group practices and structure.

Global Power, Knowledge, and the Politics of Difference in the Representations of Female Suicide Bombings

Introduction

In this chapter we draw on postcolonial and critical race theories[1] to critically analyse racialized and gendered politics of difference in problem-solving literature on female suicide bombings and expose the ways in which knowledge produced by mainstream scholarship sustains inequality and domination in global power relations. We argue that gendered Western-centric articulation of sexual, racial, and cultural difference in the problem-solving research reduces female suicide bombings to a single dimension of orientalized patriarchy and is complicit in (re)producing postcolonialism. A critical gender approach requires that we acknowledge up front that our understanding of female suicide bombings and of the social realities that influence this violence are largely constituted by the tightly imbricated discourses of gender, sex, religion, culture, and race (Kinsella 2007, 227). These discourses are neither innocent nor neutral. They are bound up with dominant configurations of colonial/imperial power that reproduce social hierarchies through borders, oppositions, and exclusions at the same time as they obscure their own demarcating function.

The objective of this chapter is thus twofold: first, we recognize the entanglement of the issues of gender, sex, race, and colonialism in the occidentalist epistemology that weaves together the images, symbols, and representations of the Western Self and the Other; and second, we disclose the essentializing nature of the gendered constitution of alterity of Oriental societies in the problem-solving representations of female suicide bombings. That is, we reveal the deforming effects of mainstream discursive constructions of female suicide bombings and expose the ways in which they produce images of these women's socio-cultural contexts as irrational, putatively oppressive, archaic, savage, and violent Other contrasted with the rational, morally, culturally, racially, and sexually superior Western Self – the United States being the dominant referent for the West (Brunner 2007; Coronil 1996).

We are mindful, of course, of the fact that female suicide bombers, even within any given cultural context, are not a homogeneous category. Individual female suicide perpetrators do not experience general social and cultural conditions uniformly. There are serious internal differences, splits, discontinuities, and fractures within their cohort, as mediating factors such as class, age, ethnicity, religion, marital status, etc., interfere with, intensify, and mitigate individual experiences of cultural and socio-political contexts. Still, despite their diverse experiences, female suicide bombers share important similarities in how they are positioned in relation to the masculinized centres of power, whether at the societal (patriarchy) or global (Western domination) levels. Thus, bearing in mind the specificity of individual women's journeys to suicide bombings and the complexity of their multilayered realities, we maintain that social opportunities available to them are affected by their subordinate position vis-à-vis the centres of power, both internal/domestic and external/global.

These masculinized centres of power are associated with various violences, which are inescapably intertwined in mutually reinforcing, synergetic dynamics. While problem-solving scholars tend to look inside female suicide bombers' societies and specifically emphasize gendered insecurity and male structural violence against women under conditions of indigenous patriarchy, a critical gender approach chips away at the monolithic Western-centrism of problem-solving representations. We do so by drawing attention to the relationship between orientalized patriarchy and gendered/sexualized and racialized hierarchy in the extant world order. We begin this chapter by asking how the process of the constitution of identity unfolds and carefully explore the representations of cultural/sexual difference in the problem-solving literature on female suicide bombings. We then inquire about the implications of such representations and demonstrate the ways in which they relate to Western interests and global power asymmetries.

We would like to make a quick note on the terminology. We do recognize the crude inadequacy of the oppositional categories of "Western" and "Eastern/Oriental" – however potent and important political identities and gendered/racialized boundaries of power they denote. Indeed, we are acutely aware of the historical specificity and social complexity that these terms obscure and of the essentialism, homogenization, and preconceived totalities that they embody. We are convinced, however, that a commitment to historical particularity should not preclude general theorizing. Thus, we follow Robbins's (1992, 175) advice to eschew "easy generalizations," but keep the difficult ones. We retain the general categories, without predetermining the character and scale of the "worlds" to which they refer. Our use of these terms in no way reflects fetishism with homogeneity, unity, or naturalness of either Western or non-Western space. Rather, in spite of their seemingly slippery malleability, we use these categories to acknowledge the complex, contested, and ever-changing heterogeneity of these political spaces.

The Politics of Problem-Solving Epistemology: Mapping the Discursive Field

In the process of constructing a particular identity, social collectivities develop understandings of the Other that at the same time constitute the Self through the production and reproduction of cultural representations of the Other. Discursive representations of the Other are thus encoded in social identity. The formation of one's subjectivity as a Self and the historical engraving of one's identity are accomplished "by way of a detour through the other" (Yeğenoğlu 1998, 1). The process of becoming a Self thrives on the carefully and skilfully cultivated imagination that connects individuals to each other and to a particular place. Although conceived by imagination, a Self and the place she or he inhabits are nevertheless real. That is, the fictive character of a Self "produces material effects by constituting the very bodies of the subjects that it subjects" (3–4). Moreover, a potentially infinite reinvention, reification, and refashioning of one's Selfhood unfolds through a dialectical-dialogical relationship with the Other. Not only does one become a Self via the Other, but one's ongoing existence as a Self is inescapably underwritten by one's representations of the Other.

Much of the recent debate around the question of dominant discursive representations of cultural difference springs from Edward Said's *Orientalism* (1978). Competing representations are frequently framed in dichotomous categories of Orientalism and Occidentalism. The former, as Said (1978) explains, refers both to the study of the Orient by Western academics and to the mode of thinking rooted in the epistemological and ontological distinction between contrasting entities of the Orient/East/ periphery/them and the Occident/West/centre/us. Significantly, Orientalism captures prevailing Western attitudes and biases towards the Orient. It invests Westerners with rationality, logic, peacefulness, liberal values, etc., while portraying Arabs/Orientals as devoid of all of these characteristics. Said is critical not only of the separate and opposed entities generated by Western thought, but also of the essentialism vested in the image of the Orient as an unchanging closed system. The Orient-ness of the Orient is not given. Rather, it is the product of the essentializing discourses of Orientalism. The Orient is orientalized through Western representations that transcend historical time and place for ontological reasons. Therefore, the Orient can never be removed or modified.

While pointing to the economic, political, social, and intellectual factors essential to understanding the development and implications of orientalist discursive practices, Said also reveals less tangible reasons for the othering of the Orient. Such othering helps the Western mind "to intensify its own sense of itself by dramatizing the distance and difference between what is closer to it and what is far away" (1978, 55). Orientalism thus shapes and reflects a deep-seated Western sense of cultural and racial superiority. It exemplifies the partiality of Western discursive constructions as well as their intimate linkage with colonialism, racism, and sexism.

Occidentalism, conversely, is frequently understood in simplistic terms to represent a dialectical response to Orientalism – an inverted construct that vilifies the Occident and reifies moral superiority of the Orient. The dialectical orientalist and occidentalist discourses shape the construction of alterity on the basis of mutual fear and distrust. Once internalized by the actors, these modes of thinking lead to social alienation and political confrontation, treating the "Other" as a threat. Moreover, insofar as the representations are not detached from power, these categories provide important insights into the understanding of global power dynamics.

Despite their frequently postulated opposition, the categories of Occidentalism and Orientalism share significant affinity in that they have originated within Western intellectual tradition. Subject to critical scrutiny, Occidentalism is not the opposite of orientalism any more than the dialectical-dialogical Self-Other, or centre and periphery are opposites (Roth-Seneff 2007, 450). Concerned with the stereotypical conceptions of the West/Occident underwriting representations of the

Orient, Occidentalism is not a simple "reverse of Orientalism but its condition of possibility, its dark side" (Coronil 1996, 56). It produces a gendered and racialized Western Self via orientalist conceptions of non-Western Others. As Carrier (1992, 199) put it, Occidentalism is "the essentialistic rendering of the West by Westerners." Fernando Coronil (1996) insightfully elucidated how "the politics of geohistorical categories" (55) shaped relational co-production of both categories, blending together conceptions of geography, history, and personhood. He demonstrated how Occidentalism and Orientalism were then reified as polarized "bounded units" – a move that erased their relational histories and locked cultural difference into a rigid, ethnocentric, and hierarchically organized binary that reflects and sustains unequal global power relations. Most importantly, Occidentalism shifts emphasis away from the epistemological dualism set by Said between the "true" Orient, on the one hand, and the Orient as the embodiment of a particular discursive production (ibid.). Occidentalism refocuses our attention away from the problematic and incomplete nature of Western representations of non-Western societies to the unequal power relations that give rise to and are sustained by such representations.

Much of the problem-solving works on female suicide bombings display a pronounced tendency towards Occidentalism through the articulation of subordinating discourses that other one billion Muslims in the world as supporting militant Islamism and oppressing women (Gentry 2011b, 179). These discourses produce twofold gendering effects by discursively subordinating Muslim societies and relegating their struggles to the peripheral status of asymmetric conflicts (see Gentry and Whitworth 2011; Barkawi and Laffey 2006). Mainstream scholars tend to engage with societies in which female suicide bombers originate as the objects, rather than the subjects of research. Common in most problem-solving works is a thinly veiled refusal to consider these societies on their own terms or to recognize their ability to represent themselves. For problem-solving scholars, exceptionalism and essentialism substitute for comparative, historicized research. Description and analysis of Oriental societies are often based on biased journalistic, intellectual, and literary sources, rather than direct and impartial observation. Western epistemic constructions are presumed to adequately capture static and uniform orientalized patriarchal societies, ignoring the constant reconstitution of social (including gender) norms, relations, and boundaries, as well as the changing social self-images in each discrete society at different points in time. Such orientalizing methodologies and discursive representations they produce are ideologically charged and overtly political. Distorted by cultural and political considerations, these representations do not merely reflect the objective, neutral knowledge of the Other. Rather, such practices of representation conjure "a paradigmatic chain of conceptions of geography, history, and personhood that reinforces each link and produces an almost tangible and inescapable image of the world" (Coronil 1996, 52), perpetuating a gendered power relationship in which weakness is a rudimentary element of Otherness.

Orientalized Patriarchy and Islam

The most common mode of occidentalist othering in the problem-solving literature on female suicide bombings draws on the notion of orientalized patriarchy in its close conjunction with Islam.[2] Problem-solvers deploy their authoritative authorship to erase all Muslim women as political subjects by emphasizing their domesticity, lack of rights, freedoms, and opportunities, while concurrently reinforcing the boundaries of orientalized patriarchy. Bloom, for example, begins her analysis of female suicide bombings by setting Western-centric referential terms of comparison. She states that the "women's movement in the 1970s brought men and women in the first world to a level of relative parity in most areas of employment, status, and opportunities. However, in the rest of the world, the position of women remains seriously disadvantaged compared to that of men" (2007, 142). There is much at stake in this dogmatic assertion. Bloom explicitly refers to the second-wave women's movement in the West to contextualize female suicide bombings by juxtaposing the achievements of Western liberal feminism and the oppressive nature of orientalized patriarchy. The notion of orientalized patriarchy allows Bloom to blend together such culturally and historically diverse societies as Tamil, Sri Lankan, Chechen, Kurdish, Turkish, and Palestinian. Bloom notes that even though the extent of women's participation varies from place to place, "a patriarchal structure dominates all ... societies" outside the Western world (147).

Bloom's terms of comparison present the conditions of modern Western women in progressive terms as advanced, democratic, and emancipated in stark contrast to that of Oriental women who are drawn as backward, secluded, and oppressed. Her narrative is, at one and the same time, differentiating and exclusive: it makes the other-ness of Oriental women an integral part of Western identity. Oriental women, in other words, represent an inferior exteriority against which the identity of the Western Self is defined. They are the essential element in the production of the Self, for Western women's status "is contingent upon the representation of the Oriental woman as her devalued other and this enables Western woman to identify and preserve the boundaries of self for herself" (Yeğenoğlu 1998, 102). Dichotomizing and juxtaposing oppressive orientalized patriarchy and liberating Western feminism helps Bloom to create a very specific context for explaining female suicide bombings and the broader political struggles of which these acts of violence are part. The political agency of female suicide bombers is relegated to sexualized and orientalized patriarchy, which depoliticizes these women's involvement in suicide bombings, as well as the acts of bombings themselves (Brunner 2007, 962–3).

Bloom's presumed and unequivocal standard entails a gendered articulation and hierarchical ordering of cultural difference. Equal rights and opportunities for men and women are set as a yardstick against which similarities and differences are judged. To be sure, the rendering of the difference does not actually mean its recognition. Quite the contrary, the establishment of the difference entails a disquieting, yet firm refusal to accept it. Unsurprisingly, this standard is associated with the West, as it represents Western feminists' achievements and reflects the conditions and rights of modern Western women. Despite its origin and development in the West, Bloom presents this standard as universal. Conflating the "Western" with the "universal" effaces the particular and specific nature of the Western. The Western is promoted as *the norm*, while the particularity of the "Others" is feminized/demoted. Bloom's narrative thus registers cultural difference through a gendered ordering of the universal and the particular. Secular, modern, egalitarian Western societies are represented as superior to the traditional, patriarchal, orientalized ones. Within Bloom's framework of oppositional and hierarchical ordering, gender inequality and the absence of women's rights are interpreted as indications of general backwardness of Muslim cultures and societies. Such backwardness is then used to establish a temporal distance between Oriental and Western societies, relegating traditional Oriental societies to the past and eliminating their culturally distinct ways of life as a source of critical reflection on the West.

Indeed, Bloom's temporalizing gesture is intended to demonstrate the irreconcilability of non-modern ways of life with Western models of progress and understandings of modernity. She deploys the categories of orientalized patriarchy and Western liberalism to create a gendered ideological message that privileges the Western perspective and legitimizes its civilizing mission as a benevolent act of liberation – an act that frees Oriental women from oppressive indigenous patriarchy and offers them a chance to participate in liberated Western universalism, concurrently reiterating their status as a distinct, separate, and inferior "Other" (Yeğenoğlu 1998, 102). Being "Western" implies a responsibility, even a duty, to universalize one's particular accomplishments. Unsurprisingly, neither category has fixed spatial coordinates, so there is a fluidity and ongoing expansion and contraction of their boundaries, as well as the elision of any internal heterogeneity. For example, the discursive representation of the Chechen wars as part of the Global War on Terror enabled and legitimized closer links between Russia and the West (the United States, in particular). The discursive invention of a common enemy – "global terrorism" – facilitated the image of Russia as a modern state with Western values and norms similar to that of the West threatened by global radical Islamism. At the same time, gendered language within such representations drew a link between the desperation of Chechen society, as well as the irrationality and hysteria it connotes (all feminine qualities), on the one hand, and global militant Islamism, on the other, to delegitimize political causes behind the Chechen struggle (Gentry and Whitworth 2011, 149).

In the context of Bloom's argument, the notion of orientalized patriarchy is ambiguously intertwined with Islam. On the one hand, the author is careful to differentiate between the religious and secular nationalist groups that utilize the practice of suicide bombings. Bloom also presents specific case studies of Palestinian-Israeli, Tamil-Sinhalese, and Kurdish-Turkish conflicts in an attempt to capture and explain specific conditions endogenous to each particular struggle. She notes, for example, that the role of religion in the Tamil-Sinhalese conflict in Sri Lanka has been rather marginal. So the Tamil-Sri Lankan conflict "has never contained the ideology of war of *all against all* as it has in Palestine" (Bloom 2007, 46). On the other hand, when devising a general theory of suicide terrorism, Bloom points to the role of ethnic, linguistic, and religious factors in extremist organizations' decisions to resort to the tactic of suicide bombings. She cautions about a potential negative boomerang effect of targeting members of one's own societal group. As an example of empirical evidence, Bloom points to the 2003 attacks by Al Qaeda in Riyadh and Istanbul and the 2004 Beslan school hostage crisis. She concludes that these attacks resulted in "significant Muslim casualties, ... demonstrate[d] that such 'collateral damage' is unacceptable to the larger Muslim community ... [and] caused a self-examination and reconsideration of violence throughout the Muslim world" (Bloom 2007, 80).

Discussing in more detail the consequences of the attacks in Riyadh and Istanbul, Bloom draws on quotes from "intelligence sources" that state that "al Qaeda loses the war of public opinion in the Islamic world by targeting Muslim women and children" (Bloom 2007, 81). Against her own caution, Bloom conflates the heinous violence of suicide terrorism with a specific culture and religion, extending the barbaric nature of the former to Muslim culture and the religion of Islam. In line with long-standing Western tradition, she deploys discursive representations of a uniform, monolithic, Islam ("Islamic world") and of cultural (Muslim) traditions in Oriental societies, as profoundly determining, in a negative way, women's conditions and lives. Bloom's one-sided account is deeply damaging in the sense that it blends non-Muslim societies (e.g., Tamil's mainly Hindu society) with Muslim ones, equates Muslim societies with Islam, ignoring their sizeable Christian, Baha'i, Zoroastrian, secular, and other minorities, and essentializes Muslim women, societies, and Islam.

Along the same line, in an effort to explain female suicide bombings using a comparative perspective, Skaine (2006) clearly privileges the Palestinian-Israeli case and emphasizes the role of Islam in inspiring female suicide bombers. Despite her observation that female suicide bombers of the LTTE were not motivated by religion (14), Skaine proceeds with a discussion of the "elements of the Islamikaze makeup" (15). This move helps Skaine to diminish the role of non-religious motivations and add an additional weight to the imbrications between Islam and female suicide bombings. An Islamic dimension of bombings is then extended to the society at large through the claim that "religion symbolically embodies society itself. It is a power greater than individual people. It gives energy, asks for sacrifice and suppresses selfish tendency" (13). Hence, Skaine's comparative framework is narrowly construed to blend female suicide bombings stemming from various struggles with those of the Palestinian case and with Islam.

Other problem-solving authors have also emphasized a link between Islam and female suicide bombings. Zedalis (2008, 50), for example, notes that "religious terrorism is a particular potent form of violence" and stresses the role of religious sanctioning of female suicide bombings by Islamic clerics as well as the blurring of the lines between nationalism and Islam in the escalation of this practice. In a similar vein, Nivat

(2008, 130) posits that Chechen women are actively participating "in the separatist-turned-jihadist struggle." Cunningham (2008) has specifically focused on the evolution of women's violence from secular to Islamic religious settings, especially female involvement in the global jihadi movement.

The quintessential link between the problem-solving constructions of orientalized patriarchy and Islamic essentialism warrants some further analysis, even though we cannot do justice to the complex debates generated on this issue. Many problem-solvers blame the absence of gender equality and women's rights in Muslim communities on the religion of Islam. Islamic practices, especially those regarding women, are often claimed to be rigid because they are authorized by the Qur'an. Indeed, these problem-solving authors, feminists and non-feminists alike, attribute differences in understanding between the Western Self and Oriental Other concerning gender mainly to the Qur'an, Islamic tradition, and holy law – a tendentious link, considering that the extent and origin of gender inequality in parts of the Muslim "world" is highly disputed. While there may be some truth to that, such representations conceal the "breaking and bending of Quranic admonitions throughout Muslim history" (Keddie 1991, 5).

It is true that Islamist-influenced legislation and a series of practices based on sharia law and the honour code have been (re)introduced in several Muslim countries, including Iran, Pakistan, Afghanistan, Sudan, Algeria, and Egypt. Integration of Islamic law into the state's legal system legalized such practices as stoning to death of men and women accused of committing adultery, equating a woman to half a man as witness to and for compensation in criminal acts, the right for men to unilaterally divorce their wives, and the right of a man or his family to claim custody of his children in the event of a separation or divorce from his wife. The honour code, in particular, presents a grave predicament for women in some parts of the Middle East. Historically not part of Islamic law, but of tribal origin, this code equates the honour of men with the purity of patrilineal female relatives, especially daughters, sisters, and wives (Keddie 2007, 24). Even minor violations of the code – based solely on gossip about female immodesty or doubt about their purity – could lead to honour killing, an unpunished murder of girls and women by their male relatives to restore the family's honour. However, the rise of the Islamist laws and practices in some societies should not be used to make generalized statements about the conditions of women in the Muslim "world."

It is crucially important to interrogate the references to religion in problem-solving analyses that situate the violent practice of female suicide bombings within the framework of Islam and imply a potential motivation for the actions of female suicide perpetrators. In line with the established Western tradition of pointing to the conditions of Muslim women in order to declare Western superiority, many problem-solving works produce a flattened image of Muslim societies by drawing a direct link between women's precarious conditions and Islam. The analytical framework developed in the problem-solving works downplays both the complexities of various discourses on women and gender issues within Islam, as well as the continuing reinvention of Islam through the confrontation between traditionalism and modernism. It blurs Islam as religion with the political use of Islam by and in the interests of particular social groups (Salime 2008; Aslam 2012) and interprets the rise of Islamism with its concomitant turn to reveiling in purely cultural terms. As such, the problem-solving approach fails to acknowledge political and socio-economic factors behind the rise of Islamist movements, including disillusionment with national liberation projects and lack of success in delivering socio-economic development (Moghadam 2012). In addition, it fails to probe how different interpretations of Islam have developed within particular Muslim communities, how collective responses to these interpretations evolved over time, and what the challenges and opportunities of intra-Islamic dialogue on matters of sex and gender are. Instead, it creates a perception of Islam as a fixed system of rules and practices grounded in the belief that there are natural differences between women's and men's capacities resulting in men being superior and having authority over women (Salime 2008; Yaqoob 2008; Keddie 1999). For example, such representations ignore the tensions that surround issues of sex and gender in the interpretive tradition of Islamic revelatory sources and the extent to which the Qur'an has been misinterpreted (Stowasser 1994, 2001; Ali 2006). Fatima Mernissi (1991), a Moroccan sociologist, argues, for instance, that the Qur'an mentions the veil only as a divide between a married couple and an outside world, not as a barrier between women and men. Barbara Stowasser (1994) provides a communitarian and gender egalitarian reading of the Qur'anic vision.

These critical insights notwithstanding, the occidentalist framework enables problem-solving authors to settle a string of deeply contentious and complex issues regarding gender, agency, religion, morality, and ethics in a simplistic summary fashion that privileges an unquestioned exceptionality of the Western Self vis-à-vis the orientalized Other. Thus, most problem-solving works on female suicide bombings assume that "women affiliated with *any* form of Islam are incapable of making choices – such as political, nationalistic ones" (Gentry 2011b, 186) and collectively convey condemnation of orientalized patriarchy and Islam. This assumption, as Gentry (2011b) notes, is subordinating, while condemnation implicit in such an assumption represents "the way in which we establish the other as nonrecognizable or jettison some aspects of ourselves that we lodge in the other whom we then condemn" (Butler 2005, 46).

The Veil

Conflation of orientalized patriarchy with Islam in the problem-solving analyses of female suicide bombings is solidified through the imagery of the veil as a symbol of women's oppression. Here, we refer to the veil as the marker of Muslim women's difference, rather than as a specific article of attire used by Muslim women. As Moghadam (1994, 2–3) put it, "Representations of modernity and national progress include the unveiled, educated, and emancipated modern woman, whereas the woman who is veiled signifies cultural and economic backwardness." When discussing the tactical advantages of Palestinian secular militant groups in deploying female suicide bombers, Bloom (2007) casually introduces the image of a veiled Arab woman. She makes a plangent claim that the organizations' leaders are not "gripped by a burning desire to see all females locked behind black veils" (144). In view of the opposition between the Western liberal Self and the Oriental patriarchal Other, which Bloom laid out at the beginning of her analysis, the implications of her assertion are far reaching. The mapping of Islam onto orientalized patriarchy extends the symbolism of the veil far beyond Islamic societies. Bloom's narrative suggests that all females "in the rest of the world" are trapped behind the veils, both literally and metaphorically. The author may or may not have wished to suggest this inference, but the representational framework that blends orientalized patriarchy with Islam connotes and conditions such an extension. Bloom's reference to the veil is hardly incidental. In fact, it reflects the common tendency among problem-solving authors who write on the topic of female suicide bombings to evoke the imagery of the veil as a complex signifier of everything Oriental – it denotes a particular article of Muslim women's attire, represents the elusive and deceptive mysticism of the Orient, symbolizes Muslim women's oppression, etc.

Writing about the women of Al Qaeda and their indoctrination into the ideology of Salafi Jihad, Von Knop (2007, 409) notes that these women "perceive the *hijab* (veil) not as repression, but as an act of liberation and faith that endows a female Muslim's life with honor, an aura of respect and dignity. It is also a symbol of power over their husbands as being a good Muslim who follows the 'true' Islam." Von Knop makes it clear in her narrative that the "true" symbolism of the veil is not liberation at all, but repression and control. In doing so, she oversimplifies the conditions of women in conservative Muslim societies. To amplify the "truthfulness" of this suggestion, Von Knop makes her statement about the hijab within the context of the discussion about religious girls' schools. Girls "start every day [in these schools] with songs praising the glory of being a Shahid and by stepping on the flags of Israel and the United States" (410). Similarly, Skaine bluntly conflates the veil with oppression and Islamist militancy. While discussing the novel ways of online training and indoctrination of female suicide bombers, Skaine (2006, 19) quotes from the jihadist cyber-magazine *Al-Khansaa*: "We will stand covered by our veils and wrapped in our robes, weapons in hand, our children in our laps, with the Koran and the Sunna of the Prophet Allah directing and guiding us."

These references to the veil within the problem-solving accounts may seem marginal, however their significance and symbolism should not be underestimated. As Yeğenoğlu (1998, 42) puts it, "There is always more to the veil than the veil." On the one hand, the veil is emblematic of the prevalent Western perception of Muslim women's invisibility in the public sphere – the invisibility conditioned by female inferior sexual status in orthodox Muslim societies either as totally repressed or as erotic objects. The veil, in other words, is perceived as determining Muslim women's physical place and symbolic position within the structure of society and represents masculine power and superiority over the feminine. As such, it is central to the occidentalist constitution of the Orient. The image of a veiled woman is used to demonstrate the extent of female victimization by sexist Islamic orthodoxy, as well as to reinforce racial and sexual othering of Muslim women and societies. On the other hand, we have noted earlier the progressivist emphasis on modernity in the problem-solving representations of cultural difference. Modernity is associated with a particular form of institutional governance based on transparency. From the colonizer's perspective, the literal unveiling of Muslim women and the symbolic unveiling of Oriental societies through the establishment of transparent forms of governance are an integral part of the conquering and reforming of the country and people, in general. This political doctrine has not changed since the French colonization of Algeria. Ironically, such a doctrine often results in the strengthening of indigenous patriarchy, as the recent Western attempts at the "liberation" of Afghanistan and Iraq amply demonstrate.

At times, the very names coined in reference to female suicide bombers betray the racialized nature of occidentalist practices of representation. A number of scholars highlighted racist overtones in the vague term "black widows," popularized by the media, academics, and allegedly the Russian Federal Security Service (Banner 2006; Eichler 2006; Sjoberg and Gentry 2007). That term ostensibly refers to the Muslim Chechen women veiled in traditional black Muslim dress, who carry out suicide bombings to avenge the deaths of male relatives at the hands of Russian military and security forces. It may also have originated in the notion of the "black Arab" (Banner 2006, 239), in which case it conveys the perception of black widows as the double Other, being Muslim and non-white. The term thus reflects conventional racialization of Chechens in the history of the long-standing Chechen resistance against Russian imperial domination. Discursively, Chechens have long been racialized by Russians as *chernye* (blacks), their skin colour being associated with lawlessness, criminality, and more lately terrorism and Islamic fundamentalism (Eichler 2006, 499; Sjoberg and Gentry 2007, 93–4). Thus, the veil becomes a marker of double othering – veiled women are other-ed vis-à-vis Western women and vis-à-vis men in their own culture. The symbolic meaning of the practice of veiling extends far beyond the mere reference. The veiled woman is the metaphor for the Oriental culture, a signifier of cultural difference. It enables the Western subject to "postulate a place that can be delimited as its own and serve as the base ... while simultaneously erasing the very process of this production" (Yeğenoğlu 1998, 41). Problem-solving discourses deploy gender, race, and religion to portray women wearing the veil as little more than slaves of patriarchal aggressive and misogynistic Islamic conservatism. Clearly concerned with conveying the "truth," this discourse popularizes sensationalist and essentialist assumptions about "alien" cultural practices and generates, perhaps unwittingly, racist hostility towards Muslim societies. The constructed imagery of the veil is evoked to truncate our understanding of its cultural significance and its complex political effects.

Problem-solvers' assertions about the invisibility of veiled Muslim women is the result of incomplete knowledge of the importance of

Muslim women's domestic power, as well as their social and political activism. A critical gender approach enables us to see the religion of Islam as both a major site for justifying women's oppression in Muslim societies, as well as the source of their empowerment. This approach allows us to reinstate non-Western, including Muslim, women as historical and political actors by recognizing their agency amidst structural constraints of orientalized patriarchy and reconceptualizing their nodes of oppression "as terrains of struggle and powerful sites for women's collective identity" (Salime 2008, 202–3). It grapples with the difficult and highly controversial question of increasing women's involvement in militant Islamist movements as agents within the masculine domain of political violence (Sabbagh 2002; Aslam 2012). For example, in 2007 under Taliban patriarchal dictates, female students of Jamia Hafsa seminary in Islamabad resorted to vigilantism against other local women in the name of upholding "the Muslim way of life" (Aslam 2012, 263). Their actions demonstrated agential capacity to act amidst widespread social mobilization in support of Islamism. Jamia women used their black burqas as a distinctive religious symbol that gave them higher moral ground vis-à-vis other local women (266).

A critical gender approach invites us to resist essentialist constructions of the veil by highlighting the complexity and diversity of Muslim women's reasons for wearing it. These range from fashion and pragmatism to religious conviction to overt coercion (Secor 2002). Seeing the veil as the symbol and tool of gender oppression in Islam belies diverse practices of veiling and obscures the fact that many Muslim women do not veil at all, either because they choose not to or because they are not allowed to do so in public spaces, as in Turkey. We argue that there is a plethora of historical and cultural meanings of the veil, as well as the broad scope of social norms pertaining to women's decision to veil. For example, in Afghanistan under the Taliban, the practice of veiling signified serious restrictions on women and was intertwined with the power politics of patriarchy (Hirschmann 2003). In other contexts or within other temporal limits, however, women upheld and defended the practice of veiling voluntarily.

Moreover, against the backdrop of a long history of gendered struggle between Muslims and Westerners, "the home [and the veil representing woman's place at home] has become a last line of defence against a West that has won out in political and economic spheres" (Keddie 1991, 2). For example, the most veiled, urban, middle- and upper-class Muslim women are more likely to enjoy Qur'anic inheritance rights, holding and managing any amount of property. This shatters the myth about disadvantaged veiled women having no or fewer rights (6). Even within the same Afghani context, during the Soviet occupation and Western "liberation," many women upheld the practice of veiling as a symbol of resistance against forceful de-veiling by foreigners. Therefore, general statements about veiling in the "Muslim world" are admittedly problematic, for "the universalism such terminology seems to endorse denies these cultural variations and specificity" (Hirschmann 2003, 171). It is not the practices of veiling, but rather the Western reaction to them that appears "fairly universal" (175).

A critical gender approach cautions against seeing all indigenous practices in negative terms and points out that the custom of wearing the veil may, but does not have to, be as harmful and denigrating as it appears to outsiders. If studied in proper context, the veil may be discovered to have a positive side. For example, Nikki Keddie's work (2007, 1999) demonstrates how in the Iranian context wearing a traditional dress has expanded women's personal autonomy and their ability to forge a space outside the private sphere. In particular, Keddie illuminates the complex and contradictory dynamics within Islam regarding women's status and rights, arguing that Islamism, a distinctive political ideology on the basis of the particular interpretations of Islam (Aslam 2012, 12), is both a reaction against women's violation of traditional gender roles and a way for traditionally dressed *bazaari* women to enter into the public life. Examining women's status in Iran in the aftermath of 1979 revolution, Keddie (2007, 1999) notes a considerable resurgence of women's activities in the media, literature, education, and the arts, and a far broader participation of Iranian women in the labour force than in several other Middle Eastern countries that do not have Islamist governments. Fundamentalists, as Keddie (1999, 27) astutely notes, "commonly accept many contemporary, and even Western-oriented, changes in women's status, including education, companionate marriage, and, de facto, a place in the workforce. Their family ideal is often only a few decades old." Indeed, for fundamentalist Muslim women in Iran, participation in religious political organizations loosened overt family control to the point where they could attend the mosque unescorted or even reject marriage partners proposed by their parents. Some women claimed greater respectability and pride from devoting their lives to family and home; others embraced the opportunity to work outside home. Perhaps, in light of Keddie's work, the results of the survey conducted by the Union of Women of the Don Region (Russian

Federation) in 1999 are not so wholly surprising. The poll revealed that two out of three Chechen women favoured the idea of establishing an Islamic state in Chechnya and one in four respondents supported sharia courts (Joseph and Najmabadi 2005, 601). To some Chechen women, the veil represents a sense of, and membership in, community, identity, and faith, to others it is a mark of agency and resistance.

Last, but not least, a critical gender approach also urges us to question the gendered meanings and applicability of Western dichotomous categories of public and private, Westernization and Islamization, in analysing the current revival of veiling in the Middle East, as well as the pertinence of these concepts to the historical and cultural contexts that determined the meanings of the veil. Elizabeth Thompson (2003), for example, argues that the conceptual framework of public and private did not appear in the medieval and early modern Middle Eastern women's history and that the topography of women's experiences is more adequately captured by the terms of seclusion and mobility.

Historical specificity and contextual sensitivity do not offer some privileged access to "accurate" knowledge, but they do provide a useful starting point for research, as they allow for a more nuanced understanding of how ideas and practices function within their respective contexts. Making space for discussing these contexts in an intellectually honest manner presents a double challenge. On the one hand, it entails producing fuller and more complex understandings of the veil as a symbol with various cultural meanings. On the other hand, it means moving away from the specific focus on *Muslim* women, societies, and Islam to the complex intersection of broader questions of gender, race, religion, and power in the discursive representations of female suicide bombings. Responding to the first challenge, Decker's (1990–1) excellent investigation of the use of terrorist violence as a political strategy in the campaign for decolonization in Algiers emphasizes the agency of Algerian women in their revolutionary struggle. His work conveys the extraordinary capacity of the Arab women to manipulate the veil for political ends and sustain resistance of both women and men against the colonizer. Drawing on Frantz Fanon's 1959 essay "Algeria Unveiled" (Fanon 1967, 35–63) Decker moves beyond the essentialist image of an Arab woman as a victim of Muslim orthodoxy. On the basis of Fanon's "historic dynamism of the veil" (63), Decker distinguishes three stages in the Algerian revolutionary struggle, each characterized by a different form of indigenous resistance in response to French strategies of colonization. The first stage is marked by "the cult of the veil" (Decker 1990–1, 190), i.e., the tighter covering of Algerian women in the veil as a reaction against France's efforts to remake Arab women through unveiling and conversion to the European value system. Celebrating the veil was perceived by Algerian women (and men) as a liberating response to the colonizer's sexist culture. The tightening of the veil symbolized resistance against the common colonial formula, which prescribes victory over the women as an inevitable precondition for successful colonization (189). During the second stage, the veil disappears and Algerian women actively join the public struggle. This "coming-out process," driven by strategic considerations, is "a radically *anti*-essentialist gesture that allows the Arab woman to lift the veil of colonial uniformity and to exercise a potentially heterogeneous form of power" (191). The veil appears again during the third stage of the struggle in response to the colonizer's overwhelming suspicion that everybody is involved in terrorist activity. In response, the Algerian women re-veil themselves, allowing themselves to evade detection while remaining actively engaged in the revolutionary struggle. Reclaiming of the veil during the third stage of the revolution manifested unabated resistance against the invasion of Algerian culture and conscious determination to preserve cultural authenticity. The manipulation of and control over the veil sustained Algerian resistance, enabling the Algerian women to become the historical agents who, even if only temporarily, challenged the conventional notion of femininity in Algerian society and contributed significantly to the unsettling of colonial order.

Decker's analysis expands conventional Western understanding of the veil and its complex effects on the revolutionary struggle of Arab women by demonstrating that the veil can simultaneously be oppressive and liberating (1990–1, 185). The veiled space is at once the signifier of power and a site of oppression. It is oppressive in that it positions Arab women in a subordinate position against the centres of patriarchal and neo-imperial power. Yet concurrently, it is liberating in that it brings out the revolutionary agency of Arab women that disturbs the dominant orders of patriarchy and neo-imperialism based on masculinity. A veiled Arab woman is both concealed/invisible and visible, which in Decker's words (1990–1, 188), "gives the simultaneous and undecidable effect of power and lack, presence and absence." Decker's complex and nuanced account of the veil within the context of Algerian revolutionary struggle not only reinstates Algerian women as an important revolutionary agent, but also restores what has been skilfully erased from Western historical memory, i.e., the link between terrorist violence and successful decolonization campaigns.

The case of the Algerian women using cultural norms and gender expectations to participate actively in nationalist struggles is not an exception. To many women in Palestine, Chechnya, Afghanistan, Iraq and Sri Lanka, their hijabs, niqabs, dupattas, chadors, burqas, purdahs, and saris have provided an opportunity to preserve their cultural authenticity and certain constancy in the face of external instabilities and pressures. Some of these women have used gender and cultural stereotypes about "appropriate" behaviour and dress to assert actively their agency by smuggling ammunition and fake identity cards, collecting intelligence, and even gaining access to enemy targets as suicide bombers. A famous example of using traditional dress by female perpetrators to evade detection is a 1991 assassination of the former Indian prime minister Rajiv Gandhi by a female LTTE member "Dhanu," which was discussed in chapter 2. Dressed in a new white sari usually worn by pregnant women, Dhanu had a harness of six grenades on a belt strapped snugly around her stomach. As Gandhi walked by, Dhanu knelt to kiss his feet as a sign of respect. She activated the bomb as the prime minister reached out to raise her up, killing them both instantly. Chechen and Palestinian female suicide bombers are also known to have manipulated the veil to take advantage of the stereotypical profiling, traverse through checkpoints, and successfully carry out their missions. For example, Chechen women participating in the 2002 Moscow theatre hostage operation were dressed in the Middle Eastern–style burqa. A year later, two Chechen females who blew themselves up at the Tushino rock festival near Moscow wore Western-style T-shirts and short skirts.

Postcolonial Subjectivity

The second challenge, as mentioned earlier, is to move away from the specific focus on *Muslim* women, societies, and religion to the complex intersection of broader questions of gender, sex, race, culture, religion, and power, especially how they pertain to the construction of (post)colonial subjectivities. The discursive dynamics within much of the problem-solving literature on female suicide bombings reproduces a gendered dualistic, categorical distinction between the West and the Orient – a distinction that constitutes the hegemonic colonial identity with its multiple and cross-cutting determinants. Problem-solving narratives position women in non-Western societies as faceless, voiceless, helpless victims in need of Western intervention in order to gain their rights. Such discourse implicitly upholds a familiar dichotomy that pits feminized "tradition" against "modernity," and relegates women's domesticity to the realm of conservatism/tradition. It focuses on the conditions and rights of women to support Western interventionism and militarized masculinity (this issue is discussed in more detail in chapter 6).

A close reading of the problem-solving literature reveals that gendered representations of sexual, racial, and cultural difference are potently mapped onto each other in recreating (post)colonial subjectivity. Problem-solving analyses of female suicide bombings are intimately interlocked with the West's will to power in that they justify (post)colonialism and function as an element of masculine, (post)colonial domination. For example, Christine Sixta (2008) deploys occidentalist discourse in her analysis of female terrorism in developing countries. She grounds her argument within a comparative framework in which contemporary women terrorists in Colombia, Kurdistan, El Salvador, Sri Lanka, Chechnya, and other "developing societies" are judged against American "new women" from the first wave of feminism. While arguing that today's women terrorists are the "new women" of developing societies, Sixta notes an important distinction: these women "do not want to throw open the gate of Western modernity to their traditional societies" (263). She finds their position "ironic," because "Western imperialism would most likely bring Western democracy and Western capitalism to their countries" (283). This, in turn, would lessen the patriarchal grip on the lives of women in developing societies. What is striking in Sixta's framework is her pronounced emphasis on Western modernity, which reiterates the distinction between the Western Self and the non-Western Other, as well as her overt defence of Western imperial expansion. The emphasis on Western modernity is embedded in the occidentalist practices of representations. Dichotomization of identities allows Sixta to introduce the Western perspective as the only normatively acceptable and desirable option. The author cautions that "for humanity's sake, we must find ways to stop the violence ... While Western democracy is not appropriate everywhere, most western capitalist democracies have succeeded in reducing terrorism" (Sixta 2008, 284).

A critical gender approach emphasizes that the discursive and political realms of (post)colonialism are inseparable. As Yeğenoğlu (1998, 16) notes, "The production of the knowledge of the Orient and the process of its subjugation by colonial power do not stand in an external relation to each other." Western power, understood in a Foucauldian sense, induces problem-solving discourse and knowledge. However, the process of knowledge production and the very act of representing is concealed by claims of objectivity and epistemological superiority. Assuming "truth," moral high ground, and authority, problem-solving authors exercise important productive power to construct gendered explanations of world order that reflect and reify Western interests and power. They *"create* not only *knowledge* but also the very reality they appear to describe"* (Butler 1993, 94). The perspectives and interests of the women these authors purport to represent, if noted at all, are dismissed "as false consciousness, the final effects of patriarchal colonization" (Hirschmann 2003, 171). The body of knowledge produced by problem-solving authors generates material effects when it is put in the service of (post)colonial expansion, as in the recent Global War on Terrorism, in which one of the justifications for invading Afghanistan, for instance, was the deplorable conditions and victimhood of Muslim women (Aslam 2012, 263).

The popular analogy between women's oppression and colonization underscores the feminine character of the dominated and the masculine nature of the colonizer (Decker 1990–1; Pettman 1996). Symbols, imagery, codes, and representations in the problem-solving works on female suicide bombings not only connote women's oppression outside the Western world, but also signify the Orient as feminine, concealed behind the veil, out of control, and threatening. The problem-solving discourses produce essential equality between the nature of the feminine and the nature of the Orient, create "a chain of equivalence in which woman is the Orient, the Orient is woman; woman like the Orient, the Orient like the woman, exists veiled" (Yeğenoğlu 1998, 56). At the same time, the binaries of the problem-solving representational model constitute the identity of the Western subject in antithetical terms as masculine and imperialist. Borrowing from Yeğenoğlu's observation made in a different context but highly relevant here, the imagery of the veil marks the production of an "exteriority," a "threat" (41). This threat, as well as the fear and hostility associated with it, persists in the problem-solving inquiry into the female suicide bombings.

In their endeavours to *"explain the unexplainable"* (Bloom 2007, 17, original emphasis) and by posing the questions, as Bloom (1) does, "Are they scared, are they angry, do they fully understand what they are about to do?" and "How bad must your life be if you think that it is better to be a sacrifice than to live?," problem-solvers betray deep-seated fear of and latent hostility towards cultural, racial, and sexual difference. Viewed through the gendered/sexualized lens, the imagery of the veiled Muslim woman upholds the discourse of the imperial masculine Western Self. The veil obscures transparency, stands in the way of control. Therefore, unveiling opens up access to reforming and controlling the feminized orientalized Other. The recourse to raced/gendered othering offers a way out of the trap of "the unexplainable," "intranslatability" (Rajan 2012, 16), incomprehensibility, and confusion. Employing raced/gendered othering, problem-solving scholarship produces the Orient as a unique and exceptional socio-cultural space, separated by the temporal/historical walls and social distance from and contrasted with an emancipated, enlightened, rational Western Self (Said 1978). This discourse frames Oriental Other in subordinating terms as the feminine space of inferiority and danger (Cockburn 2007; Gentry and Whitworth 2011; Wilcox 2013). Female suicide bombers are cast as an inevitable attribute and symbolic representation of the putatively oppressive patriarchal Orient. At the same time, strong racist overtones – Oriental, Third World, Muslim/Arab – denote hierarchization and disempowerment, and effectively reinforce masculine practice of domination based on racial, territorial, cultural, and religious associations (Cockburn 2007, 7).

Discursive production of essentialized, orientalized patriarchy glosses over the distinct political agendas of the groups employing female suicide bombers and discards the geopolitical, socio-economic, and cultural specificities of different conflicts in which females commit suicide bombings. Orientalized patriarchy produces a paradigmatic space without clear boundaries, embracing places and people far removed from each other. This discursively constructed space is at the same time real and imagined. It is malleable enough to accommodate Islamist and secular terrorism on the basis of threats, physical and discursive, that they posit to the moral, tolerant, and cosmopolitan West. Indeed, "the presumed irrationality, insanity, immorality and otherness of 'suicide terrorism' … [take] us back to the presumed rationality and naturalness of wars on terror, of the logic of the legitimate use of physical violence by nation states and international bodies, and of the masculinist, racist, and occidentalist nature of International (power) Relations as such" (Brunner quoted in Brown 2011, 208).

The struggle between the West and "global terrorism" manifests itself not only in physical violence but, perhaps more so, in the discursive battles over establishing and controlling dominant interpretive frames, over the ability to feminize resistance by rendering certain world views illegitimate, and over the power of naming and names (Duvall and Varadarajan 2003; Bhatia 2005). Attempts to manage and control violent resistance through naming can be observed, for example, in the politics of the "terrorist" label the Sri Lankan government deployed against the LTTE to pursue its strategic goals. This label denied the LTTE international legitimacy, discredited the political project of Tamil independence (Nadarajah and Sriskandarajah 2005), and was central to the government's implementation of the "final solution" to exterminate the LTTE altogether (Slee, Senewiratne, and Karunarathne 2009). Similarly, the politics of naming has been deployed by both sides in the Palestinian-Israeli conflict in their respective national projects to construct places, identities, and international imageries (Peteet 2005). Discursive focus on "Palestinization" and "terrorism" discredited Chechen nationalism as impotent, erased all legitimacy from Chechen postcolonial resistance, and framed the Chechen struggle as "part of escalating global Islamisation" (Gentry and Whitworth 2011, 156). Indeed, the conflict over names and naming between insurgent groups and states became exceedingly pronounced with the launching of the Global War on Terror. The power of established names is such that it commands the monopoly on truth, obscures their contentious nature by concealing the disputes through which the names were attached to specific subjects in the first place, defines these subjects, their relational positions, and relative power, and dictates inclusions and exclusions. Identifying a "terrorist" or a "female suicide bomber" is therefore a gendered exercise of power that adds confusion in both legal and political realms. At the same time, frequent lack of information about perpetrators and the political aspects of their violence "creates its own subordination" (Gentry 2011b, 184).

By silencing alternative discourses in academic and political circles and by ostensibly serving particular interests in global power relations, terrorism studies scholarship produces a series of subordinating binary juxtapositions, inscribing "others" with negative characteristics and motives, assigning the brutality of "their" acts to the fundamentally evil character of the actors, and contrasting "them" with "us." For terrorism studies scholars, a terrorist is always "the other" who directs violence against "us." While "us" takes on different meanings in specific contexts, ranging from innocent individuals to Western civilization as a whole, "them" is invariably presented as an "objective" threat. In this way, terrorism studies defines a terrorist threat without acknowledging its constructed nature. The result of this process is a web of discursively produced linkages whereby "us versus them" dichotomy is subtly woven into an intricate net of other oppositions, i.e., innocent-vicious, stability-chaos, friends-enemies, progressive/superior/civilized-backward/inferior/savage. Terrorism studies scholarship on female suicide bombings is, therefore, a particular way of attaching meanings, stereotypes, moral connotations, and labels to acts, groups, individuals, and societies using a highly politicized and gendered process of name-giving. The structure of knowledge produced by mainstream research combined with the focus on the practical relevance of their analyses serves as a self-reinforcing foundation for the preservation of the global power-relational status quo.

In view of the constructed nature of knowledge and productive power it generates, the social positioning of knowledge producers bears profound essentializing and exclusionary implications. As Prugl (1999, 8) put it, it matters who "the knower [is]." Acknowledging social embeddedness of knowledge invariably invites the charge of relativism and may undermine the legitimacy of one's knowledge claims. However, an alternative to relativism does not have to be a single, totalizing, scientific vision with coercive consequences. A critical gender approach calls for the need to unearth historical contingency and contestability of objective knowledge claims about our "fully textualized," socially negotiated reality (Haraway 1988, 577). It calls for "a conception of truth [that is] situated, perspectival, and discursive" (Hekman 1997, 356). It is important to be aware of the "'eye/I' ... that constructs the 'world-as-picture' and makes the 'world-as-target'" (Kinsella 2007, 227), to be aware of the vantage point from which the explanations about female suicide bombings are produced, and of the moral significance of discursive violence implicit or explicit in such explanations. Such awareness enables one to see the sheer complexity of the geopolitical, linguistic/epistemic, and moral subtleties that circumscribe analytical judgments of this violent practice.

Conclusion

Problem-solving rationalizations of the practice of female suicide bombings embody implicit gendered notions of the world order based on Western moral, cultural, racial, and sexual superiority. They intertwine discourses of gender, race, sex, and religion in the differentiating and hierarchizing articulation, constitution, and ordering of difference. The notion of orientalized patriarchy occupies a central position within this discursive othering. It marks the boundaries of difference and denotes a specific inscription of the gendered relationship between masculine West and feminized East that is grounded in the persistent colonial legacies and power imbalance. This literature constructs, mobilizes, and enforces a series of dichotomies – self/other, security/insecurity, masculine/feminine – and as the next chapter demonstrates, these dichotomies determine the meaning of security and the objectives of security practices whereby Western masculine states are to be secured against the ever-threatening feminized Other.

Our critical gender approach scrutinizes discursive representations, value biases, knowledge interests, and political orientations that are found within problem-solving analyses. It illuminates the tropes of gendered modes of differentiation, whether through the emphasis on Muslim women's domesticity, their lack of political rights, or veiling practices. Articulated in contradistinction to modern Western societies, all of these differentiations conjure the feminized images of Oriental societies on the basis of Western terms. These conjectures frame female suicide bombers, their societies, and the broader political struggles of which these acts of violence are part in a very specific light, as an attribute of sexualized and orientalized patriarchy. At the same time, gendered ordering of cultural difference effectively shields Western societies from critical self-reflection and obscures tight imbrications between Western power and problem-solving practices of representation.

Chapter Six

Counterterrorism, Gender, and Human Security

Introduction

Beyond essentialized distortions and stereotypical generalizations, discussed in the previous chapters, analyses of female suicide bombings produced by problem-solving authors are geared towards justifying and endorsing counterterror measures. Therefore, the validity of mainstream knowledge should be scrutinized against its relationship to specific political actors, interests, and counterterror policies. Such scrutiny leads to questions about the preoccupation of mainstream terrorism studies literature with state counterterrorism. We argue that ontological, epistemic, and political claims advanced by problem-solving authors are tightly interconnected in that ostensibly apolitical, independent, and objective knowledge they produce is, in fact, informed by the goal to guide policymaking in the West, and more specifically in the United States. Such knowledge is quintessentially political and gendered in that it is attuned to governmental positions of hegemonic masculine states and their allies and fulfils the ideological function of justifying and legitimizing coercive U.S./Western actions against groups and collectivities deemed suspect, aggressive, and threatening not only the West but global peace and security more generally (see Raphael 2009; Jackson, Breen Smyth, and Gunning 2009).

A critical gender approach requires that we ask how such knowledge is used to explain and support certain foreign policies. We need to carefully examine existing policies to counter the spread of female suicide bombings as well as mainstream academic recommendations to improve them, and contemplate with all seriousness, credible alternatives that are gender-sensitive, morally appealing, and practically feasible. This requires an acknowledgment of the essential contestability and gendered character of security and the state as its exclusive and privileged referent object within problem-solving analyses. We need to remember, as Hurrell reminds us, that there is nothing natural or "self-evident about the statement that the greatest threat to peace and security comes from international terrorism. Indeed, from a variety of contexts, moral positions, and analytical perspectives, such a statement is manifestly wrong" (Hurrell 2007, 182).

In this chapter, we address overwhelming concern of the problem-solving authors with counterterrorism and underscore the critical importance of formulating an alternative to the gendered state-centric counterterrorism approach based on the emancipatory notion of human security. Our approach to addressing the violence of female suicide bombings eschews a gendered distinction between terrorism and counterterrorism by reorienting the analytical lens from the policymakers to the "policy-takers" (Neufeld 2001, quoted in Toros and Gunning 2009, 105). It calls for a fundamental shift in the referent object of security and recognizes individuals and communities, rather than states, as bearers of rights, duties, entitlements, and capabilities. A gender-sensitive human security approach can inform strategies not only to protect would-be victims of the acts of female suicide bombings but also to address insecurities that lead to these acts of violence in the first place.

Gendered State and Security in the Problem-Solving Approach to Countering Female Suicide Bombings

The framing of female suicide bombings as a state security issue is widely accepted and taken for granted / un-theorized in the problem-solving analyses. The mainstream approach is heavily statist, concerned with the question of how states can prevent and respond, in cases where prevention fails, to the acts of female suicide bombings. Embedded in this conceptual framework are fundamental political, normative, and gender issues that not only circumscribe the referent object and scope of security, but more importantly reflect a particular understanding of politics. In asking "security for whom?," this approach ontologizes sovereign nation states as a fixed and immutable form of collective existence and elevates states, gendered as masculine, above other forms of collective existence. It locates agency and legitimacy exclusively within states, specifically Western states, and feminizes other collectivities. Privileging of the states through prior theoretical assumptions of their primacy and the irrelevance/illegitimacy of other collective actors influences how counterterrorism is studied, understood, and pursued.

Importantly, the problem-solving argument rests on the uncritical acceptance of the enduring validity of the monopoly of sovereign states on the legitimate use of violence and presents counterterrorism as an attribute of the state, "a response to terrorism" (Skaine 2006, 151), which threatens to rupture and destabilize the state. This often boils down to the normalization of state coercion, which is viewed and defended as an inevitable solution to terrorist violence. At the same time, intrinsic gender bias serves to determine whose violence counts as terrorist and counterterrorist. This bias, as Sjoberg (2011, 237) observed, can be traced to the gendered understanding of security in global politics – an understanding inherently linked to the gendered "constitution of authority in speaking/enacting security" (Aradau 2004, 391). More specifically, problem-solving authors focus on the strategic choices that Washington has made in the past or might make in the future with regard to countering suicide bombings. Thus, the issue of contemporary counterterrorism has been conceived from the perspective of hegemonic, masculine Western states and through the lens of the strategic interests of the United States in the immediate context of the American occupation of Iraq and the NATO counterterrorism strategy in Afghanistan. The increasing spate of suicide bombings and the deliberate targeting of American soldiers in Iraq, who *"appear* as occupiers" (Bloom 2007, 173, emphasis added), were presented as a direct threat to U.S. national security (168). In addition, problem-solvers are increasingly concerned about the expanding geography of female suicide bombings with the intensification of terrorist activity of ISIL in Syria and Iraq, and Boko Haram in Nigeria, as well as the eventuality of this violence reaching American soil.

Against the analytical focus on the U.S. Global War on Terror, problem-solving authors support the strategy of war, coupled with "other elements of national power such as diplomacy, intelligence and economic policy" (Skaine 2006, 151), as a legitimate and rational response to female suicide bombings. Such war is clearly framed in civilizational terms – it is led by the United States on behalf of "civilized societies and countries and individuals [who realize increasingly] that we have got to bond together" (Mazzetti 2006, quoted in Zedalis 2008, 63) – reinforcing occidetalist framing of female suicide bombers and their societies. In other words, problem-solvers' proposed solution to the violence of female suicide bombings is counter-violence, or more violence and increased insecurity among those subjects affected by counter-violence. Effectively, the problem-solving approach justifies and perpetuates the politics of exceptional measures (see Aradau 2004) that entails a suspension of normal democratic politics, invokes masculine logic of urgency and survival, and is based on hegemonic masculine domination. The most common policy recommendation advanced by problem-solving scholars is "*to outbid the outbidders,*" that is to obtain tactical advantages over the terrorist groups employing female suicide bombings (Bloom 2007, 191). These include, inter alia, disrupting the recruiting, fundraising, and financial networks of the terrorist organizations engaged in this practice, collecting intelligence about prospective perpetrators and pre-empting successful execution of future attacks, developing strong ties with local communities, rewarding moderate leaders and populations for their cooperation, and undermining support for extremism through socio-economic programs. The last are not understood in terms of deep structural changes, but rather as short-term measures to improve relations with local communities so as to obtain the "most useful intelligence," the "foreknowledge" about terrorist groups, "for whoever has better intelligence is the winner" (Hoffman 2003 quoted in Zedalis 2008, 63).

Problem-solvers generally accept that military counterterrorism may be effective in the short term but is highly problematic in the long run. They admit that coercive counterterrorism measures may actually be implicated in sustaining and fuelling both male and female suicide bombings. Scott Atran, a recognized authority on state counterter-rorism, has criticized intelligence practices derived from the analysis of positivistic/rational choice models focused on the "frequency and recentcy of past occurrences." According to Atran, the more "one looks to the ripples, the less one is prepared for a tsunami" (Atran 2006a, 286). And, as Bloom (2007, 181) put it, "Military force is a hammer, but not every problem is a nail." The broad use of checkpoints and curfews, barbed wiring of villages, bulldozing of homes, transfers of popula-tions, targeted assassinations, and arbitrary detentions fuel deep feel-ings of resistance, unleash reprisals, and inflame reaction. In many cases, indiscriminate suicide bombing attacks provoke frustration and overreaction, including acts that seriously violate human rights and curb civil liberties. This, of course, is exactly what some terrorist organizations hope to accomplish. Terrorist groups employing suicide bombings are perfectly aware of the human rights dilemma, and of the fact that it is aggravated by counterterrorism measures. Jeffrey Simon (1994) calls it "the terrorist trap" – an overreaction that entails the use of maximum military force, which in turn mobilizes resistance. Extensive security measures at the expense of human rights serve as a proof of the evil and uncompromising nature of the enemy and help militant groups exploit instances of human rights violations, like the abuses of Iraqi prisoners by the U.S. male and female guards at Abu Ghraib, to garner support for their tactics, ideology, and causes. For this reason, most problem-solvers criticize excessive reliance on military force and are generally sanguine about punitive, hard-line, counterterrorism measures.

Yet they also recognize that while suicide bombings are exceedingly difficult to defend against, states are not completely defenceless. States can increase their security by improving border protection (Pedahzur 2005), introducing a policy of "offshore balancing," thus ending foreign military occupations, while making sure that the "others" have no capacity to disrupt the status quo (Pape 2005), applying a measured policy response through the closure of foreign funds for terrorist-sponsoring organizations, improving the socio-economic conditions of the local "target" population (Bloom 2007), channelling political solutions to conflicts (Pedahzur 2005), and relying on policing, rather than military force (Gambetta 2006). In line with the logic of rational choice, these recommendations, once applied, are meant to undermine popular support for suicide bombings and strategically outmanoeuvre the "other" side. Thus, suicide bombings are assumed to wither away. However, even some problem-solvers are sceptical about the potential of these policy recommendations to put an end to suicide bombings. If successful, the proposed measures could stimulate "learning" by terrorist organizations, rather than abandonment of the tactic (Crenshaw 2007, 162), trapping the states in the endless cycle of the "outbidding of the outbidders" (Bloom 2007).

To mitigate the negative effects of coercive counterterrorism, some problem-solvers recommend that military measures be supplemented by the provision of political and economic opportunities through general reform of "closed political systems and economies" (Bloom 2007, 181; Zedalis 2008; Skaine 2006). Thus, the export of democracy and the market economy by Western liberal states becomes another central element of counterterrorism alongside coercive, military force. As Zedalis (63) puts it, "The use of all elements of national power (e.g., diplomatic, economic, military, and intelligence) is ... required" to counter suicide bombings. This recommendation represents profoundly gendered, quintessential liberal thinking encapsulated in the idea of neo-liberal globalization and the Democratic Peace thesis. The former allows problem-solving authors to ignore inequality as a systemic and structural feature of the global political economy and the role of the global arms trade in sustaining contending masculinities. Mainstream scholars, as Runyan put it, "background or evacuate the issue of inequality-producing nature of the global economy and its role in enabling money and weapons to circulate freely among competing masculine subjects as well as the role of the West, and particularly the US, in supporting a variety of ... patriarchal regimes gone mad" (2002, 363). The latter justifies exclusionary practices by masculine liberal states and their allies of coercing non-liberal states and stateless collectivities into the liberal political framework. It makes the war between liberal states and non-liberal subjects "appear 'normal,'" deflects criticisms from liberal states, and "implicitly accords both 'responsibility' and 'absolution'" for their violence (MacMillan 2006, 55).

Such a recommendation obscures the extent to which a commonly accepted view – that, regardless of their actions, the presence of non-liberal subjects posits a "problem" (MacMillan 2006), in this case a security threat – shapes permissive attitudes towards coercive counterterrorism measures by Western liberal states and their allies. Indeed, while expressing concerns over excessive reliance on coercion, the core literature fails to provide extensive and adequate analysis of the disproportionate destruction and significant human costs wrought by the counterterrorist actions of the U.S./Western and U.S.-backed governments. The victims of counterterrorism are sidelined to the margins of mainstream analyses. For instance, leading problem-solving scholars often praise the policies of the Turkish government vis-à-vis the PKK, emphasizing a successful implementation of a stick-and-carrot approach by Istanbul authorities, which combined repressive measures with a string of socio-economic reforms. The latter included the creation of governing structures for Turkish Kurds, improvements in agriculture and education, and sizeable investments in infrastructure. At the same time, the issue of systematic and aggressive use of state coercion during Turkish counterterror campaigns in the 1990s, and U.S. complicity in it, is largely silenced. Similarly, Israel's widespread and protracted use of terrorist methods in the Occupied Territories receives very little treatment (see Otto 2012). Consistent violations of human rights by Israel led former UN Secretary General Kofi Annan to declare that while terrorist acts are grave violations of human rights, "to pursue security at the expense of human rights is short-sighted, self-contradictory, and in the long-run self-defeating" (quoted in Catignani 2005, 259).

Such emphasis on state coercion and disregard of structural violence highlights an important aspect of gender dynamics within the problem-solving narrative about countering female suicide bombings. Framing counterterrorism as a traditional state security issue implies that the content of security can be determined only from a statist, masculine position of power and privilege. The emphasis on the state as an exclusive referent object of security circumscribes the scope of issues rendered as security problems. Abstract definitions of security from above mean that everyday insecurities of ordinary people from the "bottom up," including food, health, lack or absence of economic means to sustain oneself and one's family, and inability to participate in the life of one's community are not part of the security equation. Such an analytical framework conflates security of individuals and groups with that of the state. "Security is," as Buzan and Hansen aptly summarized (2009, 9), "about crucial political themes such as the state, authority, legitimacy, politics, and sovereignty." The state is rendered as the protector of individuals because it has the masculine identity of security provider. The state reserves the privilege not only to respond to threats and insecurities, but also to identify them. Crucially, the provision of security by the state entails "the expectation of subservience on the part of the subject. The power relations upon which the state relies disavow human agency; they reject the abilities of humans to identify in/securities and to contribute to the creation of security" (Hoogensen and Stuvoy 2006, 211).

Indeed, gendered statist bias translates into a general disinclination or outright refusal by leading scholars in terrorism studies to give serious consideration to the histories and conditions of continual occupation, social marginalization, deprivation, underdevelopment, and other encroachments on human dignity and integrity generated by the global structures that favour liberal capitalist states at the expense of the non-liberal subjects. Problem-solvers' state-centric, materialist, and political-military approach reduces female suicide bombings to the traditional security issue. Consequently, the mainstream narrative on the subject is one of danger, threat, control, and coercion. This narrative profoundly shapes mainstream recommendations on how to tackle the violence of female suicide bombings. Even when the shortcomings of violent counterterrorism are acknowledged, problem-solvers remain generally resistant to any meaningful and systematic incorporation of structural violence into their analyses. For instance, concerned that Israeli-type counterterror practices, emulated by the American forces in Iraq, have ignited resentment against the occupying forces, Bloom (2007, 191) suggests that there is need to meet "legitimate aspirations and grievances of people who have been deliberately or unknowingly wronged in the past." This is strikingly out of tune with her overall position and with specific counterterrorism recommendations she advocates. Aside from this brief remark, the issue of remedying past wrongs receives little or no treatment in her analysis. Framing female suicide bombings as a violent tactic profoundly shapes the content and boundaries of Bloom's work. It dictates how counterterrorism should be pursued and precludes Bloom (and other problem-solving authors) from engaging with the issues of structural violence. "*Complete* analyses," as Zedalis (2008, 54; emphasis added) observes, require only a consideration of individual characteristics of the perpetrators and a focus on the organizations. Therefore, "individual motivations and organizational processes must be equally studied to exploit 'soft spots' and stop suicide bombings" (ibid.). Not surprisingly, such analyses are in the vanguard of sustaining militaristic counterterror policies, leaving little, if any analytical space for the inclusion of structural violence and its explosive potential to ignite physical violence.

We argue that although interest-driven calculations at the level of organizations play an important role in female suicide bombings, the view that this violence can be reduced to an insurgent tactic overlooks social relations of domination based on culture, race, ethnicity, class, and gender. It also downplays violence – physical, discursive, and structural – against and resistance by the marginalized groups. The societies from which female suicide bombers come are beset by years, sometimes decades, of humanitarian crises and human rights abuses resulting from civil war, state repression, foreign occupation, localized political violence, and patriarchal as well as global structural domination. The critical challenges confronted by women individually and collectively in places like Sri Lanka, Turkey, Chechnya, Palestine, Iraq, Afhganistan, and elsewhere include gender oppression, socio-economic marginalization, continual deprivation, poverty, and experiences or perceptions of discrimination and injustice. These experiences form the basis for the underlying conditions that lead to resistance and undoubtedly influence women's engagement in political violence, since individual women's conditions and status are affected by the social life of their communities and the body politic. Therefore, revealing relations of dominance and illuminating inequalities that are generally obscured within the dominant discourses on female suicide bombings posits a way of escaping easy generalizations and addressing those ambiguities in problem-solving analyses. Challenging the problem-solving approach to counterterrorism requires "emancipatory visions of security" geared towards understanding "how the security of individuals and groups is compromised by violence, both physical and structural, at all levels" (Tickner 2001, 48). It requires a vision of security that goes beyond the strict masculine logic centred on fear, threat, and violence. It requires a vision of security that reveals the vulnerabilities, while recognizing the capabilities of individuals and communities to chart their own security. It requires a vision of security that accounts for the politics of identity and difference and is sensitive to the historical contexts in which insecurities are played out. It requires a vision of security that moves beyond gendered state-centric bias and can meaningfully account for and address myriad insecurities found within multilayered social relations.

Human Security, Women, and Gender

In searching for the ways to address and remedy weaknesses in the problem-solving approach to countering female suicide bombings, the primary challenge is to find a concept of security that brings into focus security needs and the interests of feminized subjects who are routinely marginalized, exiled, or silenced within the mainstream paradigm of national/state security. That is, formulating an alternative counterterrorism approach requires a significant shift in focus away from the state as the referent object of security and from the discourses and practices that centre on status quo management. It requires an non-hierarchical understanding of security from the perspective of individuals and communities, as well as recognition of the need for major social, economic, and political changes within intersecting gendered structures of oppression at all levels, from local to global. We suggest that the notion of human security offers an analytical framework for rethinking state-centric counterterrorism.

Human security made a potent entrance into the policy and academic lexicon in the early 1990s.[1] Crucially, articulation of the broader conception of human security reflected growing concerns over the conceptual and analytical limits, as well as problematic normative and political agenda of traditional statist-military thinking about security.[2] Human security concerns itself not only with the material dimension of security, but also with the attainment of human dignity, thus stressing the importance of personal autonomy, control over one's life, and unhampered participation in the life of a community (Thomas and Wilkin 1999, 3). Understood as "freedom from fear" and "freedom from want," human security represents the kind of normative and theoretical reasoning that simultaneously recognizes the complexity of socio-cultural contexts and posits the universality and indivisibility of human security. Stemming from this concept is the notion that forms of violence and threats to the everyday lives of individuals ought to be examined within the particular contexts in which they emerge. At the same time, no human insecurities in any context are insulated. Therefore, the concept ought to be understood holistically: it cannot be pursued by or for one group at the expense of others. The attainment of human security in one part of the world is contingent upon the security of people elsewhere.

Like other critical security concepts that evolved in the late 1980s and 1990s, human security compounded academic and political-activist agendas. Unlike these other concepts, it benefited from the advantage of a strong institutional foundation when the UN Commission on Human Security embraced the concept, and from the adoption of human security by a number of states as a guiding element of foreign policy (Buzan and Hansen 2009). In 1999 a Human Security Network was formed by Canada, Norway, and twelve like-minded states to advance the concept. This advantage notwithstanding, the discussion on human security in both policymaking and academic circles fractured across the widening and deepening divide. This led to increasing disagreements over what human security is, how it relates to state security, and whether or how it can be operationalized.[3]

Feminist scholars generally welcomed the broad approach, although their encounter with human security produced mixed reactions – from willingness to embrace the concept on the basis of numerous points of convergence with feminisms of various strands (Hoogensen and Stuvoy 2006) and its potential to draw attention to specific gender-based insecurities (Fox 2004), to rejecting the concept because it failed to reconceptualize security (Wibben 2011). This encounter, as Marhia (2013, 20) put it, has been "decidedly ambivalent in its slippage between celebration and critique." At the same time, the influence of gender-informed perspectives on the general understandings of and debates on human security has been marginal at best.[4] When acknowledged as pertinent to matters of human security, gender was rarely included as a category of analysis. Instead, the category of "women" has been added to the discourse of human security to invoke gender-based vulnerabilities and insecurities, including domestic violence, wartime rape, human trafficking, and ethnic cleansing.[5] For example, in the mid-1990s the UN introduced two major indices for measuring gender inequality and women's empowerment on the global scale – the Gender-Related Development Index (GDI) and the Gender Empowerment Measure (GEM). Both indices were used extensively to implement a string of measures to empower women. The first focused on inequality in achievement between men and women, while the second provided a measure of agency evaluating progress in women's advances in political and economic forums. Both measures have been used for advocacy and monitoring purposes and have become key in the fight for gender equity as an important element in human development. However, both indices have serious flaws, especially in poor conceptualization of gender, labour, power, and empowerment, as well as their disregard of crucial gender-related issues, such as childcare, sexuality, and women's rights (see Bardhan and Klasen 1999; Dijkstra 2002; Charmes and Wieringa 2003). Culturally specific social and political dimensions of gender relations were unaccounted for in these indices (Wieringa 2006). As a result, many of the development projects based on these measurements left out gendered religious and socio-cultural constraints on economic development, including sexual division of labour, control over women's mobility and sexuality, and women's substantive involvement in non-waged work.

Similarly, engendering human security in conflict resolution and peacebuilding translated within programmatic and operational realms into the attempts by liberal donors to increase women's presence and participation in the formal arenas of decision-making. The inclusion of women in the formal structures of governing was meant to recognize female contribution to the struggle and consolidate women's gains during war (Abeysekera 2006). Thus, the solution to gender-based exclusion from the positions of political power was found in the simple increase of the number/proportion of women in parliaments by introducing a quota system for female representatives. This approach ignored gendered power outside the often corrupt and sometimes powerless formal governing structures, masked the persistent state of women's subordination, and dismissed a full range of important concerns with which women are overwhelmingly confronted daily. It neglected sexuality and security of the body, domestic violence, forced marriages, reproductive health, polygyny, inheritance rules, and numerous violations of women's rights, many of which are considered to be in the private domain. As Wieringa (2006, 219) observed, "[Wo]men's political power spans many more areas than national parliaments … Ideally, women should be accepted as full and equal partners at all levels where decisions are made about their lives." Such broader understanding of power requires a deeper appreciation for the workings of differentiated and gendered power relations, as well as strategies attuned to specific contexts, while focused on the common goal of gender equality and equity. In this context, Blanchard's (2003, 1292) observation that "critical security discourse has generally invoked, but not engaged, feminist scholarship" adequately captures the relationship between gender and human security perspectives.

Indeed, both examples – mainstreaming gender on the basis of GDI and GEM and engendering human security in the process of peace-building – speak to the masculinist universalizing tendencies promoted by liberal and radical feminisms (Elshtain 2000; Hudson 2005).[6] These cases prove that simply adding women to human security leaves this concept, as well as the practices informed by it, vulnerable to the risks of universalizing masculinity. This is directly relevant to female suicide bombings and sheds light on the reasons why female perpetrators of political violence are difficult to account for within the framework of human security, unless they are first victimized. As Tickner (1991) observed, a female suicide bomber is not a "woman whose common experience gives concern for human security" (quoted in Sjoberg and Gentry 2007, 4).

Despite the paucity of productive encounters, analytically and politically there is substantial convergence between human security (broadly understood) and gender perspectives in that their normative, theoretical, and activist endeavours are concerned fundamentally with freedoms that enable individuals to feel secure without threats to physical survival and dignity. Both challenge security from above as elitist, hyper-masculine, exclusionary, and unreflective of the security concerns of the people "below" (Blanchard 2003; Tickner 1992), sustain anti-statist reasoning, and are critical of the top-down articulations of security. In fact, this feature of broad human security provoked the criticism that this concept represents the feminization of security, for its "imagery as sentimental, feminine, utopian, and therefore incapable of transfer to the international arena for rigorous analysis, is powerful in the world of policy and scholarship which specializes in [security] matters" (McSweeney 1999, 15).

Feminist and broad human security perspectives emphasize the importance of context in the conceptualization and understanding of security. In contradistinction to mainstream hierarchical articulations, security is viewed "as a multiplicity of securities flowing concurrently" (Hoogensen and Rottem 2004, 168–9). Thus, security is characterized by fluidity that leaves open its specific content and makes it dependent on the concrete spatial and temporal context (Uvin 2004). Moreover, security should be understood as a dynamic process, rather than an objective practice (or set of practices) captured and enclosed within the rigid structures of masculine sovereign states. Security as a process cuts across levels (individual, household, community) and sectors (gender, class, race, ethnicity) and ties them in a complex and synergetic dynamic (Hudson 2005; see also Hoogensen 2005). Feminist contestations of the politics of boundary, deconstructions of the false and constraining dichotomies (inside/outside, public/private, local/global, domestic/international), and insistent calls for the "politics of connection" (Eschle 2001) are all relevant for developing an inclusive, comprehensive, and multidimensional understanding of human security.

Rethinking security as a fluid process also highlights the significance of power and identity politics in determining security and underscores gendered power relations through which actors with particular identities are (re)produced by invoking discourses of threat and danger (see Blanchard 2003; Tickner 2001; Sutton and Novkov 2008). Such rethinking requires, among other things, that we acknowledge that "human insecurity results directly from existing structures of power that determine who enjoys the entitlement to security and who does not" (Thomas 2001, 160). Therefore, the experiences and perceptions of threats by minorities, especially those located in sub-dominant sites of gender, ethnicity, class, and religion, differ from those of majorities (Thakur 2004).

Despite these commonalities, the feminist perspectives on security and broad human security approach part ways in significant respects. While the concept of human security with its origin in the liberal tradition is broad enough to accommodate gender considerations, it explicitly stresses the importance of understanding, conceptualizing, and responding to threats, insecurities, and vulnerabilities of the individual, *regardless* of gender identity. Specific mention of gender is deemed counterintuitive for singling out gender above all other catego-ries of identity. This is contrary to our position in that, like most feminist scholars, we assert that the universalizing aspect of the human security approach runs a substantial risk of perpetuating "a false holism" (Hud-son 2005, 162). That is, we argue that human security with the focus on the individual is not immune to the androcentric mode of reasoning, but is deeply gendered. Engaging critically with human security entails questioning the seemingly gender-neutral term *human* within this con-cept that obscures gendered undercurrents of security discourse and practice (Keeble and Smith 1999; Tickner 2001; Hudson 2005; Marhia 2013). Reflective deconstruction of this category reveals at once a funda-mentally gendered nature of the abstract "human" within the human security framework, as well as the gendering effects – discursive, material, and political – of human security in reproducing dominant norms, identities, and power relations. These effects are manifested in excluding or insecuring some groups of humans. Since gender repre-sents a dynamic analytical instrument that helps to uncover inequali-ties and insecurities across, between, and within often overlapping collective identities (McKay 2004), leaving gender out of the human security framework obscures one of the most fundamental and wide-spread relations of domination that underscores other unequal power relationships based on race, ethnicity, culture, or class. As Hoogensen and Stuvoy (2006, 218) put it, the "power relations of gender illuminate the nature of all identity relationships." Since gender traverses all areas related to human security, gender identities and parameters should be viewed as crucial signifiers of the security needs of the individual.

Equally problematic from a critical gender perspective is the reference to community security within the human security approach. Commu-nity security is defined as security deriving from "membership in a group – a family, a community, an organization, a racial or ethnic group that can provide a cultural identity and a reassuring set of values" (UNDP 1994, 31). Community security emphasizes the collective/identity dimension of security and cannot be underestimated for understanding security dynamics below the state (whether at the level of an extended family, tribe, or ethnicity). It rightly points to the embeddedness of individu-als within broader communities and recognizes that one's experiences of insecurity are influenced in important ways by the dynamics within and among groups. Incorporation of the relational aspects of security into the framework of human security registers the importance of inter-dependence of individual and group security: both individuals and communities are recognized as important agents of security. Still, omission of the analytical category of gender obscures the ways in which gender interferes in and shapes interactions between individuals and communities, how gender works to produce and reproduce collective identity, and how it determines intra-communal marginalizations, exclusions, and insecurities (Sutton and Novkov 2008).

In the UNDP's formulation, community security overemphasizes ethnic tensions and discriminations. But the UNDP report neglects to recognize the entanglement of ethnicity with gender and other identities. It faces the danger of "purifying" ethnicity and constructing ethnic hyper-identity (Hoogensen 2005, 128). Consequently, community security either relegates gender-based inequalities within and among ethnicities to the margins, or does not recommend how to overcome them. For example, the 1994 UNDP report points to the experiences of gender-based insecurity, when harsh treatment and oppressive practices, such as genital mutilation endured by women in traditional cultures, are mentioned under the rubric of community security. However, within the parameters of the presumably "gender-neutral" human security approach, solutions to gender-based insecurities boiled down to an expression of hope that "these traditional practices [will] break down under the steady process of modernization" (UNDP 1994, 31).

Engendering Human Security

A critical gender approach to engendering human security attempts to avoid universalizing tendencies of liberal and radical feminisms. Engendering human security entails critical reflection on its normative assumptions and political implications, especially the politics of difference and social relations that this approach sustains. In regards to female suicide bombers, while recovering commonalities and continuities in the security needs and interests specific to women and femininity, it recognizes the intersectionality of gender with numerous other identities within specific contexts. This leads to an emphasis on the difference and the importance of creating analytical space for structurally marginalized actors to elaborate localized approaches to human security. Such a framework develops contextual understandings of human security by asking whose freedom from fear and want is at stake, "which human beings we are talking about, in what context, where and to what effect." Rather than sustaining "false holism," such an approach stresses "broken," "fractured," or "fractious" holism

(Hudson 2005; Runyan 1992), in which "universality" of human security does not mean "uniformity." Human security informed by a critical gender approach creates analytical space for accommodating heterogeneity of everyday experiences, captures the complexity of multiple and diverse roles played by women and men in times of war, and allows us to uncover insecurities experienced by female perpetrators of suicide bombings.

Conceptualized as "fractured holism," human security is vulnerable to three major critiques. First, any contextualized, gender-sensitive human security approach can be criticized for being excessively concerned with differences across multiple socio-historical spaces. The disadvantage of the framework that attempts to synthesize differences is that while working to dismantle the master narrative of human security, it unwittingly promotes a different kind of universalism in the form of contextualized narratives. Conversely, the second critique is that the analytical focus on the plurality of experiences and identities opens the door to relativism, thus preventing the possibility of developing a general knowledge of the world "out there." We believe both critiques reflect the fallacy of dichotomous logic whereby universalist underpinnings of human security cannot but exclude particularities. The challenge here is not necessarily to force a choice between either the general or the concrete, but to recognize that "differences are relational" (Hudson 2005, 169). Therefore, we need to find a way to balance the universal and the particular and to move away "from hierarchical to relational thinking" (ibid.). Such thinking promotes dialogue on what we do, how we think, and who we are. It contributes to a deeper understanding of the social practices and structures, ideas and ideologies, as well as individual and collective identities that inform our understanding of such practices and structures. Relational thinking, as discussed in chapter 1, creates analytical space for understanding female suicide bombings as an act of resistance embedded within and directed against power relations of domination and subordination. Resistance, as Hoogensen (2005, 130) rightly observes, is "a product" of these relations and should be recognized as such by a gender-sensitive human security perspective. And since identities are the driving force behind domination and resistance, in the case of female perpetrators, suicide bombings "can be seen as a moment of identity choice" (ibid.), of contestation of the imposed identities and structural positions that come with these identities.

The third concomitant critique is that the study of difference and attention to identities may preclude the development of practical policies aimed at addressing existing insecurities. We recognize that this proposed approach is not easy to implement. However, the embrace of difference, if not treated as absolute, can become an instrument of a larger process of emancipation, that is of "the freeing of people (as individuals and groups) from those physical and human constraints which stop them from carrying out what they would freely choose to do" (Booth 1991, 319). Embracing difference as an instrument of emancipation invites researchers to question entrenched socio-political boundaries that determine inclusions and exclusions in all their forms, to contest the norms and institutions that produce difference in order to subordinate and exclude the different, and to seek a genuine dialogue with the "other" (Linklater 2006).

How does one implement such an approach in practice? General principles of human security cannot be applied without consideration of particular socio-historical contexts and individual needs and experiences. Counter-terrorism informed by a gender-sensitive human security perspective needs to be culturally relevant, without becoming culturally relative. It cannot be packaged in the West as a "perfectly controlled, coherent security policy" (Blanchard 2003, 1290) and projected outward. Rather, it should be developed through dialogue as a joint political undertaking that recognizes and respects differences, while seeking "to avoid both the enforced abandonment of differences in the construction of agreement and the unreflexive entrenchment of differences that allows no agreement at all" (Eschle 2001, 206). Counter-terrorism built on the respect for difference and geared towards emancipation means that individuals should be empowered "to negotiate and develop a form of human security that is fitted to their needs – political, economic, and social, but also provides them with the necessary tools to do so … [It is] therefore focused on emancipation from oppression, domination, and hegemony, as well as want" (Richmond 2007, 461).

In practical terms, female suicide bombings need to be addressed on different levels – family, community, society, and beyond. All measures would have to adhere to the principles of respect for human dignity, the promotion of social welfare and justice, the protection of civil liberties, and pacific settlement and non-violence. On the last point, it is important that peaceful means be used to address the structural conditions and underlying grievances that facilitate the emergence of female suicide perpetrators in the first place. In the long run, this approach can be successful only if it is part of a broader initiative that views the violence of female suicide bombings as a signal that the existing power relations and structures of domination need to change. Accordingly, any discussion of "counterterrorism" should "draw attention to silences in the dominant discourses on the emerging world order and in the practices ... that flow from them" (Chaturvedi and Painter 2007, 388). It is important to ask how a world order based on non-domination and non-exclusion as the fundamental principle of governance can be achieved (Cox 1996). Since gendered discourses and practices of power cultivate both domination and resistance, the enduring practices and dominant structures of power ought to be challenged and resisted. What this means in the particular contexts is to be decided case by case. To illustrate this approach, we demonstrate specific gendered relationships of domination as well as insecurities and vulnerabilities they generate in Chechnya, and the North Caucasus more broadly. We argue that all of these insecurities should be accounted for in formulating gender-sensitive responses to female suicide bombings in this context.

Counterterrorism operations in Chechnya officially ceased in April 2009. Since then, eleven female suicide bombings took place on the territory of the Russian Federation, most of them in Dagestan neighbouring with Chechnya, with four women blowing themselves up in 2012 and two in 2013. With the end of large-scale military operations by the federal forces, pro-Moscow Chechens, initially headed by Akhmad Kadyrov, and, following his assassination, by his son Ramzan Kadyrov, were charged with the task of directing counter-insurgency. This counter-insurgency relied overwhelmingly on militarism and male domination, reflecting the hegemonic masculine tendency to resolve conflicts with violence and control. Kadyrov's heavy-handed approach to quelling the rebellion in Chechnya, to which Moscow acquiesced, seemed to have been relatively successful. Yet, although overall rates of violence decreased, pervasive unemployment and endemic corruption are constant features of everyday life. Combined with a large younger demographics and brutality of law enforcement officials, socio-economic and political conditions in Chechnya provide an ideal environment for fuelling radicalization and insurgency.

In a carefully documented anthropological study of Chechen wars, Valery Tishkov conveyed insecurities experienced by local Chechens in their own words: "My brother in Moscow, when he visits helps me with money. My wife's relatives from Shalazhi village help with wheat meal, meat and sour cream. At current prices, we need about 1,000–1,200 rubles a month for food ... allowing for meat once a week. It is possible to live on tea and bread, and one can eat potatoes for weeks but it is hard" (Tishkov 2004, 187).

Economic insecurity and the lack of employment opportunities reinforced informal income-generating practices and reliance on familial and clan connections. As one interviewee put it, "Officially, there used to be 200,000 unemployed Chechens before 1990. In fact all of us were working. We made money, and we also always helped each other in time of need" (Lieven 1999, 36, quoted in Standish 2006, 20–1). At the same time, adherence to religion brings material benefits: "For my acceptance of the new purified faith, the Arabs gave me money as a gift and told me that if I brought round two more followers, they would give me $5,000 for each of them. So I brought two of my relatives from Dagu-Barzoi" (Tishkov 2004, 174).

Intolerance and suppression of dissent, widespread lawlessness, as well as impunity for grave and massive violations of human rights in Chechnya, Dagestan, and Ingushetia committed by state military and law enforcement authorities, as well as by non-state groups, remain routine. These hegemonic masculine practices include forced evictions of internally displaced people, punitive house burnings, disappearances, torture, abductions, imprisonment, detention in the "filtration camps," extrajudicial killings of civilians, and degrading treatment of the relatives of those who were killed or disappeared (Amnesty International 2012). Allegedly, President Kadyrov and law enforcement officials under his control have been implicated in these violations (Lokshina 2012). Additional insecurity experienced by women in the North Caucasus include domestic violence, high unemployment rates, and punitive house burnings by state authorities and non-state groups. The practice of torching houses started in early 2000 as a way to punish families whose members joined the armed groups. It is now being used by both the Chechen government against those suspected of having links with insurgency and by insurgents targeting pro-Moscow Chechen officials. In many cases, house burnings also lead to illegal detentions and enforced disappearances.

The use of gender violence and threat of rape to obtain testimonies is common. Civilians can be detained by the authorities that do not identify themselves or tell the relatives where detainees will be kept. For example, in April 2010 the European Court of Human Rights ruling recognized the responsibility of the Russian Federation in the presumed death of a twenty-year-old Luiza Mutayeva, whose elder sister was involved in a Moscow theatre hostage crisis in 2002. Mutayeva disappeared after being detained by Russian servicemen at home in Assinovskaya village in Chechnya (Amnesty International 2010). A widespread culture of impunity for human rights abuses is compounded by reprisals against the individuals who were targeted and sought justice, as well as their advocates, spreading fear and reluctance to report violations and/or press charges against abusers. At a conference on combating extremism in November 2008, the interior minister of Dagestan stated that members of the non-governmental organization Mothers of Dagestan for Human Rights that investigates allegations of enforced disappearances should receive "a bullet to the head" (Amnesty International 2010, 9).

Women have been the targets of abuses both during the war and in its aftermath. In November 2008, the bodies of six women shot at point-blank range in the head and chest were discovered in different districts in Chechnya (Amnesty International 2010, 11–12). The ombudsperson's explanation was that family members killed them for "immoral behaviour." At least two women were married, with children. Following their deaths, they were given large funerals by their husbands and buried in the family plots – all indicators that they did not disgrace family honour. In addition, federal prosecutors found no evidence that relatives were involved in their deaths. Official investigations yielded no outcomes or arrests. In another similar episode, seven women were found shot and killed in Grozny, prompting a comment from Chechnya's President Ramzan Kadyrov that the women were guilty of indecent behaviour (ibid.).

The above instances of violence against women and the failure to find and bring perpetrators to justice speak to the changes in the social norms that reinforced gender discrimination in Chechnya. Since 2007, President Kadyrov has introduced a number of measures, known as the "virtue campaign," geared towards "Chechenization" of society or the revival of "Chechen traditions." These traditions, according to Kadyrov, entailed support for polygamy, honour killings, bride-kidnapping, and the view of women as men's property. Despite these practices being expressly prohibited under the laws of the Russian Federation, the federal government in Moscow has not addressed the issue of deteriorating women's rights brought by the Chechenization. The quasi-official and extra-legal "virtue campaign," supported by Chechen public officials and enforced by security forces, introduced "modesty laws" whereby women, Muslim and non-Muslim, are expected to dress conservatively (Lokshina 2012). Moral policing of women also entailed a mandatory headscarf policy, initially applied to all females over the age of ten in public institutions, such as schools, government offices, and hospitals. Later, this policy extended to streets, parks, shops, and entertainment centres. Women refusing to cover their heads and limbs were increasingly subject to harassment and even shot at close range with a paintball gun (Amnesty International 2010; Lokshina 2012). Increased discrimination and violence against women is widely tolerated, leaving women with little to no support. Any dissent against "modesty laws" is forcibly suppressed. Women subject to harassment and paintball attacks are often unwilling to file official complains for fear of retribution against them and their families.

The gender-sensitive human security approach allows us to understand insecurity in Chechnya from the perspective of people and community, rather than states and governments. It reveals a consistent pattern of endemic violence, directed by state and non-state actors against feminized subjects, and demonstrates multiple gaps between Russian and Chechen governmental policies, their inability to provide adequate security, physical and social infrastructure and public goods, on the one hand, and local needs, on the other. It also highlights that physical violence, weak laws and entrenched institutional ineffectiveness, socio-economic hardship, and newly introduced cultural norms are intertwined in mutually reinforcing synergetic dynamics, producing a volatile context in which multiple gender relations amplified by race, sex, ethnicity, and religion are implicated in human insecurity in Chechnya. While, as we demonstrated in the previous chapters, the individual motives for engaging in violence, including suicide bombings, are inherently complex and often contradictory, the broader conflict blurs the lines between different insecurities and creates an environment conducive to different forms of violence. Crucially, human insecurity in Chechnya and the North Caucasus is related directly to the ways in which multiple masculinities are enacted within complex relationships between the Russian federal government, the Chechen government, Chechen society, militant/insurgent groups, as well as ordinary men and women in Chechnya. The conflict in Chechnya, then, represents a struggle in which multiple masculinities, i.e., superior hegemonic masculinity of the Russian federal government, subordinate loyal masculinity of the Chechen government, fundamentalist masculinity of militant groups, and emasculated Chechen men, compete for power and in the process perpetuate patriarchal social structures and violence.

Our approach to human security also illustrates that power differentials work against local females who bear a significant weight of insecurity in Chechnya as a result of their gender and concomitant subject positions within the relationships with local men, Chechen and Russian officials, as well as state and non-state militaries. The long-term violent conflict coupled with the reinvention of religious, ethnic, and cultural traditions in Chechnya resulted in the encroachments of women's personal autonomy, privacy, freedom of conscience and expression, as well as increased physical violence towards women. Combined, these developments speak to the dramatic deterioration of human security in Chechnya. State-centred counterterrorism policies and measures provide an inadequate platform to address socio-cultural, economic, and political challenges facing feminized subjects, i.e., local women and civilian population more generally. Concerned primarily, if not exclusively with creating a stable state and the right kind of patriarchy in Chechnya, which would be instrumental to Russia's security, official policies offer little to no opportunities for the genuine engagement of individuals and communities within Chechnya in a state-building project in their own country. It effectively precludes a political solution to violence based on societal support and consensus. Eleven female suicide bombings after the official end of counterterrorist operations by Russian federal forces suggest that these policies solve little in the short run and appear unsustainable in the long run.

Conclusion

In this chapter, we examined a gendered state-centric approach to female suicide bombings within mainstream scholarship and questioned its inordinate focus on U.S./Western counterterrorism, as well as the recommendations to improve counter-terrorism policies. We argued that the problem-solving approach to counterterrorism, which stresses militaristic government responses, elides multiple relations of domination inherent in the conflicts in which some women blew themselves up and is generally counterproductive. We proposed an alternative approach to addressing the violence of female suicide bombings that is gender-sensitive and social relational. Analytically located at the intersection of gender and human security, our approach recognizes that female suicide bombings can be dealt with fruitfully only if we find ways to emancipate individuals and groups from gendered social structures that oppress and subordinate them. While thinking about alternative approaches to countering female suicide bombings, we should be careful not to impose totalizing clichéd prescriptions, but remain attuned to local voices, dynamics, and practices. A human security approach sensitive to the considerations of gender enables us to accomplish such a task. It makes a shift from a statist framework by embracing a "bottom-up" perspective that shares a common concern about the quotidian security, safety, and well-being of individuals and communities. A gender-sensitive human security approach also points to the effects of differentiated gendered power structures on individual and collective experiences of (in)security. Thus, gender is important not only for understanding gendered representations of female suicide perpetrators, but also for thinking about the ways of dealing with this violent social practice.

"Lady Parts," Naida Asiyalova's Bombing, and the Shattering of Gender Stereotypes

In September 2013, *Newsweek Pakistan*'s cover featured a headline "Lady Parts" accompanied by a provocative image of a pair of tampon applicators, one of which was lit up as a fuse leading to a bomb. The full headline of the inside story read, "Lady Parts: More and More Women Are Finding Their True Calling – as Suicide Bombers" (Shah, Ul Islam, and Taseer 2013). Sensationalism in the media is not new; unfortunately, neither is the gendering and sexualization of women's political violence. Indeed, while the controversial cover image conveyed a highly simplistic story of the complex dynamics behind women's increasing involvement in suicide bombings, the inside article sought to elucidate the "problem posed by terror's homicidal women" by developing two sets of familiar, well-scripted, and presumably objective explanations. On the one hand, it portrayed women as expendable instruments in the hands of terrorist groups and pointed to the operational exigencies and tactical advantages of employing female suicide bombers. These include disproportionate media attention, shaming effects, and ability to evade security where "a bearded man with wild eyes could be a dead giveaway" (ibid.). On the other hand, the article stressed a complementary set of reasons beyond the purely instrumental value of women suicide bombers to the organizations employing them. These are personal loss, rape, desperation, and trauma as primary motivations that drive "mothers and wives and daughters ... to end their lives for some sort of justice" (ibid.). In other words, the authors of the article argued that women must be driven to the path of violence by exceptional reasons. They do not make a choice to become suicide bombers within the context of broader political violence. Rather, they become suicide bombers, because – as mothers, wives, and daughters mediated by their sexuality and relationships with men – they have no choice.

The emphasis on the personal motives gave deeper meaning to the wording in the headline for the article. It may not be immediately obvious why suicide bombings would be considered a "true calling" for anyone, unless one takes into account women's horrific personal circumstances, emotional reaction to the bad things that happened to them during war, and options left to them within their societies. Consideration of personal motives therefore has far-reaching implications. It allows one to dismiss the significance of women's political violence on the basis of sex and to reaffirm female suicide bombers as perpetual victims, i.e., aberrations and exceptions among politically violent perpetrators. The cover image leaves no doubt about the centrality of sex and sexuality in female suicide bombings, ensuring readership fascination with the story and subject matter more generally. This image rules out the slightest possibility of acknowledging that female suicide bombers may play an important, sometimes even decisive role in political violence by blowing themselves up. Such dismissal remains intact even when, as deviant exceptions, female suicide bombers pose a security threat significant enough to raise the concerns of Pakistan's officials and militaries. The article concludes by briefly considering how the Pakistan army can address the increasing spate of female suicide bombings in this country, offering a simple, if not simplistic suggestion that the "only solution ... is better intelligence, and more women in the services."

This is the story, which, albeit in a more sophisticated form, permeates the problem-solving approach to female suicide bombings. Significantly expanded in the post-9/11 political and normative climate, this approach directs theoretical and practical attention towards explaining female suicide bombings in an ostensibly value-neutral manner so as to authorize, justify, improve, and normalize state counterterrorism. This scholarship combines self-professed commitment to objectivity with heavy reliance on the essentialist conception of gender that ties violence or lack thereof with naturally predetermined behavioural attributes of men and women. By this simple, binary logic men are naturally predisposed towards violence, whereas women are destined to be nurturing and peaceful. Gender essentialism directs problem-solving scholars' attention disproportionately towards individual psychology in explaining why some women engage in suicide bombings. However difficult, if not impossible to validate empirically, the sweeping, dichotomous registry of male and female behavioural propensities is cemented by the conventional heteronormative codes, which, in turn, sustain binary gender logic. In this sense, problem-solving works serve more as a metaphorical device, rather than analytically refined and empirically substantiated explanatory frameworks. They present female suicide bombings either as an extension of motherhood, in which case politically violent women are seen as conforming to the ideal typical femininity, or as an extreme deviation from the norm. In both scenarios, this approach elicits the image of women defined by their sex and culture as paradigmatic victims. Female perpetrators may violate conventional social, cultural, and religious constraints on women's participation in suicide bombings. They may even disturb the stereotypical understanding of suicide bombings or terrorism and political violence more broadly as authentically masculine, distinctly unfeminine, and exceptionally male, but such disturbance is only temporary. For the most part, female suicide bombers remain within problem-solving analyses "pawns and sacrificial lambs" (Schweitzer 2006, 9). This logic further influences how we understand various forms of political violence, its victims and perpetrators, as well as normative character and rationale for (counter)-action.

While the narrative of victimhood permeates journalist accounts and mainstream academic literature on female suicide bombings, the actual cases do not fit easily into this uncomplicated framework and often challenge the underlying logic of female victimhood. This leaves problem-solving authors at a loss for explanations. The 21 October 2013 female suicide bombing in the southern Russian city of Volgograd illustrates the challenges to explanations based on essentialist understanding of gender. On that day, at around 2 pm, a woman wearing a hijab boarded city bus N29. Local residents call route N29 a student route, for it runs between the southern neighbourhoods of Volgograd and the state university (Galochka 2013). Almost immediately after the woman boarded the bus packed with students, she detonated the explosives. Russian authorities quickly identified the perpetrator as Naida Asiyalova, only four days away from her thirty-first birthday, born in the city of Buynaksk in the North Caucasus Republic of Dagestan. Her passport and the remains of the ticket in Asiyalova's name from Makhachkala, Dagestan, to Moscow were found after the attack (Dubnov 2013). Seven people, excluding the bomber, died, and over forty others were wounded as a result of an explosion (Krupneishie terakty v Rossii 2013).

A series of biographical and other details surfaced after this act of violence. Naida Asiyalova grew up in the mountainous village of Gunib, where her mother, Ravzat Asiyalova, still works at the post office. As one of the hubs of Dagestani militant activities, Gunib has been subject to regular *zachistki* (clean-up operations) during the last fifteen years. About a decade ago, Naida Asiyalova left for Moscow, where she found employment at the Turkish Construction and Industry company ENKA and met her first husband (Yeliseyev 2013; Galochka 2013). Later, Asiyalova found a new job at the large recruiting company Coleman Services UK (Yeliseyev 2013). Around 2010 she broke all connections with her kin and friends in Gunib. Russian NTV reported that she stopped phoning her relatives and did not come to her father's funeral (Magomedov 2013). At about the same time, authorities noticed her as an active and experienced recruiter into Wahhabism, even though her neighbours back in Gunib did not remember Asiyalova as a devout Muslim. Official reports indicate that since 2010, Asiyalova had been wearing a hijab and become a sharia wife of ethnic Russian Dmitri Sokolov, twenty-one, from Dolgoprudny, not far from Moscow.

Sokolov was born and raised in the family of a member of the Russian military. His mother, Olga, shared in an interview that the family lost contact with him about a year before the attack, when Dmitri went missing in July 2012 (Yelenin and Boyko 2013). The media dubbed Sokolov, aka Abdul Jabar, a "Russian wahhabi" and attributed his conversion into Wahhabism to Asiyalova. Interviews with his mother and school teachers reveal that he was baptized and wore a cross at school (Andreyev 2013). By different reports, the two met either in an online chat room or studied together at university. Prior to his disappearance, Dmitri Sokolov attended Arab language courses in Moscow (Newsru.com 2013). Allegedly, under Asiyalova's influence, Sokolov moved to Dagestan and joined a militant group in Makhachkala. There he became an expert on improvised explosive devices. Media speculated that it was Sokolov who may have made an explosive belt for Asiyalova, as well as for Aliyeva, who blew herself up in Makhachkala on 25 May 2013 (Malykh and Rybina 2013). In November, the National Anti-terrorist Committee reported that Murad Kasumov, a leader of the militant group to which Sokolov belonged, was a mastermind behind Asiyalova's bombing, while Dmitri Sokolov and Ruslan Kazanbiyev prepared the explosives and instructed the bomber (Polit.ru 2013). All three militants were killed during Russian counterterrorism operations in November 2013. Russian media also drew a link between the videotaped July 2013 statement by Doku Umarov, a top militant leader in the North Caucasus, and Asiyalova's bombing. In this statement, Umarov called on Islamist militants to use any means to disrupt the 2014 Winter Olympic Games in the Russian city of Sochi (Akhmirova 2013).

It is tempting to cast Naida Asiyalova as yet another Russian black widow, but we have something important to learn by paying close attention to the details surrounding her life and death. Considering these details seriously, we can realize, for example, that she does not fit easily into the image of a woman driven to her deadly act by the personal motive of revenging male relatives lost in the wars between Chechnya and Russia. Naida Asiyalova simply did not have a lost loved one to avenge. Neither did the militants compromise her sexually, so that rules out the possible desire to restore her family's honour through martyrdom. In the years and hours prior to her death, she exhibited skills and resourcefulness that make it hard to conceive of her as a help-less, hopeless iconic female victim. Asiyalova's schoolteacher remembered her as an active, independent, and social girl who got along very well with other children (Newsru.com 2013). Having left Dagestan, Asiyalova studied and made an adequate living in Moscow. As one Russian journalist put it, "Russia had not robbed her of her home or her chance at a decent life" (Yuzik 2013). In time, Asiyalova steered her life in a direction that surprised many who knew her and even caused fallout with her mother (Malykh and Rybina 2013). She began to wear a hijab and engaged in active recruiting into Wahhabism, persuading others to embrace radical Islamism. Employment at a recruiting company provided multiple opportunities for her own recruiting efforts. For the last three years, Asiyalova belonged to the so-called women's *jamaat*, comprising females whose male relatives had joined militant groups. Beyond her recruiting activities, she served as a courier and a manager of *jamaat*'s funds in support of militants' wives and widows (Malykh and Rybina 2013).

Another important detail is the absence of a chaperon to closely supervise the bomber on the day of the attack. Chaperons, often males, typically accompany female suicide bombers in Russia to ensure the attack proceeds as planned. As it appears from the news and official reports, on the day of the bombing Asiyalova acted alone and seemed in charge of her mission. Russian media reported that she purchased a bus ticket to Moscow but unexpectedly asked the driver to stop the bus as it was leaving Volgograd and got off. When investigators reconstructed her actions in Volgograd, they found that she spent some time wandering around the city, as if looking for the best place to strike. Russian media even posted surveillance footage of Asiyalova in the mall before she headed for the bus stop (Life News 2013).

Even though Asiyalova's actions displayed her ingenuity and resourcefulness, Russian media described her as a frail, terminally ill, and desperate woman and an easy target for Islamic extremists. It is interesting that her mother dismissed allegations about Asiyalova's illness. Physical and moral weakness were claimed to "have made her a useful if expendable weapon in someone else's war" (Yuzik 2013). There is no denying that Asiyalova's act of violence was part of a larger war that was itself part of a long historical struggle. Perhaps coincidentally, the village of Gunib, in which Asiyalova grew up, is a symbolic site of this struggle's historical continuity. It was the place of the last brutal battle in the nineteenth-century Caucasian war between the Russian Empire and the highlanders of the North Caucasus. The highlanders were defeated and their legendary leader, Imam Shamil, surrendered to the Russians in Gunib.

Both recent wars and a longer historical struggle between Russia and the peoples in the North Caucasus were permeated with layers of gendering in which contending masculinities manipulated gendered beliefs, practices, institutions, and structures, thus influencing how Asiyalova's bombing, as well as the war of which it was part, is understood and will be remembered. It is a script centred on men – a script that puts Umarov, Kasumov, even Sokolov into a spotlight and effectively effaces the protagonist, Asiyalova. She vanishes in the vortex of gendered logic that links militancy with manly characters and masculinity. In the story about her own act of violence, Asiyalova is reduced to a mere accessory. It is also a script that through the gendered narrative and manipulative control over masculinity and femininity constructs the meaning of all political violence in the North Caucasus as illegitimate, corrupt, and criminal.

Mainstream academics and journalists serve as a medium for crafting gendered understandings and memories that tilt the balance of power towards Russian hegemonic masculinity. Consider the following. Russian journalist Yulia Yuzik (2013) refers to a witness of Asiyalova's bombing who recalled that "the bomber stared out the window before the explosion, not drawing attention to herself, acting calm. It is as if she were oblivious, not a black widow but a blank slate." It may be convenient to call a female bomber who does not fit into an established image of a black widow a blank slate, except, as Enloe (2010, 9) reminds us, acts of violence do not erupt on a blank slate. The subjects and contexts of violence are always already gendered. Far from being a blank slate, Naida Asiyalova was a site of intense political contestations. She was gendered by virtue of the fact of being a woman, a wife, a Muslim, and a North Caucasian. Her act of violence was intricately woven into the gendered fabric of the recent Russian-Chechen wars that spilled into Dagestan and other neighbouring republics and represented a current phase of the centuries-long violent resistance in the North Caucasus against Russian domination. Over the last decade, this struggle also acquired a global dimension, having been constructed as part of the Global War on Terror.

It takes "feminist curiosity" (Enloe 2004) to see that just like the black widows, a blank slate represents an intellectual construct by which those in the service of patriarchy and hegemonic masculinity manipulate ideas about women and femininity, squeezing them "into narrow molds" (Enloe 2010, 1). Driven by feminist curiosity, we set out in the preceding chapters to engage in a dialogue with mainstream scholarship in the hope of deepening our understanding of female suicide bombings. Feminist curiosity invites us, on the one hand, to take women seriously without valorizing them and, on the other, to look deep into presumably gender-neutral ideas, values, institutions, practices, and structures in order to unearth the logic and political workings of gender that sustain systemic domination of masculinity (Enloe 2004, 3–5). Embracing feminist curiosity, therefore, means challenging conventional ways of understanding and acting towards the world around us that privilege the masculine and trivialize the feminine. In the case of female suicide bombings, feminist curiosity enables us to expose the logic and politics of multiple and often overlapping gendered hierarchies in places where problem-solving authors have seen only women victims, backward societies, illegitimate violence, and the clash of incompatible values and principles. Critically engaging with the violence of female suicide bombings means that patriarchy in all its manifestations "must always be on the analytical couch" (6).

So what have we learned from the dialogue with problem-solving scholars? First, we have learned that mainstream scholars put inordinate emphasis on female suicide bombers as *women*. As we have demonstrated in the case of Naida Asiyalova, this emphasis erases female perpetrators as purposeful, autonomous, and conscious agents of violence. A central theme in Asiyalova's biography reconstructed immediately after the bombing was her romantic and family life, especially her marriage to a Russian man who was ten years her junior. This theme drew disproportionate public and media attention. Vadim Dubnov (2013), Russian political commentator, observed that "there are tens, if not hundreds of women" like Asiyalova in Dagestan today. Many of them, according to Dubnov, begin their journey to suicide bombings by becoming girlfriends or wives of male militants. Each is driven by "inner impulse, which may drastically change the life of otherwise successful young woman ... unsuspected of any psychological or mental deficiency" (ibid.). In this sense, an extraordinarily intense public discussion centred on the digital copy of Asiyalova's passport that went viral in the media and social networks is unwarranted, according to Dubnov. In his own words, "What difference does it make what her name was?" (ibid.). Suffice to know that she is a woman married to a "Russian Wahhabi."

Second, the problem-solving approach frequently portrays female perpetrators as victims of orientalized patriarchy that restricts women exclusively to the private domain of family and home, attaches male/ family honour to women's modesty and sexual purity, and sees women's principal responsibility as obeying and serving their husbands and other male relatives, giving birth, and raising children. Within the social environment of orientalized patriarchy, a feminine woman accepts and internalizes her subservient, subordinate position and conforms to behavioural expectations associated with her "naturally" and culturally predetermined roles. From a Western liberal perspective, orientalized patriarchy provides a framework for understanding women's oppressed, dependent, and marginal status outside Western democracies. At the same time, a discursive move that paints female suicide bombers as victims of orientalized patriarchy not only effaces individual female perpetrators, but also marginalizes their societies as backward and inferior Others of the progressive and superior Western Self. Often blended with Muslim culture and Islam, orientalized patriarchy adds a racialized dimension to mainstream representations. Young's (2003, 19) observation that Western feminist optics of Afghan women's subordination under Taliban constructs "these women as exoticized others and paradigmatic victims in need of salvation by Western feminists" captures the general depiction of women within orientalized patriarchy in the problem-solving literature. It seems to matter little to problem-solving scholars that Muslim women themselves contest the internal logic and normative benchmark for female agency and gender equality measured in women's rights and visibility in the public realm in the liberal West. Problem-solving representations and their contestations "emanate from very different discursive universes ... evolving on parallel tracks" (Kandiyoti 2009, 1).

Third, we have also learned that gender essentialism combined with representations of orientalized patriarchy provides both a matrix for understanding security and an algorithm for assessing the threat posed by female suicide bombings. The meaning of security within problem-solving accounts of female suicide bombings is centred on the idea of masculinist protection brilliantly elaborated by Young (2003). This logic explicates theoretical linkages between masculinity, protection, sovereign states, and political violence, all of which are centred on the image of a "good" man, i.e., a man who guards the safety of his household against the threatening, aggressive "bad" men. Those protected by a "good" man find themselves in a subordinate position and are expected by their protector to remain loyal and obedient. As Young puts it, "When a household lives under a threat, there cannot be divided wills and arguments about who will do what, or what is the best course of action. The head of the household should decide what measures are necessary for the security of the people and property, and he gives the orders that they must follow if they and their relations are to remain safe" (4–5). Even though a more benign protective masculinity of a "good man" is defined against aggressive dominative masculinity of a "bad" man, both sustain unequal power relations based on gender.

The logic of masculinist protection illuminates the relationship between sovereign states / the "good" men and its citizens / the protected when facing the threat of terrorist violence / the "bad" men who use their women as suicide bombers. Sovereign states manipulate fear of female suicide bombing attacks among its citizens and accentuate their own role as security providers and protectors of the population to justify repressive authoritarian policies that vastly expand state executive and surveillance power and criminalize dissent, while mobilizing popular support for coercive counterterrorism. The logic of masculinist protection ensures that the "state's identity is militaristic, and it engages in military action but with the point of view of the defendant rather than the aggressor" (Young 2003, 8). Despite the appearance of its identity as more virtuous and ethically appealing than the dominative masculine identity of terrorist groups, sovereign-state exploitation of fear to subordinate, intimidate, and repress nonetheless reinforces a gendered power imbalance.

Thus gender shapes the prevalent meaning of security and guides masculine states' practices of legitimating a set of well-rehearsed, soft, and hard security policies. These include increased limitations of citizens' rights and freedoms, arbitrary use of surveillance and detentions, recourse to coercive military actions against female suicide bombers' groups and communities, and other measures to strengthen state sovereign power. The practical relevance of a problem-solving approach in the context of the ongoing and in some places increasing spate of female suicide bombings makes critical scrutiny not just an analytical imperative, but also a political one, especially given the potentially detrimental counterterrorism measures this approach sustains politically. Critically reflecting on the overlapping dynamics of the essentialist notions of gender and mainstream conceptions of security reveals both the problematic construction and analytical inadequacy of each. At the same time, tracking down the logic and politics of multiple femininities and masculinities sheds light on the ways in which their intricately complex relationships sustain prevalent understandings of violence and security.

In the preceding chapters we articulated a comprehensive critique of the problem-solving scholarship that deals with the violence of female suicide bombings. Employing a combination of feminist security and postcolonial perspectives, we discussed in detail a fairly consistent pattern of the unscrupulous replication of contentious myths and partial truths that substantially misconstrue and misrepresent individual female suicide perpetrators, their societies, and their cultures. We traced the tropes of raced-gendered othering crystallized in the problem-solving canon and found that these representations reduced the complex socio-political character of female suicide bombings to a single dimension of orientalized patriarchy. Such representations victimize individual perpetrators and delegitimize their political claims, while projecting (sub)liminal West-centrism. A critical gender approach alerts us that the violent social practice of female suicide bombings is complicated in a number of ways, i.e., geopolitical, epistemic, and moral. Such complexity circumscribes analytical judgments of this practice. This is why it is important when examining this violence to be suspicious of the categorical claims that mainstream scholars make about female suicide bombings. We argued that despite impressive and commonly recognized expertise of many problem-solving authors, as well as the widespread acceptance of their knowledge claims, the sophisticated accounts of these scholars are contestable in both theory and practice.

Finding problem-solving analyses of female suicide bombings analytically and normatively puzzling, and we might add solving very little in practical terms, we elaborated an alternative approach anchored in critical theory, broadly understood, and developed around explicit recognition of the centrality of gender in the object of knowledge called "female suicide bombings" and its entanglement with existing power relations and social hierarchies. One primary goal of this book was to open up key assumptions and explanations of the problem-solving analyses by raising important political, analytical, and normative questions that challenge the core constructions of gender, legitimacy, and security within mainstream representations. Unlike problem-solving scholars, we treat gender as a set of fundamental, socially (re)produced ideas and values about femininity and masculinity built into the matrix of power. Gender, in other words, is not an explanatory variable, but rather, as Young (2003, 2) observed, an element of "interpretation ... a certain logic of gendered meanings and images ... [that] organize the way people interpret events and circumstances, along with the positions and possibilities for action within them." As for security, our analytical and political commitment in this book is expressly to solidify the conceptual shift towards critical conceptions of security, which is currently dominated by the political and ethical prerogatives of gendered sovereign states. Such reconstruction inevitably moves away from the state-centrism embedded in mainstream conceptualization of security and troubles a series of gendered identities and boundaries (re)produced by the problem-solving analyses, i.e., male and female suicide bombers, masculine sovereign states and feminized stateless nations, illegitimate terrorist violence and legitimate coercive counterterrorism, the liberating, progressive West and subordinating, aggressive global terrorism.

Following Enloe's recommendation, we took female suicide bombers seriously and explored their violence, as well as the gendered representations it animates without reducing it to individual motives. That is, in examining female suicide bombings and their representations we were less concerned with the question of what drives individual women to engage in this violence, and focused primarily on gender dynamics within and around such violence and on how these dynamics play out in the politics of representation. In other words, we asked questions about the role of the discourses of gender in shaping "common" understandings of female suicide bombers' conditions, relations, struggles, and violences. Such questions complicated static binary logic of gender

in problem-solving analyses by shifting analytical focus beyond individual female suicide bombers' motivations towards multiple social
relations and layered forms of masculinity and femininity (Young 2003;
Eisenstein 2007). For example, we traced the overlap between patriarchal hegemonic masculinity of sovereign states, on the one hand, and
patriarchal feminized masculinity of stateless groups and terrorist
organizations, on the other, in their competition to (re)assert patriarchal
power through aggressive militarism and control over women. Equally
important, the emergence of female suicide bombings in various conflicts resulted in women entering into and becoming visible within the
new site of political violence, thus prompting uneasy reconfigurations
of patriarchal norms within their communities.

In our analysis we steered towards social relational explanations of
female suicide bombings. This shift does not mean the replacement of
the structuralist account with the individualist one. On the contrary, a
social relational framework, as we demonstrated in the preceding chapters, escapes the entrapment of false dichotomies by explaining female
suicide bombings as a violent social practice resulting from complex
interactions between individual agents and various structural forms.
A social relational approach to structure/agency begins with the basic
assumption that structures are not immutable; they are continuously
reproduced through social practices and transformed historically by
and through agency. We recognize and accept that women may engage
in the violence of suicide bombings from gender positions that are different from those of men. However, we maintain that ethnicity, class,
race, age, religion, and culture also condition individual female suicide
bombers. That is, the intersections of gender with other socially weighty
signifiers of identity affect fluctuations in individual agential power and
structural limitations. In this respect, female suicide bombers do not
represent a homogeneous category, even within the same cultural context. These women do not experience social and cultural conditions in
the same way, as their realities and opportunities available to them are
mediated by their multiple identities. Many female suicide perpetrators actively sought contact with the secular organizations, while others
seem to have been indoctrinated and probably coerced into carrying
out acts of suicide terrorism. The extent of agential choice and structural constraints is a matter of relative power available to individual
agents within particular socio-historic contexts.

The question of relative power is central to our analysis. More
specifically, it is the question of the different forms of power, i.e., the

power to represent and determine meanings of political violence, and shape subjectivities of those who engage in it, as well as its relation to the power to use actual physical violence and legitimate it. Female suicide bombings are shocking and incomprehensible at first sight. The illusiveness of their meaning creates possibilities for multiple interpretations, opening room for interpretive contestations. In the West, the perplexing, obscure character of female suicide bombings enables problem-solving scholars to authoritatively determine their meaning for Western audiences and to create raced gendered silences. Problem-solving analyses of female suicide bombings treat violence as an exclusive sovereign right and a legitimate means to sovereign ends. These representations reinforce a major tradition of thinking about global politics, which subordinates political violence to state sovereignty. In this sense, they are more than simply representations, for they are linked directly to the actual physical violence. The authoritative character of problem-solving analyses derives from and is sustained, at least partially, by the close links between mainstream academe and the state. It is founded on the ability of problem-solving scholars to justify and guide state counterterrorism. As we have argued in this book, these two forms of power are an attribute of the masculine position and condition the possibilities for action for those on whose behalf they speak, as well as those against whom they are directed.

Another goal of our analysis was to re-embed female suicide bombers in their respective social, political, cultural, and historical contexts in order to move beyond the widespread essentialized image of the Arab/ Muslim/oppressed female suicide perpetrator. We demonstrated that female suicide bombers come from various backgrounds, ethnicities, religions, and ideologies. They blew themselves up in such distant and distinct spaces as Lebanon, Sri Lanka, Turkey, Russia, Palestine, Israel, Uzbekistan, Pakistan, and now Afghanistan and Iraq. Their religious backgrounds included Christian, Shi'a, Sunni, and Hindu. Some of the perpetrators were as young as thirteen years old, others like a "suicide granny" – Fatima Omar Mahmud al-Najara, a sixty-four-year-old woman with nine children and forty-one grandchildren – were older; some were single, others were married; some had no children, others were mothers. They represent a full range of social statuses and levels of education. Some had their identities revealed in highly public commemorations and are celebrated as martyrs; others remain anonymous. Many seem to have had a wide range of ideological commitments (communist, socialist, nationalist, etc.). In fact, the empirical data demonstrate that the overwhelming majority of female suicide bombings were carried out in the context of military campaigns against foreign occupying forces. Many female martyrdom operations in the Middle East have targeted Israeli forces specifically with the aim of getting those forces out of the Occupied Territories or out of South Lebanon. Similarly, female suicide bombers have targeted U.S. and British occupying forces in Iraq and NATO forces in Afghanistan after major counter-insurgency campaigns. Some female suicide perpetrators were involved in self-determination or nationalistic struggles. For example, the women of the Black Tigers were well known for their willingness to die for the cause of creating an independent state called Tamil Eelam in the north and east of Sri Lanka. Other women seem to have carried out acts of self-sacrifice because of humiliation suffered at the hands of a dominant regime or at the hands of someone in their own family.

A kaleidoscope of factors has contributed to the emergence and sustenance of the violence of female suicide bombings. There is clearly no single demographic profile of female suicide bombers. The commonly perceived link between Islamic fundamentalism and female suicide bombers stretches the facts when one examines the empirical data. With the recruitment of Western women (Jihad Jane) into Islamist terrorist organizations, there are increasing concerns in Western capitals that we may be witnessing another tactical move by these organizations. Regardless, it is hoped that the empirical information in this book have laid to rest some of the widespread misconceptions about female suicide bombers.

Last, but not least, we argued that the only effective response to the violence of female suicide bombings entails finding the ways to emancipate individuals from overlapping gendered social structures and oppressive relationships. Promoting such emancipatory change means identifying, questioning, and challenging the structures implicated in the perpetuation of female suicide bombings. To do so, we proposed to replace the state-centred notion of national security with gender-sensitive human security. Engendering human security entails self-reflection on one's normative assumptions and political relevance, as well as the need to address the politics of difference and the relations of domination such politics sustains. In practical terms, a response to the violence of female suicide bombings should be contextual and multi-level. It should address context-specific structural conditions and underlying grievances, while adhering to the principles of respect for human dignity, the promotion of social welfare and justice, and non-violence. On a global level, it requires transcending neoliberal economic arrangements in favour of a more redistributive and equalizing framework, as well as reconfiguration of top-down liberal governance in a way that more clearly reflects the interests and particularities of the feminized subjects. Measures informed by a gender-sensitive human security approach may be criticized for being attractive, yet implausible, too far ahead of the curve, or even policy irrelevant. While acknowledging practical challenges to its applicability, we nonetheless insist on the need to create analytical space and hold open the possibilities for alternative approaches such as this one. This insistence stems from the recognition of the mutually constitutive dynamics of knowledge and praxis and reflects fundamental concern with emancipatory change through epistemic reconstruction of counterterrorism strategies. This is a critical theoretical "guide" for action in dealing with the violence of female suicide bombings.

Notes

Introduction

1 A number of scholars, including Schweitzer, Pape, and Davis, agree that between 1980 and 2003, women accounted for about 15 per cent of all suicide bombings (see Davis 2013, 280). Upon including more recent information about female suicide bombings till 2012, Davis calculated that these attacks amounted to approximately 4.2 per cent annually (281).

2 Upon examining the propaganda value of female suicide bombings, Stack (2011) concluded that the stories about individual perpetrators generated by states and terrorist organizations are more important than the actual reasons and motives of individual women.

3 For the discussion on the morality of suicide bombings from the perspective of just war theory and how gender of female perpetrators affects the general moral equation, see Friedman (2009). Also Sjoberg and Gentry (2007) and Marway (2011) discuss the issue of proscibed vs morally legitimate violence and the role of gender in this distinction.

4 This approach has recently made a comeback in the works of Merari (2010) and Kobrin (2010), both of which engage in psychological profiling of suicide bombers in an attempt to distil their unique psychological make-up. Kobrin, for example, argues that Islamic suicide terrorism is the by-product of domestic violence. It is, in her own words, a form of "displaced violence about the Early Mother in life, especially the Early Muslim Mother and the disavowed wish to murder her because she is experienced as engulfing and smothering" (13). Her book perpetuates the kind of racial othering and stereotypical misrepresentation of Islam we critique in this book. The most relevant part of Merari's book for our analysis focuses on psychological profiles of fifteen Palestinian would-be suicide bombers. Merari argues

that they are more likely than non-suicide terrorists to have a diagnosis of avoidant-dependent personality disorder. In approach and analysis, both authors have been criticized on numerous grounds (see, for example, McCauley and Moskalenko 2010). Paul Gill's (2012) analysis of the shift from psychopathological approaches to psychoanalytic period in studying suicide terrorism is interesting in this context.

5 Illustrative works on female suicide bombings include Bloom (2007, 2011), Pape (2005), Pape and Feldman (2010), Berko (2012), Cragin and Daly (2009), Zedalis (2008), Schweitzer (2001, 2006, 2007, 2008).

6 The only possible exception here is a 2014 female suicide bombing by a Kurdish woman and a member of People's Defence Units in Syria against Islamic State (IS). Since the Kurds took the side of the Syrian state, this act of violence was in defence of the state and against a jihadi militant group. From a state-centric perspective, an act of female suicide bombing by a Kurdish female fighter can be construed as more legitimate than all the other female suicide bombings.

7 Terrorism studies' preoccupation with U.S. counterterrorism precluded any meaningful engagement with the issues of structural violence (Galtung 1969) in its multiple dimensions. This is despite the fact that even some terrorism studies scholars have been receptive of the idea that collective experience of structural violence may be linked directly to the rise of suicide bombings. Kalyvas and Sanchez-Cuenca (2006, 228), for instance, maintain that "what matters is not that the individual personally experiences political repression or economic deprivation but, rather, that the living conditions of the community are so grim and hopeless as to move people to extreme acts." This is not to reinstate a simplistic notion that poverty, social exclusion, inequality, human rights abuse, foreign occupation, alienation, and demographic factors are the root causes of female suicide bombings. These factors alone do not explain specific incidents of female suicide bombings (see Newman 2006), but they are significant for understanding the phenomenon. Dismissing them, therefore, leads to a failure to recognize important links between the acts of female suicide bombings and structural violence, which may result in less than adequate counterterror recommendations and policies.

8 Qazi (2011, 43), for example, while noting that the study of female suicide bombers as a category is limiting, nonetheless speaks about "the Muslim woman," "her participation in suicide attacks," and "her individual contribution."

9 The title of Cragin and Daly's book, *Women as Terrorists: Mothers, Recruiters, and Martyrs*, speaks to the generally perceived contradiction entailed in the term *women terrorists*.

10 "President Bush on the Middle East," PBS Newshour.
11 Individual stories have been cited of both female and male suicide bombers. The key question in our analysis is what kinds of motivations have been inferred from these individual stories. Mainstream terrorism studies literature displays a strong tendency to link individual stories of male and female suicide bombers to political and personal motivations respectively.
12 Tickner and Sjoberg (2006) distinguish between IR feminist realism, liberalism, constructivism, critical theory, postcolonialism, and postmodernism.
13 Some feminist works on women's involvement in political violence include Sylvester (2013), Sjoberg and Gentry (2007, 2011), Sjoberg and Via (2010), Gentry and Whitworth (2011), Ahall (2012), Ahall and Shepherd (2012), Parashar (2009), Shepherd (2007, 2009), Brunner (2005, 2007), and Alison (2004, 2009).
14 For more about the possibilities and challenges of dialogic engagement between positivist and post-positivist scholarship, see Hellmann (2003).
15 While acknowledging that discourse may be understood to include non-linguistic elements, such as visual images, in our analysis we treat discourse narrowly, primarily as a written text. Our understanding of discourse is broadly consistent with Jennifer Milliken's (1999: 229) concept of discourse as "structures of signification which construct social realities" producing subjects with different abilities to speak and act, and shaping different knowledge and political practices by stabilizing dominant meanings.
16 It is noteworthy that while the academic literature analysed in our book was published in English, empirical information about the attacks was collected from the news sources in English, French, Hebrew, and Russian.

Chapter 1

1 These limitations are not unique to research on female suicide bombings, but plague the entire field of terrorism studies. Against this backdrop, a robust and relatively novel analytical approach to the study of political terrorism – critical terrorism studies – was undertaken by Jackson, Smyth, Gunning (2009) and their colleagues.
2 Despite a significant history of scholarly explorations, the study of terrorism in general has resulted in only two major attempts to develop a comprehensive consensus definition of the term – one undertaken by Alex Schmid (Schmid and Jongman 1988) in the 1980s, and another in a more recent collaborative work by Weinberg, Pedahzur, and Hirsch-Hoefler (2004). Both attempts focused on the sphere of academic discourse, leaving

out official state statements, public debates, and discussions among terrorism supporters. The above two undertakings yielded a number of "definitional elements" ranked in accordance with the frequency of their appearance either in responses to a questionnaire (as was the case in Schmid and Jongman 1988, 28) or in the contributions to the leading academic journals in the field of terrorism (in Weinberg, Pedahzur, and Hirsch-Hoefler 2004). The two studies also registered significant differences in the relative strength of definitional elements.

3 For a theoretically informed argument that denies the existence of state terrorism, see Wight (2009).

4 Berko (2012), for example, in considering if suicide bombers can be driven by altruism, simply states, "In my opinion, they cannot. Suicide bombers usually act on impulse and the desire for immediate gratification, expecting sexual and material rewards immediately after explosion" (3).

5 We offer this rather generalized definition as an analytical guide only. We acknowledge that this definition is contested and contestable and, therefore, will acquire specific meanings in particular contexts. In some contexts and for some individuals and social groups the meaning of this type of violence is captured by the notion of martyrdom, whereas others will see it as suicide terrorism.

6 Sylvester defines it as "a unit that has agency to target and injure others in war and is also a target of war's capabilities" (2013, 5).

7 Cragin and Daly (2009, vii, viii) demonstrate uneasiness over categorical confusion when they use moral language to confess that they feel "a certain degree of empathy ... [to] women who continuously attempted to find their place in the midst of male-dominated terrorist groups ... [However,] one cannot set aside the fact that these women actively sought the death of innocent civilians."

Chapter 2

1 This argument is often used in the context of the Chechen-Russian conflict. The gendered language of the "Palestinization" thesis is discussed in chapter 5.

2 Muriel Degauque, a Belgian convert to Islam, blew herself up in Iraq on 9 November 2005.

3 On average, female suicide bombings have been more lethal than male suicide bombings (see Davis 2013, 282).

4 Testimonials, such as Mehaidli's, are routinely dismissed by terrorism studies scholars for being scripted by the organizations behind the attacks

for propaganda purposes and containing little, if any, information about individuals carrying out the bombings. In contrast, we treat these testimonials seriously, for we see an important parallel between the dismissal of the testimonials left by female suicide bombers and traditional invisibility of women terrorists in general, as well as the downplaying of the political significance of the acts of violence perpetrated by female suicide bombers. Such dismissal is symptomatic of and perpetuates a gendered (and misleading) approach towards female suicide bombers, and violent women more generally.

5 Some researchers speculate that the perpetrators were under the influence of narcotics at the time. The LUPA database for classifying suicide bombings in Israel, Palestine, and Lebanon categorized these two cases as SM3p, or "probably suicidal" attacks (Ricolfi and Campana 2005, 44).

6 Both ethnicities contain Christian minorities that make up about 7 per cent of the overall population. Also, Sri Lanka's Muslim population speaks Tamil but does not consider itself ethnic Tamils.

7 We explain the gendered and racialized meanings of this term in chapters 4 and 5.

Chapter 3

1 This problem is often framed in epistemological and/or methodological terms. However, we agree with Colin Wight that epistemological and methodological issues are the result of different theoretical approaches to this essentially ontological problem. See Wight (2006).

2 Similar "feminist warrior" accounts focusing on toughness, smartness, beauty, sexuality, and defiance were produced by Western media. See Marway (2011), Berkowitz (2005).

3 Israeli (2004) makes the same argument.

Chapter 4

1 It has been suggested that the "Black Fatima" is a character fabricated by the Russian government to deflect criticism from coercive counterterror tactics that could have pushed many more women to become suicide bombers. Whether a real person or a discursive construct, the "Black Fatima" underscores the importance of the politics of representation discussed in chapter 5.

2 *Narodnaya Volya* is translated into English as "people's will," although *volya* in Russian may mean "will" or "freedom."

Chapter 5

1 While detailed discussion of the postcolonial and critical race theories falls beyond the scope of this book, we would like to point out that they share a close affinity with feminist theory in that they theorize linkages between the discursive and material production of identity and practices of domination. In demonstrating that interlocking political constructions of race and gender undergird colonialism, postcolonial, critical race, and feminist theorists denaturalize oppressive social hierarchies, roles, and stereotypes, expose the foundational role of mainstream scholarship in sustaining racialization and gendering, and are deeply committed to the emancipatory project of socio-political transformation.

2 See Aslam (2012, 11–14) on the use of the language of political Islam and distinctions between Muslim, Islamic, and Islamist.

Chapter 6

1 A series of transformative developments contributed to the emergence of human security. These include the end of the Cold War and the attendant retreat of the dominant approaches to security, the decades of advocacy by civil society groups in support of human rights, the increasing salience of intra-state violence that targeted individuals who were not necessarily combatants and resulted in huge losses of lives, increased instances of genocide, mass rape, ethnic cleansing, and terrorism, as well as the acknowledgment of insecurities generated by the rapid acceleration of globalization.

2 For adaptations of human security, see Christie (2010).

3 Traditionalists were sceptical about its analytical value and rejected its practical relevance and efficacy altogether (see Paris 2001). Other critics challenged the wisdom of replacing societal/identity security with human security, of mixing up the agendas of international and societal security, and of including what they deemed to be essentially a human rights agenda in the framework of security (see Buzan 2004). Concerns over operationalization of the concept led several authors to suggest the need to narrow the focus of human security exclusively to the protection from violence – i.e., the "freedom from fear" agenda – and to advocate a greater convergence of human security and state security (see Suhrke 1999, Liotta 2002, Thomas and Tow 2002). Others defended the broadening of the scope of security, arguing that the narrow approach simply co-opts human security into the statist framework, entrenches state-centric

understanding of security, and dilutes the emancipatory potential of human security (Bellamy and McDonald 2002). Coalescence of human security with humanitarian foreign policies was critiqued for serving international ambitions and solidifying middle-power status of certain states, for disguising the Eurocentric nature of human security, and for reinforcing the dominance of the global North (Hudson 2005).

4 Having examined twenty-one contributions to the human security debate by leading security scholars in the special section of *Security Dialogue* (2004), Hoogensen and Stuvoy (2006, 210) concluded that the discussion did "not incorporate gender very significantly."

5 Note that the 1994 *Human Development Report* makes references to women, but clearly leaves out gender as an analytical category. For example, it mentions threats directed against women (rape, domestic violence, etc.) under the rubric of personal security, but refers to community security that derives from membership in a group only in terms of race and ethnicity. This implies that any direct reference to gender would be superfluous because the insights of gender have already been integrated within the *human* security approach.

6 In an attempt to remedy women's subordination and achieve gender equality, liberal feminism stresses the importance of removing obstacles to women's participation in the public realm. In other words, more women taking on men's roles and becoming visible (that is, become more like men) brings us closer to the ideal of equality. In terms of security, liberal feminism adds women to the human security paradigm without questioning either the meaning of *human* or the positivist foundation of liberal epistemology. Gender identity is therefore reduced to masculinity, disguised as humankind. This leads to the reiteration of more inclusive, but nonetheless masculinist hegemonic universalism (Hudson 2005, 159). Radical feminism, too, is complicit in perpetuating masculinist universalism, albeit of a different kind. Emphasizing difference between men and women, radical feminism maintains that men's dominant position distorts understanding of security, which is inevitably incomplete. A non-dominant/women's perspective is argued to inform a less distorted and more reliable understanding. "The voice of the victim," as Elshtain (2000, 252) puts it, "gains not only privilege but hegemony – provided she remains a victim, [which] ... can be part and parcel of an explicit power play." This type of radical feminist discourse essentializes women's victimhood, perpetuates "the ideology of victimization" (ibid.), and posits a dichotomized universalism that pits female subordination and peacefulness against men's domination

and aggressiveness. It overlooks differences in the complex overlapping experiences and identities of both men and women and settles for easy generalizations by neglecting that femininity and masculinity "are not mutually exclusive but in relation, which permits more than the two possibilities posited in either-or constructions" (Peterson 1996 18).

Bibliography

Abdullayev, Nabi. 2003. "Suicide – or Staged – Bombings?" *Transitions Online*, 16 July. http://www.fpa.org/newsletter_info2497/newsletter_info_sub_list. htm?section=Chechnya, accessed 18 May 2010.

Abeysekera, Sunila. 2006. "Gendering Transitional Justice: Experience of Women in Sri Lanka and Timor Leste in Seeking Affirmation and Rights." In *Engendering Human Security: Feminist Perspectives*, ed. Thanh-Dam Truong, Saskia Wieringa, and Amrita Chhachhi, 3–35. London: Zed Books.

Ahall, Linda. 2012. "The Writing of Heroines: Motherhood and Female Agency in Political Violence." *Security Dialogue* 43 (4): 287–303. http://dx.doi.org/10.1177/0967010612450206.

Ahall, Linda, and Laura Shepherd. 2012. *Gender, Agency, and Political Violence.* Basingstoke, UK: Palgrave.

Ahmad, Muhammad. 2014. "Shocker: Kano Suicide Bomber Says Father Donated Her to Boko Haram." *Premium Times*, 25 December. www. premiumtimesng.com/news/top-news/173769-shocker-kano-suicide-bomber-says-father-donated-boko-haram.html.

Ahmed, Mohamed. 2011. "Al Shabaab Trains 70 Female Suicide Bombers." *Somalia Report*, 14 March. http://www.somaliareport.com/index.php/post/258/Al_Shabaab_Trains_70_Female_Suicide_Bombers.

Ahmetbeyzade, Cihan. 2007. "Negotiating Silences in the So-Called Low-Intensity War: The Making of the Kurdish Diaspora in Istanbul." *Signs* (*Chicago, IL*) 33 (1): 159–82. http://dx.doi.org/10.1086/518315.

Akhmirova, Rimma. 2013. "On, Ona i … terakt. Kto i Kak na Samom Dele Zaverboval Volgogradskuyu Smertnitsu Naidu Asiyalovu." *Sobesednik*, 28. www.sobesednik.ru/investigation/20131028-ona-i-teract-kto-i-kak-na-samom-dele-zaverboval-volgogradskuyu-smertnitsu-nai, accessed 1 November 2013.

Ali, Farhana. 2005. "Muslim Female Fighters: An Emerging Trend." *Terrorism Monitor* 3 (21). http://www.jamestown.org/single/?no_cache=1&tx_ttnews[tt_news]=603.

Ali, Kecia. 2006. *Sexual Ethics and Islam: Feminist Reflections on Qur'an, Hadith, and Jurisprudence*. Oxford: Oneworld Publications.

Alison, Miranda. 2004. "Women as Agents of Political Violence: Gendering Security." *Security Dialogue* 35 (4): 447–63. http://dx.doi.org/10.1177/0967010604049522.

– 2009. *Women and Political Violence: Female Combatants in Ethno-national Conflict*. London: Routledge.

Amnesty International. 2010. "Russian Federation: Briefing to the Committee on the Elimination of Discrimination against Women." July. www2.ohchr.org/English/bodies/cedaw/docs/ngos/AI_RussianFederation46.pdf.

– 2012. *Annual Report 2012 – Russian Federation*. http://www.refworld.org/docid/4fbe391569.html.

Andreyev, Sergey. 2013. "Pochemu Dmitriya Sokolova Ne Vziali Zhyvym." *Komsomolskaya Pravda*, 17 November. www.kp.by/daily/26160.7/3047580/.

Ankersen, Christopher. 2007. *Understanding Global Terror*. Edited by Michael O'Leary. Cambridge, UK: Polity.

Aradau, Claudia. 2004. "Security and the Democratic Scene: Desecuritization and Emancipation." *Journal of International Relations and Development* 7 (4): 388–413. http://dx.doi.org/10.1057/palgrave.jird.1800030.

Arendt, Hannah. 1969. *On Violence*. New York: Harcourt.

Aslam, Maleeha. 2012. *Gender-Based Explosions: The Nexus between Muslim Masculinities, Jihadist Islamism, and Terrorism*. Tokyo: United Nations University Press.

Associated Press. 2005. "Female Suicide Bomber Kills Six Iraqi Recruits." *USA Today*, 28 September. http://usatoday30.usatoday.com/news/world/iraq/2005-09-28-iraqi-recruits-killed_x.htm.

– 2007. "Female Suicide Bomber Kills at Least 16 in Iraq." *CTV.ca*, 10 April. http://www.ctvnews.ca/female-suicide-bomber-kills-at-least-16-in-iraq-1.236834.

– 2008. "Four Female Suicide Bombers Kill 57 in Iraq." *USA Today*, 28 July. http://usatoday30.usatoday.com/news/world/iraq/2008-07-28-iraq-pilgrims-monday_N.htm.

Atilla, Toygun. 2015. "Suicide Bomber Who Attacked Istanbul Police Was Married to Norwegian ISIL Jihadist." *Hurriyet Daily News*, 16 January. www.hurriyetdailynews.com/suicide-bomber-who-attacked-istanbul-police-was-married-to-norwegian-isil-jihadist.aspx?PageID=238&NID=77070&NewsCatID=509.

Atran, Scott. 2006a. "A Failure of Imagination (Intelligence, WMDs, and 'Virtual Jihad')." *Studies in Conflict and Terrorism* 29 (3): 285–300. http://dx.doi.org/10.1080/10576100600564166.

– 2006b. "The Moral Logic and Growth of Suicide Terrorism." *Washington Quarterly* 29 (2): 127–47. http://dx.doi.org/10.1162/wash.2006.29.2.127.

Banerjee, Sikata. 2006. "Armed Masculinity, Hindu Nationalism and Female Political Participation in India: Heroic Mothers, Chaste Wives and Celibate Warriors." *International Feminist Journal of Politics* 8 (1): 62–83. http://dx.doi.org/10.1080/14616740500415482.

Banner, Francine. 2006. "Uncivil Wars: 'Suicide Bomber Identity' as a Product of Russo-Chechen Conflict." *Religion State & Society* 34 (3): 215–53. http://dx.doi.org/10.1080/09637490600819358.

Bardhan, Kalpana, and Stephan Klasen. 1999. "UNDP's Gender-Related Indices: A Critical Review." *World Development* 27 (6): 985–1010. http://dx.doi.org/10.1016/S0305-750X(99)00035-2.

Barkawi, Tarak, and Shane Brighton. 2011. "Powers of War: Fighting, Knowledge, and Critique." *International Political Sociology* 5 (2): 126–43. http://dx.doi.org/10.1111/j.1749-5687.2011.00125.x.

Barkawi, Tarak, and Mark Laffey. 2006. "The Postcolonial Moment in Security Studies." *Review of International Studies* 32 (2): 329–52. http://dx.doi.org/10.1017/S0260210506007054.

Barnett, Michael, and Raymond Duvall. 2005. "Power in Global Governance." In *Power in Global Governance*, ed. Michael Barnett and Raymond Duvall, 1–33. Cambridge: Cambridge University Press.

Barri Flowers, Ronald. 1987. *Women and Criminality: The Woman as Victim, Offender and Practitioner.* New York: Greenwood.

BBC News. 2003. "Iraq Says Women Killed Troops." 5 April. http://news.bbc.co.uk/2/hi/middle_east/2917107.stm.

– 2007a. "Belgian Iraq Terror Trial Begins." 15 October. http://news.bbc.co.uk/2/hi/europe/7045282.stm.

– 2007b. "Woman in Pakistan Suicide Bombing." 4 December. http://news.bbc.co.uk/2/hi/south_asia/7126637.stm.

– 2009. "Iraq's 'Female Bomber' Recruiter." 4 February. http://news.bbc.co.uk/2/hi/middle_east/7869570.stm.

Bellamy, Alex, and Matt McDonald. 2002. "'The Utility of Human Security': Which Humans? What Security? A Reply to Thomas & Tow." *Security Dialogue* 33 (3): 373–7. http://dx.doi.org/10.1177/0967010602033003010.

Berko, Anat. 2012. *The Smarter Bomb: Women and Children as Suicide Bombers.* Lanham, MD: Rowman and Littlefield.

Berko, Anat, and Edna Erez. 2007. "Gender, Palestinian Women, and Terrorism: Women's Liberation or Oppression." *Studies in Conflict and Terrorism* 30 (6): 493–519. http://dx.doi.org/10.1080/10576100701329550.

Berkowitz, Dan. 2005. "Suicide Bombers as Women Warriors: Making News through Mythical Archetypes." *Journalism & Mass Communication Quarterly* 82 (3): 607–22. http://dx.doi.org/10.1177/107769900508200308.

Beyler, Clara. 2003a. "Chronology of Suicide Bombings Carried Out by Women." *Herzlia: International Institute for Counter Terrorism.* https://www.ict.org.il/Article.aspx?ID=855.

– 2003b. "Messengers of Death: Female Suicide Bombers." *International Institute for Counter-terrorism.* https://www.ict.org.il/Article.aspx?ID=854.

Bhatia, Michael. 2005. "Fighting Words: Naming Terrorists, Bandits, Rebels and Other Violent Actors." *Third World Quarterly* 26 (1): 5–22. http://dx.doi.org/10.1080/0143659042000322874.

Biersteker, Thomas. 2010. "Interrelationships between Theory and Practice in International Security Studies." *Security Dialogue* 41 (6): 599–606. http://dx.doi.org/10.1177/0967010610388211.

Blanchard, Eric. 2003. "Gender, International Relations and the Development of Feminist Security Theory." *Signs (Chicago, IL)* 28 (4): 1289–312. http://dx.doi.org/10.1086/368328.

Bloom, Mia. 2007. *Dying to Kill: The Allure of Suicide Terror.* New York: Columbia University Press.

– 2008. "Women as Victims and Victimizers." *America.gov.* http://iipdigital.usembassy.gov/st/english/publication/2008/05/20080522172353srenod0.6383936.html#axzz3yITfBhSB.

– 2010. "Death Becomes Her: Women, Occupation, and Terrorist Mobilization." *PS, Political Science & Politics* 43 (3): 445–50. http://dx.doi.org/10.1017/S1049096510000703.

– 2011. *Bombshell: The Many Faces of Women Terrorists.* Toronto: Penguin. http://dx.doi.org/10.9783/9780812208108.

Bloom, Mia, Bradley A. Thayer, and Valerie M. Hudson. 2010/11. "Life Sciences and Islamic Suicide Terrorism." *International Security* 35 (3): 185–92. http://dx.doi.org/10.1162/ISEC_c_00027.

Booth, Ken. 1991. "Security and Emancipation." *Review of International Studies* 17 (4): 313–26. http://dx.doi.org/10.1017/S0260210500112033.

– 2005. *Critical Security Studies and World Politics.* Boulder, CO: Lynne Rienner.

– 2013. "Foreword." In *Critical Approaches to Security: An Introduction to Theories and Methods,* ed. Laura Shepherd, xv–xvii. London: Routledge.

Brown, Katherine. 2011. "Blinded by the Explosion? Security and Resistance in Muslim Women's Suicide Terrorism." In *Women, Gender, and Terrorism,* ed. Laura Sjoberg and Caron Gentry, 194–226. Athens, GA: University of Georgia Press.

Brunner, Claudia. 2005. "Female Suicide Bombers – Male Suicide Bombing? Looking for Gender in Reporting the Suicide Bombings of the Israeli-Palestinian Conflict." *Global Society* 19 (1): 29–48. http://dx.doi.org/10.1080/1360082042000316031.

– 2007. "Occidentalism Meets the Female Suicide Bomber: A Critical Reflection on Recent Terrorism Debates. A Review Essay." *Signs (Chicago, IL)* 32 (4): 957–71. http://dx.doi.org/10.1086/512490.

Butler, Judith. 1990. *Gender Trouble: Feminism and the Subversion of Identity.* New York: Routledge.

– 1993. *Bodies That Matter: On the Discursive Limits of Sex.* London: Routledge.

– 2005. *Giving an Account of Oneself.* New York: Fordham University Press. http://dx.doi.org/10.5422/fso/9780823225033.001.0001.

Buzan, Barry. 2004. "A Reductionist, Idealistic Notion That Adds Little Analytical Value." *Security Dialogue* 35 (3): 369–70. http://dx.doi.org/10.1177/096701060403500326.

Buzan, Barry, and Lene Hansen. 2009. *The Evolution of International Security Studies.* Cambridge: Cambridge University Press. http://dx.doi.org/10.1017/CBO9780511817762.

Carrier, James. 1992. "Occidentalism: The World Turned Upside Down." *American Ethnologist* 19 (2): 195–212. http://dx.doi.org/10.1525/ae.1992.19.2.02a00010.

Catignani, Sergio. 2005. "The Security Imperative in Counterterror Operations: The Israeli Fight against Suicidal Terror." *Terrorism and Political Violence* 17 (1–2): 245–64. http://dx.doi.org/10.1080/09546550490520718.

Center for Strategic and International Studies. 2010. "Violence in the North Caucasus: Not Just a Chechen Conflict." http://csis.org/publication/violence-north-caucasus-7.

Charmes, Jacques, and Saskia Wieringa. 2003. "Measuring Women's Empowerment: An Assessment of the Gender-Related Development Index and the Gender Empowerment Measure." *Journal of Human Development* 4 (3): 419–35. http://dx.doi.org/10.1080/1464988032000125773.

Chaturvedi, Sanjay, and Joe Painter. 2007. "Whose World, Whose Order? Spatiality, Geopolitics and the Limits of the World Order Concept." *Cooperation and Conflict* 42 (4): 375–95. http://dx.doi.org/10.1177/0010836707082646.

Chicago Project on Security and Terrorism (CPOST). http://cpost.uchicago.edu/.

Christie, Ryerson. 2010. "Critical Voices and Human Security: To Endure, to Engage or to Critique?" *Security Dialogue* 41 (2): 169–90. http://dx.doi.org/10.1177/0967010610361891.

Clothia, Farouk. 2014. "Boko Haram Crisis: Nigeria's Female Bombers Strike." *BBC Africa*, 6 August. www.bbc.com/news/world-africa-28657085.

Clutterbuck, Lindsay. 2004. "The Progenitors of Terrorism: Russian Revolutionaries or Extreme Irish Republicans?" *Terrorism and Political Violence* 16 (1): 154–81. http://dx.doi.org/10.1080/09546550490457917.

CNN. 2005. "Belgian Paper IDs 'Suicide Bomber.'" 1 December. http://www.cnn.com/2005/WORLD/europe/12/01/belgium.iraq/.

– 2007. "Bombs Target Police, Awakening Council North of Baghdad." 31 December. http://cnnwire.blogs.cnn.com/2007/12/31/bombs-target-police-awakening-council-north-of-baghdad/, accessed 25 May 2009.

– 2008. "Female Suicide Bomber Strikes Soccer Fans in Iraq." 14 June. http://www.cnn.com/2008/WORLD/meast/06/14/iraq.main/index.html.

Cockburn, Cynthia. 2007. *From Where We Stand: War, Women's Activism and Feminist Analysis*. London: Zed Books.

Connell, Raewyn. 1995. *Masculinities*. Cambridge: Polity.

Connolly, William. 1993. *The Terms of Political Discourse*. Oxford: Blackwell.

Cook, David. 2008. "Women Fighting in Jihad?" In *Female Terrorism and Militancy: Agency, Utility, and Organization*, ed. Cindy Ness, 37–48. London: Routledge.

Cooper, H.H.A. 2002. "Terrorism: The Problem of Definition Revisited." In *Essential Readings in Political Terrorism: Analyses of Problems and Prospects for the 21st Century*, ed. Harvey Kushner, 1–16. New York: Gordian Knot Books.

Coronil, Fernando. 1996. "Beyond Occidentalism: Toward Nonimperial Geohistorical Categories." *Cultural Anthropology* 11 (1): 51–87. http://dx.doi.org/10.1525/can.1996.11.1.02a00030.

Cox, Robert. 1996. "Social Forces, States and World Orders: Beyond International Relations Theory." In *Approaches to World Order*, ed. Robert Cox, with Timothy Sinclair, 85–123. Cambridge: Cambridge University Press. http://dx.doi.org/10.1017/CBO9780511607905.007.

Cragin, Kim, and Sara Daly. 2009. *Women as Terrorists: Mothers, Recruiters, and Martyrs*. Santa Barbara, CA: Praeger.

Crenshaw, Martha. 2005. "The Name Game." *Foreign Policy* 149:88.

– 2007. "Explaining Suicide Terrorism: A Review Essay." *Security Studies* 16 (1): 133–62. http://dx.doi.org/10.1080/09636410701304580.

Cunningham, Karla J. 2003. "Cross-Regional Trends in Female Terrorism." *Studies in Conflict and Terrorism* 26 (3): 171–95. http://dx.doi.org/10.1080/10576100390211419.

– 2008. "The Evolving Participation of Muslim Women in Palestine, Chechnya and the Global Jihadi Movement." In *Female Terrorism and Militancy: Agency, Utility, and Organization*, ed. Cindy Ness, 84–99. London: Routledge.

Davis, Joyce M. 2003. *Martyrs: Innocence, Vengeance and Despair in the Middle East*. New York: Palgrave/Macmillan.

– 2008. "Gendered Terrorism: Women in the Liberation Tigers of Tamil Eelam." *Minerva Journal of Women and War* 2 (1): 22–38. http://dx.doi. org/10.3172/MIN.2.1.22.

– 2013. "Evolution of the Global Jihad: Female Suicide Bombers in Iraq." *Studies in Conflict and Terrorism* 36 (4): 279–91. http://dx.doi.org/10.1080/ 1057610X.2013.763598.

De Cataldo Neuburger, Luisella, and Tiziana Valentini. 1996. *Women and Terrorism*. New York: St Martin's. http://dx.doi.org/10.1007/978-1-349-24706-6.

Decker, Jeffrey Louis. 1990–1. "Terrorism (Un)Veiled: Frantz Fanon and the Women of Algiers." *Cultural Critique* 17 (Winter): 177–95.

De Mel, Neloufer. 2004. "Body Politics: (Re)Cognising the Female Suicide Bomber in Sri Lanka." *Indian Journal of Gender Studies* 11 (1): 75–93. http:// dx.doi.org/10.1177/097152150401100106.

Denov, Myriam, and Christine Gervais. 2007. "Negotiating (In)Security: Agency, Resistance and Resourcefulness among Girls Formerly Associated with Sierra Leone's Revolutionary United Front." *Signs (Chicago, IL)* 32 (4): 885–910. http://dx.doi.org/10.1086/512488.

De Silva, P.L. 1995. "The Efficacy of 'Combat Mode': Organisation, Political Violence, Affect and Cognition in the Case of the Liberation Tigers of Tamil Eelam." In *Unmaking the Nation: The Politics of Identity and History in Modern Sri Lanka*, ed. Pradeep Jeganathan and Qadri Ismail, 176–90. Colombo: Social Scientists' Association.

Diaz-Cotto, Juanita. 1991. "Women and Crime in the United States." In *Third World Women and the Politics of Feminism*, ed. Chandra Talpade Mohanty, Ann Russo, and Lourdes Torres, 197–211. Bloomington: Indiana University Press.

Dijkstra, Geske. 2002. "Revisiting UNDP's GDI and GEM: Toward an Alternative." *Social Indicators Research* 57 (3): 301–38. http://dx.doi.org/ 10.1023/A:1014726207604.

Dobbs, Richard. 2002. "Toward Understanding Insurgent Success: Two Cases in South Lebanon, 1968–2000." *Dissertation Abstracts International*, 63–10A.

Dubnov, Vadim. 2013. "Naida Asiyalova, ili Novyi Pasport Rosiyskoho Terrorizma." RIA Novosti, 22 October. www.ria.ru/ analytics/20131022/971897759.html.

Dunn, Shannon. 2010. "The Female Martyr and the Politics of Death: An Examination of the Martyr Discourses of Vibia Perpetua and Wafa Idris." *Journal of the American Academy of Religion* 78 (1): 202–25. http://dx.doi. org/10.1093/jaarel/lfp090.

Durkheim, Émile. 1982. *The Rules of Sociological Method*, ed. Steven Lukes. New York: Free Press. http://dx.doi.org/10.1007/978-1-349-16939-9.

Duvall, Raymond, and Latha Varadarajan. 2003. "On the Practical Significance of Critical International Relations Theory." *Asian Journal of Political Science* 11 (2): 75–88. http://dx.doi.org/10.1080/02185370308434228.

Eager, Paige Whaley. 2008. *From Freedom Fighters to Terrorists: Women & Political Violence*. Burlington, VT: Ashgate Publishing.

"Editorial." 1993. In "Nationalisms and National Identities," special issue of *Feminist Review* 44 (1): 1–2.

Eichler, Maya. 2006. "Russia's Post-Communist Transformation." *International Feminist Journal of Politics* 8 (4): 486–511. http://dx.doi.org/10.1080/14616740600945065.

Eisenstein, Zillah. 2007. *Sexual Decoys: Gender, Race and War in Imperial Democracy*. London: Zed Books.

Elshtain, Jean Bethke. 1987. *Women and War*. New York: Basic Books.

– 2000. *Real Politics at the Center of Everyday Life*. Baltimore, MD: Johns Hopkins University Press.

Elster, Jon. 2006. "Motivations and Beliefs in Suicide Missions." In *Making Sense of Suicide Missions*, ed. Diego Gambetta, 233–58. Oxford: Oxford University Press.

Enloe, Cynthia. 1983. *Does Khaki Become You? The Militarization of Women's Lives*. London: Pluto.

– 1990. *Bananas, Bases and Beaches: Making Feminist Sense of International Politics*. London: Pandora.

– 2004. *The Curious Feminist: Searching for Women in a New Age of Empire*. Berkeley: University of California Press.

– 2007. *Globalization and Militarism: Feminists Make the Link*. Lanham, MD: Rowman and Littlefield.

– 2010. *Nimo's War, Emma's War: Making Feminist Sense of the Iraq War*. Berkeley: University of California Press.

Eschle, Catherine. 2001. *Global Democracy, Social Movements, and Feminism*. Boulder, CO: Westview.

Euben, Roxanne. 2007. "Review Symposium: Understanding Suicide Terror." *Perspectives on Politics* 5:129–33.

Fanon, Frantz. 1967. *A Dying Colonialism*, trans. Haakon Chevalier. New York: Grove.

Ferber, Abby, and Michael Kimmel. 2008. "The Gendered Face of Terrorism." *Sociology Compass* 2 (3): 870–87. http://dx.doi.org/10.1111/j.1751-9020.2008.00096.x.

Fighel, Jonathan. 2003. "Palestinian Islamic Jihad and Female Suicide Bombers." *International Policy Institute for Counter-Terrorism*. https://www.ict.org.il/Article/888/Palestinian%20Islamic%20Jihad%20and%20Female%20Suicide%20Bombers.

Foden, Giles. 2003. "Death and the Maidens." *Guardian*, 18 July. http://www.theguardian.com/world/2003/jul/18/gender.uk.

Fox, Mary-Jane. 2004. "Girl Soldiers: Human Security and Gendered Insecurity." *Security Dialogue* 35 (4): 465–79.

Friedman, Marilyn. 2007. "Female Terrorists: What Difference Does Gender Make?" *Social Philosophy Today* 23:189–200. http://dx.doi.org/10.5840/socphiltoday20072310.

– 2009. "Female Terrorists: Martyrdom and Gender Equality." *Values and Violence: Studies in Global Justice* 4:43–61. http://dx.doi.org/10.1007/978-1-4020-8660-1_4.

Gallie, Walter Bryce. 1956. "Essentially Contested Concepts." *Proceedings of the Aristotelian Society* 56:167–98.

Galochka, Ekaterina. 2013. "Mat Volgogradskoy Shahidki." 22 October. www.mk.ru/social/article/2013/10/22/934091-mat-volgogradskoy-shahidki_doch-nadela-hidzhab-kogda-vyishla-zamuzh-za-russkogo.html.

Galtung, Johan. 1969. "Violence, Peace and Peace Research." *Journal of Peace Research* 6 (3): 167–91. http://dx.doi.org/10.1177/002234336900600301.

Galvin, Deborah M. 1983. "The Female Terrorist: A Socio-Psychological Perspective." *Behavioral Sciences & the Law* 1 (2): 19–32. http://dx.doi.org/10.1002/bsl.2370010206.

Gambetta, Diego, ed. 2006. *Making Sense of Suicide Missions*. New York: Oxford University Press.

Gentry, Caron. 2009. "Twisted Maternalism." *International Feminist Journal of Politics* 11 (2): 235–52. http://dx.doi.org/10.1080/14616740902789609.

– 2011a. "The Committed Revolutionary: Reflections on a Conversation with Leila Khaled." In *Women, Gender, and Terrorism*, ed. Laura Sjoberg and Caron Gentry, 120–30. Athens, GA: University of Georgia Press.

– 2011b. "The Neo-Orientalist Narratives of Women's Involvement in al-Qaeda." In *Women, Gender, and Terrorism*, ed. Laura Sjoberg and Caron Gentry, 176–93. Athens, GA: University of Georgia Press.

Gentry, Caron, and Laura Sjoberg. 2011. "The Gendering of Women's Terrorism." In *Women, Gender, and Terrorism*, ed. Laura Sjoberg and Caron Gentry, 57–82. Athens, GA: University of Georgia Press.

Gentry, Caron, and Kathryn Whitworth. 2011. "The Discourses of Desperation: The Intersections of Neo-Orientalism, Gender and Islam in the Chechen Struggle." *Critical Terrorism Studies* 4 (2): 145–61. http://dx.doi.org/10.1080/17539153.2011.586202.

Ghosh, Bobby. 2008. "The Mind of a Female Suicide Bomber." *Time*, 22 June. http://content.time.com/time/world/article/0,8599,1817158,00.html.

Giddens, Anthony. 1986. *The Constitution of Society: Outline of the Theory of Structuration*. Berkeley: University of California Press.

Gill, Paul. 2012. "Assessing Contemporary Trends and Future Prospects in the Study of the Suicide Bomber." *Negotiation and Conflict Management Research* 5 (3): 239–52. http://dx.doi.org/10.1111/j.1750-4716.2012.00101.x.

Gonzalez-Perez, Margaret. 2008a. "From Freedom Birds to Water Buffaloes: Women Terrorists in Asia." In *Female Terrorism and Militancy: Agency, Utility, and Organization*, ed. Cindy Ness, 183–200. London: Routledge.

– 2008b. *Women and Terrorism: Female Activity in Domestic and International Terror Groups*. London: Routledge. http://dx.doi.org/10.4324/9780203926550.

– 2011. "The False Islamization of Female Suicide Bombers." *Gender Issues* 28 (1–2): 50–65. http://dx.doi.org/10.1007/s12147-011-9097-0.

Gunawardena, Arjuna. 2006. "Female Black Tigers: A Different Breed of Cat?" In *Female Suicide Bombers: Dying for Equality*, ed. Yoram Schweitzer, 81–90. Tel Aviv: Jaffe Center for Strategic Studies, Tel Aviv University.

Gunning, Jeroen. 2009. "Social Movement Theory and the Study of Terrorism." In *Critical Terrorism Studies: A New Research Agenda*, ed. Richard Jackson, Marie Breen Smith, and Jeroen Gunning, 156–77. London: Routledge.

Haddad, Simon. 2004. "A Comparative Study of Lebanese and Palestinian Perceptions of Suicide Bombings: The Role of Militant Islam and Socioeconomic Status." *International Journal of Comparative Sociology* 45 (5): 337–63. http://dx.doi.org/10.1177/0020715204054155.

Hafez, Mohammed. 2007. *Suicide Bombers in Iraq: The Strategy and Ideology of Martyrdom*. Washington, DC: United States Institute of Peace Press.

Hall, Catherine. 1993. "Gender, Nationalisms and National Identities Bellagio Symposium, July 1992." *Feminist Review* 44 (1): 97–103. http://dx.doi.org/10.1057/fr.1993.23.

Haraway, Donna. 1988. "Situated Knowledges: The Science Question in Feminism and the Privilege of Partial Perspective." *Feminist Studies* 14 (3): 575–99. http://dx.doi.org/10.2307/3178066.

Harb, Mona, and Reinoud Leenders. 2005. "Know Thy Enemy: Hizbullah, 'Terrorism' and the Politics of Perception." *Third World Quarterly* 26 (1): 173–97. http://dx.doi.org/10.1080/0143659042000322973.

Hassan, Riaz. 2008. "Global Rise of Suicide Terrorism: An Overview." *Asian Journal of Social Science* 36 (2): 271–91. http://dx.doi.org/10.1163/156853108X298743.

Hekman, Susan. 1997. "Truth and Method: Feminist Standpoint Theory Revisited." *Signs (Chicago, IL)* 22 (2): 341. http://dx.doi.org/10.1086/495159.

Hellmann, Gunther. 2003. "The Forum: Are Dialogue and Synthesis Possible in International Relations?" *International Studies Review* 5 (1): 123–53. http://dx.doi.org/10.1111/1521-9488.501019_1.

Herath, Tamara. 2012. *Women in Terrorism: Case of the LTTE*. Thousand Oaks, CA: Sage Publications.

Herring, Ronald. 2001. "Making Ethnic Conflict." In *Carrots, Sticks and Ethnic Conflict*, ed. Milton Esman and Ronald Herring, 140–74. Ann Arbor, MI: University of Michigan Press.

Hird, Myra. 2002. *Engendering Violence: Heterosexual Interpersonal Violence from Childhood to Adulthood*. Aldershot, Hampshire: Ashgate.

Hirschmann, Nancy. 1989. "Freedom, Recognition, and Obligation: A Feminist Approach to Political Theory." *American Political Science Review* 83 (4): 1227–44. http://dx.doi.org/10.2307/1961666.

– 2003. *The Subject of Liberty: Toward a Feminist Theory of Freedom*. Princeton: Princeton University Press.

Hoffman, Bruce. 2003. "The Logic of Suicide Terrorism." *Atlantic Monthly*, June. http://www.theatlantic.com/magazine/archive/2003/06/the-logic-of-suicide-terrorism/302739/.

Hoogensen, Gunhild. 2005. "Gender, Identity, and Human Security: Can We Learn Anything from the Case of Women Terrorists?" *Canadian Foreign Policy* 12 (1): 119–40. http://dx.doi.org/10.1080/11926422.2005.9673392.

Hoogensen, Gunhild, and Svein Vigeland Rottem. 2004. "Gender Identity and the Subject of Security." *Security Dialogue* 35 (2): 155–71. http://dx.doi.org/10.1177/0967010604044974.

Hoogensen, Gunhild, and Kirsti Stuvoy. 2006. "Gender, Resistance and Human Security." *Security Dialogue* 37 (2): 207–28. http://dx.doi.org/10.1177/0967010606066436.

Hudson, Heidi. 2005. "'Doing' Security as though Humans Matter: A Feminist Perspective on Gender and the Politics of Human Security." *Security Dialogue* 36 (2): 155–74. http://dx.doi.org/10.1177/0967010605054642.

Huggler, Justin. 2006. "Tamil Tiger Apology for Gandhi Assassination." *New Zealand Herald*, 28 June. www.nzherald.co.nz/world/news/article.cfm?c_id=2&objectid=10388749.

Hurrell, Andrew. 2007. *On Global Order: Power, Values, and the Constitution of International Society*. Oxford: Oxford University Press. http://dx.doi.org/10.1093/acprof:oso/9780199233106.001.0001.

India eNews.com. 2007. "Female Suicide Bomber Kills Seven Policemen in Iraq." 23 July. http://www.indiaenews.com/middle-east/20070723/62059.htm.

Institute for Economics and Peace. 2014. "Global Terrorism Index 2014." http://www.visionofhumanity.org/sites/default/files/Global% 20Terrorism%20Index%20Report%202014_0.pdf.

Israeli, Raphael. 2004. "Palestinian Women: The Quest for a Voice in the Public Square through 'Islamikaze Martydom.'" *Terrorism and Political Violence* 16 (1): 66–96. http://dx.doi.org/10.1080/09546550490446063.

Jackson, Richard, Marie Breen Smyth, and Jeroen Gunning, eds. 2009. *Critical Terrorism Studies: A New Research Agenda*. London: Routledge.

Jalal, Massouda. 2013. "CSW: Voices from Afghanistan." 7 March. https://www. opendemocracy.net/5050/massouda-jalal/csw-voices-from-afghanistan.

Johnson, Michael, and Janet Leone. 2005. "The Differential Effects of Intimate Terrorism and Situational Couple Violence: Findings from the National Violence against Women Survey." *Journal of Family Issues* 26 (3): 322–49. http://dx.doi.org/10.1177/0192513X04270345.

Johnston, Hank. 2008. "Ritual, Strategy, and Deep Culture in the Chechen National Movement." *Critical Studies on Terrorism* 1 (3): 321–42. http:// dx.doi.org/10.1080/17539150802514981.

Joseph, Suad, and Afsaneh Najmabadi. 2005. *Encyclopaedia of Women and Islamic Cultures*. Leiden: Brill.

Kalyvas, Stathis, and Ignacio Sanchez-Cuenca. 2006. "Killing without Dying: The Absence of Suicide Missions." In *Making Sense of Suicide Missions*, ed. Diego Gambetta, 209–32. New York: Oxford University Press.

Kandiyoti, Deniz. 2009. "The Lures and Perils of Gender Activism in Afhganistan." SOAS. www.soas.ac.uk/cccac/events/anthonyhyman/ 16mar2009-2009-the-lures-and-perils-of-gender-activism-in-afghanistan.html.

Keddie, Nikki. 1991. "Introduction: Deciphering Middle Eastern Women's History." In *Women in Middle Eastern History: Shifting Boundaries in Sex and Gender*, ed. Nikki Keddie and Beth Baron, 1–22. New Haven, CT: Yale University Press.

– 1999. "The New Religious Politics and Women Worldwide: A Comparative Study." *Journal of Women's History* 10 (4): 11–34. http://dx.doi.org/10.1353/ jowh.2010.0533.

– 2007. "Iranian Women's Status and Struggles since 1979." *Journal of International Affairs* 60 (2): 17–33.

Keeble, Edna, and Heather A. Smith. 1999. *(Re)Defining Traditions: Gender and Canadian Foreign Policy*. Halifax: Fernwood Publishing.

Khaled, Leila. 1973. *My People Shall Live*. London: Hodder and Stoughton.

Khalilov, Roman. 2003. "Moral Justifications of Secession: The Case of Chechnya." *Central Asian Survey* 22 (4): 405–20. http://dx.doi.org/10.1080/ 0263493042000202616.

Kinsella, Helen. 2005. "Securing the Civilian: Sex and Gender in the Laws of War." In *Power in Global Governance*, ed. Michael Barnett and Raymond Duvall, 249–72. Cambridge: Cambridge University Press.

– 2007. "Understanding a War That Is Not a War: A Review Essay." *Signs (Chicago, IL)* 33 (1): 209–31. http://dx.doi.org/10.1086/518316.

Knox, Kathleen, and Daniel Kimmage. 2004. "Uzbekistan: Sifting for Clues." *Asia Times*, 2 April. http://www.atimes.com/atimes/Central_Asia/FD02Ag01.html.

Kobrin, Nancy. 2010. *The Banality of Suicide Terrorism: The Naked Truth about the Psychology of Islamic Suicide Bombing*. Washington, DC: Potomac Books.

Korchagina, Valeriya. 2004. "Zakayev Was Asked to Assist in Negotiations at the School." *Moscow Times*, 6 September. http://www.themoscowtimes.com/stories/2004/09/06/014.html.

Krupneishie terakty v Rossii v 2010–2013 godakh, RIA Novosti, 29 December 2013 at www.ria.ru/spravka/20131229/987132908.html, accessed on 2 January 2014.

Kuttab, Eileen. 1997. "The Women Studies Program in Palestine: Between Criticism and New Vision." In *Muslim Women and the Politics of Participation: Implementing the Beijing Platform*, ed. Mahnaz Afkhami and Erika Friedl, 94–100. Syracuse, NY: Syracuse University Press.

Lapid, Yosef. 1989. "The Third Debate: On the Prospects of International Theory in a Post-Positivist Era." *International Studies Quarterly* 33 (3): 235–54. http://dx.doi.org/10.2307/2600457.

Lieven, Anatol. 1999. *Chechnya: Tombstone of Russian Power*. New Haven, CT: Yale University Press.

Life News. 2013. "Volgogradskuyu Smertnitsu Pered Teraktom Zasnyali Kamery Nabludeniya." www.lifenews.ru/#!news/121710.

Linklater, Andrew. 2006. "The Achievements of Critical Theory." In *International Theory: Positivism and Beyond*, ed. Steve Smith, Ken Booth, and Marysia Zalewski, 279–300. Cambridge: Cambridge University Press.

Liotta, P.H. 2002. "Boomerang Effect: The Convergence of National and Human Security." *Security Dialogue* 33 (4): 473–88. http://dx.doi.org/10.1177/0967010602033004007.

Lobanova, Zinaida, and Anna Selivanova. 2003. "Shahidki krupnym planom." *Komsomolskaya Pravda*, 10 July. http://www.kp.ru/daily/23069/4902/.

Lokshina, Tanya. 2012. "Virtue Campaign on Women in Chechnya under Ramzan Kadyrov." *Human Rights Watch*, 22 October. https://www.hrw.org/news/2012/10/29/virtue-campaign-women-chechnya-under-ramzan-kadyrov.

Lupovici, Amir. 2012. "Ontological Dissonance, Clashing Identities, and Israel's Unilateral Steps towards the Palestinians." *Review of International Studies* 38 (4): 809–33. http://dx.doi.org/10.1017/S0260210511000222.

Mackenzie, Catriona, and Natalie Stoljar. 2000. "Introduction." In *Relational Autonomy: Feminist Perspectives on Autonomy, Agency, and the Social Self*, ed. Catriona Mackenzie and Natalie Stoljar, 3–34. New York: Oxford University Press.

MacMillan, John. 2006. "Immanuel Kant and the Democratic Peace." In *Classical Theory in International Relations*, ed. Beate Jahn, 52–73. Cambridge: Cambridge University Press. http://dx.doi.org/10.1017/CBO9780511491429.003.

Magdaleno, Johnny. 2014. "Boko Haram Plans to Massacre 100,000 Nigerians with Female Suicide Bombers." *Vice News*, 5 December. https://news.vice.com/article/boko-haram-plans-to-massacre-100000-nigerians-with-female-suicide-bombers.

Magomedov, Omar. 2013. V selo terroristki Asiyalovoy priyekhali za krovyu yeye materi. www.ntv.ru/novosti/682560.

Malykh, Yaroslav, and Yulia Rybina. 2013. "Do Volgograda Dobralas Smertnitsa." *Gazeta Kommersant*, 22 October. www.kommersant.ru/doc/2325490?isSearch=True.

Marhia, Natasha. 2013. "Some Humans Are More Human Than Others: Troubling the 'Human' in Human Security from a Critical Feminist Perspective." *Security Dialogue* 44 (1): 19–35. http://dx.doi.org/10.1177/0967010612470293.

Marway, Herjeet. 2011. "Scandalous Subwomen and Sublime Superwomen: Exploring Portrayals of Female Suicide Bombers' Agency." *Journal of Global Ethics* 7 (3): 221–40. http://dx.doi.org/10.1080/17449626.2011.635677.

Mazzetti, Mark. "Insurgent Attacks on Iraqis Soared in 2005, Report Says." *New York Times*, 29 April 2006. http://www.nytimes.com/2006/04/29/world/middleeast/29terror.html?_r=0.

McCall, Leslie. 2005. "The Complexity of Intersectionality." *Signs (Chicago, IL)* 30 (3): 1771–800. http://dx.doi.org/10.1086/426800.

McCauley, Clark, and Sophia Moskalenko. 2010. "Do Suicide Terrorists Have Personality Problems? A Review." *Terrorism and Political Violence* 23 (1): 108–11. http://dx.doi.org/10.1080/09546553.2011.533074.

McKay, Susan. 2004. "Women, Human Security, and Peacebuilding: A Feminist Analysis." In *Conflict and Human Security: A Search for New Approaches of Peacebuilding*, ed. Shinoda Hideaki and How-Won Jeong, 152–75. Hiroshima: Institute for Peace Science.

McSweeney, Bill. 1999. *Security, Identity and Interests: A Sociology of International Relations*. Cambridge: Cambridge University Press.

Meintjes, Sheila, Meredith Turshen, and Anu Pillay. 2001. *The Aftermath: Women in Post-Conflict Transformation*. London: Zed Books.

Merari, Ariel. 2010. *Driven to Death: Psychological and Social Aspects of Suicide Terrorism*. Oxford: Oxford University Press.

Mernissi, Fatima. 1991. *The Veil and the Male Elite: A Feminist Interpretation of Women's Rights in Islam*, trans. Mary Jo Lakeland. Reading, MA: Addison-Wesley.

Milliken, Jennifer. 1999. "The Study of Discourse in International Relations: A Critique of Research and Methods." *European Journal of International Relations* 5 (2): 225–54. http://dx.doi.org/10.1177/1354066199005002003.

Mitzen, Jennifer. 2006. "Ontological Security in World Politics: State Identity and the Security Dilemma." *European Journal of International Relations* 12 (3): 341–70. http://dx.doi.org/10.1177/1354066106067346.

Moghadam, Valentine. 1994. "Introduction and Overview." In *Gender and National Identity: Women and Politics in Muslim Societies*, ed. Valentine Moghadam, 1–17. London: Zed Books.

– 2012. *Globalization and Social Movements: Islamism, Feminism, and the Global Justice Movement*. Lanham, MD: Rowman and Littlefield.

Mohanty, Chandra. 1991. "Under Western Eyes: Feminist Scholarship and Colonial Discourses." In *Third World Women and the Politics of Feminism*, ed. Chandra Talpade Mohanty, Ann Russo, and Lourdes Torres, 51–80. Bloomington: Indiana University Press.

Morgan, Robin. 1989. *The Demon Lover: On the Sexuality of Terrorism*. New York: W.W. Norton.

Mukasa, Henry. 2009. "Three Ministers Killed in Somalia Attack." *New Vision*, 3 December, at www.newvision.co.ug/D/8/12/703172.

Multi-National Corps – Iraq. 2008. "Female Suicide Bomber Kills 1, Injures 13 in Baqubah," 11 August. http://www.mnf-iraq.com/index.php?option=com_content&task=view&id=21759&Itemid=128, accessed 27 May 2009.

Murphy, K. 2004. "'Black Widows' Caught Up in Web of Chechen War." *Los Angeles Times*, 16 September.

Musleh, Rose Shomali. 2008. "People behind Walls, Women behind Walls: Reading Violence against Women in Palestine." In *Violence and Gender in the Globalized World: The Intimate and the Extimate*, ed. Sanja Bahun-Radunovic and V.G. Julie Rajan, 59–73. Aldershot, UK: Ashgate.

Mutimer, David. 1998. "Reconstituting Security: The Practices of Proliferation Control." *European Journal of International Relations* 4 (1): 99–129. http://dx.doi.org/10.1177/1354066198004001004.

Naaman, Dorit. 2007. "Brides of Palestine/Angels of Death: Media, Gender, and Performance in the Case of the Palestinian Female Suicide Bombers." *Signs (Chicago, IL)* 32 (4): 933–55. http://dx.doi.org/10.1086/512624.

Nadarajah, Suthaharan, and Dhananjayan Sriskandarajah. 2005. "Liberation Struggle or Terrorism? The Politics of Naming the LTTE." *Third World Quarterly* 26 (1): 87–100. http://dx.doi.org/10.1080/0143659042000322928.

Nassar, Jamal. 2004. *Globalization and Terrorism: The Migration of Dreams and Nightmares*. Lanham, MD: Rowman and Littlefield Publishers.

National Strategy Institute. 2013. "Karta etnoreligioznykh ugroz Rossii: Severny Kavkaz and Povolzhye." www.rus.ruvr.ru/tag_24451876/.

Ness, Cindy, ed. 2008a. *Female Terrorism and Militancy: Agency, Utility, and Organization*. London: Routledge.

– 2008b. "In the Name of the Cause: Women's Work in Secular and Religious Terrorism." In *Female Terrorism and Militancy: Agency, Utility, and Organization*, ed. Cindy Ness, 11–36. London: Routledge.

– 2008c. "Introduction." In *Female Terrorism and Militancy: Agency, Utility and Organization*, ed. Cindy Ness, 1–10. London: Routledge.

Neufeld, M. 2001. "What's Critical about Critical International Relations Theory?" In *Critical Theory and World Politics*, ed. R. Wyn Jones, 127–45. Boulder, CO: Lynne Rienner.

Neumann, Iver. 2012. "Introduction to the Forum on Liminality." *Review of International Studies* 38 (2): 473–9. http://dx.doi.org/10.1017/S0260210511000817.

Newman, Edward. 2006. "Exploring the 'Root Causes' of Terrorism." *Studies in Conflict and Terrorism* 29 (8): 749–72. http://dx.doi.org/10.1080/10576100600704069.

Newsru.com. 2013. "Sledstviye ustanovilo piateryh organizatorov terakta v Volgograde," 22 October. www.newsru.com/Russia/22oct2013/boeviki.html.

Nivat, Anne. 2008. "The Black Widows: Chechen Women Join the Fight for Independence – and Allah." In *Female Terrorism and Militancy: Agency, Utility, and Organization*, ed. Cindy Ness, 122–30. London: Routledge.

O'Rourke, Lindsey. 2008. "Behind the Woman behind the Bomb." *New York Times*, 2 August. http://www.nytimes.com/2008/08/02/opinion/02orourke.html.

Otto, Roland. 2012. *Targeted Killings and International Law: With Special Regard to Human Rights and International Humanitarian Law*. Berlin: Springer. http://dx.doi.org/10.1007/978-3-642-24858-0.

Özcan, Ali Kemal. 2006. *Turkey's Kurds: A Theoretical Analysis of the PKK and Abdullah Öcalan*. New York: Routledge.

Özcan, Nihat Ali. 2007. "PKK Recruitment of Female Operatives." *Terrorism Focus* 4 (28). http://www.jamestown.org/single/?no_cache=1&tx_ttnews[tt_news]=4394.

Pape, Robert A. 2003. "The Strategic Logic of Suicide Terrorism." *American Political Science Review* 97 (3): 1–20. http://www.danieldrezner.com/research/guest/Pape1.pdf.

– 2005. *Dying to Win: The Strategic Logic of Suicide Terrorism.* New York: Random House.

Pape, Robert, and James Feldman. 2010. *Cutting the Fuse: The Explosion of Global Suicide Terrorism and How to Stop It.* Chicago: University of Chicago Press. http://dx.doi.org/10.7208/chicago/9780226645643.001.0001.

Parashar, Swati. 2009. "Feminist International Relations and Women Militants: Case Studies from Sri Lanka and Kashmir." *Cambridge Review of International Affairs* 22 (2): 235–56. http://dx.doi.org/10.1080/09557570902877968.

Parfitt, Tom. 2003. "Meet Black Fatima – She Programmes Women to Kill." *Telegraph,* 20 July. http://www.telegraph.co.uk/news/worldnews/europe/russia/1436622/Meet-Black-Fatima--she-programmes-women-to-kill.html.

Paris, Roland. 2001. "Human Security: Paradigm Shift or Hot Air?" *International Security* 26 (2): 87–102. http://dx.doi.org/10.1162/016228801753191141.

Parker, Andrew, Mary Russo, Doris Sommer, and Patricia Yaeger, eds. 1992. *Nationalism and Sexualities.* London: Routledge.

Pearson, Elizabeth. 2014. "Nigeria: Do Nigeria's Female Suicide Attackers Point to Desperation or High Ambition for Boko Haram?" *allAfrica,* 20 November. http://allafrica.com/stories/201411210494.html.

Pedahzur, Ami. 2005. *Suicide Terrorism.* Cambridge: Polity.

Peteet, Julie. 2005. "Words as Interventions: Naming in the Palestine-Israel Conflict." *Third World Quarterly* 26 (1): 153–72. http://dx.doi.org/10.1080/0143659042000322964.

Peterson, V. Spike, ed. 1992. *Gendered States: Feminist (Re)Visions of International Relations.* Boulder, CO: Lynne Rienner Publishers.

– 1996. "Shifting Ground(s): Epistemological and Territorial Remapping in a Global Context." In *Globalization: Theory and Practice,* ed. Eleonore Kofman and Gillian Youngs, 11–28. London: Pinter.

– 1999. "Political Identities/Nationalism as Heterosexism." *International Feminist Journal of Politics* 1 (1): 34–65. http://dx.doi.org/10.1080/146167499360031.

– 2008. "'New Wars' and Gendered Economies." *Feminist Review* 88 (1): 7–20. http://dx.doi.org/10.1057/palgrave.fr.9400377.

– 2010. "Gendered Identities, Ideologies, and Practices in the Context of War and Militarism." In *Gender, War, and Militarism: Feminist Perspectives,* ed. Laura Sjoberg and Sandra Via, 17–29. Santa Barbara, CA: Praeger.

Peterson, V. Spike, and Anne Sisson Runyan. 1999. *Global Gender Issues.* Boulder, CO: Westview.

Pettman, Jan Jindy. 1996. *Worlding Women: A Feminist International Politics.* New York: Routledge.

Pflanz, Mike. 2012. "Somalia's Prime Minister Narrowly Escapes Female Suicide Bomber." *Telegraph,* 4 April. www.telegraph.co.uk/news/worldnews/africaandindianocean/somalia/9186566/Somalias-prime-minister-narrowly-escapes-female-suicide-bomber.html.

Pickup, Francine, with Suzanne Williams and Caroline Sweetman. 2001. *Ending Violence against Women: A Challenge for Development and Humanitarian Work.* Oxford: Oxfam.

Polit.ru. 2013. "V Dagestane Ubity Dva Boyevika iz 'Makhachkalinskoy' Gruppirovki," 20 November. www.polit.ru/news/2013/11/20/twobandits/.

Pratap, Anita. 2003. *Island of Blood: Frontline Reports from Sri Lanka, Afghanistan and Other South Asian Flashpoints.* New York: Penguin.

"President Bush on the Middle East." PBS Newshour, 4 April 2002. http://www.pbs.org/newshour/updates/white_house-jan-june02-bush_04-04/.

Price, Richard, and Christian Reus-Smit. 1998. "Dangerous Liaisons? Critical International Theory and Constructivism." *European Journal of International Relations* 4 (3): 259–94. http://dx.doi.org/10.1177/1354066198004003001.

Prugl, Elizabeth. 1999. *The Global Construction of Gender: Home-Based Work in the Political Economy of the 20th Century.* New York: Columbia University Press.

Qazi, Farhana. 2011. "The Mujahidaat: Tracing the Early Female Warriors of Islam." In *Women, Gender, and Terrorism,* ed. Laura Sjoberg and Caron Gentry, 29–56. Athens, GA: University of Georgia Press.

Rajan, V.G. Julie. 2012. *Women Suicide Bombers: Narratives of Violence.* Abingdon, UK: Routledge.

Ramachandran, Sudha. 2004. "Uzbekistan's Femmes Fatales." *Asia Times Online,* 28 April. http://www.atimes.com/atimes/Central_Asia/FD28Ag01.html.

Ramphele, Mamphela. 1997. "Political Widowhood in South Africa: The Embodiment of Ambiguity." In *Social Suffering,* ed. Arthur Kleinman, Veena Das, and Margaret Lock, 99–118. Berkeley: University of California Press.

Ranchod-Nilsson, Sita, and Mary Ann Tétreault. 2000. "Gender and Nationalism: Moving beyond Fragmented Conversations." In *Women, States and Nationalism: At Home in the Nation?,* ed. Sita Ranchod-Nilsson and Mary Ann Tétreault, 1–17. London: Routledge. http://dx.doi.org/10.4324/9780203361122_chapter_1.

Ranstrop, Magnus. 1997. *Hizb'allah in Lebanon.* New York: St Martin's.

Raphael, Sam. 2009. "In the Service of Power: Terrorism Studies and US Intervention in the Global South." In *Critical Terrorism Studies: A New Research Agenda,* ed. Richard Jackson, Marie Breen Smith, and Jeroen Gunning, 49–65. London: Routledge.

Rechkalov, Vadim. 2003. "Devushki-delfiny." *Izvestiya*, 3 September.

Report of the Secretary-General's Internal Review Panel on United Nations Action in Sri Lanka. 2012. www.un.org/News/dh/infocus/Sri_Lanka/The_Internal_Review_Panel_report_on_Sri_Lanka.pdf.

Reuter, Christoph. 2004. *My Life Is a Weapon: A Modern History of Suicide Bombing*, trans. Helena Ragg-Kirby. Princeton: Princeton University Press.

Reuters. 2007a. "Afghan Detains Woman with Bomb under Burqa." http://sweetness-light.com/archive/afghans-arrest-first-female-suicide-bomber.

– 2007b. "Female Suicide Bomber Wounds 7 US Troops in Iraq." *LiveLeak*, 28 November. http://www.liveleak.com/view?i=787_1196235491.

– 2008. "Female Suicide Bomber Kills Iraq Tribal Head-Police." Reuters.com, 10 March. http://www.reuters.com/article/us-iraq-bomber-idUSL1071203720080310.

Richmond, Oliver. 2007. "Emancipatory Forms of Human Security and Liberal Peacebuilding." *International Journal (Toronto)* 62 (3): 459–77.

Ricolfi, Luca. 2006. "Palestinians, 1981–2003." In *Making Sense of Suicide Missions*, ed. Diego Gambetta, 77–129. Oxford: Oxford University Press.

Ricolfi, Luca, and Paolo Campana. 2005. "Suicide Missions: A New Database on the Palestinian Area." *Polena: Political and Electoral Navigations* 2 (1): 29–51.

Riley, Robin L. 2008. "Women and War: Militarism, Bodies, and the Practice of Gender." *Sociology Compass* 2 (4): 1192–208. http://dx.doi.org/10.1111/j.1751-9020.2008.00132.x.

Robbins, Bruce. 1992. "Comparative Cosmopolitanism." *Social Text* 31/32: 169–86. http://dx.doi.org/10.2307/466224.

Roggio, Bill. 2009. "Female Suicide Bomber Kills 30 in Karbala, Iraq." *Long War Journal*, 13 February. http://www.longwarjournal.org/archives/2009/02/female_suicide_bombe_1.php.

Rose, Jacqueline. 2004. "Deadly Embrace." *London Review of Books* 26:21–4. http://www.lrb.co.uk/v26/n21/jacqueline-rose/deadly-embrace.

Roth-Seneff, Andrew. 2007. "Occidentalism and the Realism of Empire: Notes of the Critical Method of William Roseberry." *Critique of Anthropology* 27 (4): 449–62. http://dx.doi.org/10.1177/0308275X07084238.

Runyan, Anne Sisson. 1992. "The 'State' of Nature: A Garden Unfit for Women and Other Living Things." In *Gendered States: Feminist (Re)Visions of International Relations Theory*, ed. V. Spike Peterson, 123–40. Boulder, CO: Lynne Rienner.

– 2002. "Still Not 'At Home' in IR: Feminist World Politics Ten Years Later." *International Politics* 39 (3): 361–8. http://dx.doi.org/10.1057/palgrave.ip.8897459.

Rupert, Mark. 2005. "Class Powers and the Politics of Global Governance." In *Power in Global Governance*, ed. Michael Barnett and Raymond Duvall, 205–8. Cambridge: Cambridge University Press.

Sabbagh, Suha, ed. 2002. *Arab Women: Between Defiance and Restraint*. New York: Olive Branch.

Said, Edward. 1978. *Orientalism*. New York: Random House.

Sakaoglu, S. 1996. "The PKK's Latest Method of Attack." *Hurriyet Daily News*, 1 November. http://www.hurriyetdailynews.com/the-pkks-latest-method-of-attack.aspx?pageID=438&n=the-pkks-latest-method-of-attack-1996-11-01.

Salime, Zakia. 2008. "Mobilizing Muslim Women: Multiple Voices, the Sharia, and the State." *Comparative Studies of South Asia, Africa and the Middle East* 28 (1): 200–11. http://dx.doi.org/10.1215/1089201x-2007-065.

Sasson-Levy, Orna, and Tamara Rapoport. 2003. "Body, Gender, and Knowledge in Gender Movements: The Israeli Case." *Gender & Society* 17 (3): 451–72. http://dx.doi.org/10.1177/0891243203017003006.

Schalk, Peter. 1994. "Women Fighters of the Liberation Tigers in Tamil Ilam: The Martial Feminism of Atel Palacinkam." *South Asia Research* 14 (2): 163–95. http://dx.doi.org/10.1177/026272809401400203.

Schmid, Alex, and Albert Jongman. 1988. *Political Terrorism: A New Guide to Actors, Authors, Concepts Databases, Theories and Literature*. New Brunswick, NJ: Transaction Books.

Scholey, Pamela. 2008. "Palestine: Hamas's Unfinished Transformation." In *From Soldiers to Politicians: Transforming Rebel Movements after Civil War*, ed. Jeroen De Zeeuw, 131–55. Boulder, CO: Lynne Rienner Publishers.

Schweitzer, Yoram. 2001. "Suicide Bombings: The Ultimate Weapon?" International Institute for Counter-Terrorism. https://www.ict.org.il/Article.aspx?ID=809.

– 2006. "Palestinian Female Suicide Bombers: Reality vs Myth." In *Female Suicide Bombers: Dying for Equality?*, 25–41. Tel Aviv: Jaffee Center for Strategic Studies. http://www.inss.org.il/uploadimages/Import/%28FILE%291188302013.pdf.

– 2007. "Female Suicide Bombers: Dying for Equality?" *Democracy and Security* 3 (2): 241–6.

– 2008. "Palestinian Female Suicide Bombers: Virtuous Heroines or Damaged Goods?" In *Female Terrorism and Militancy: Agency, Utility and Organization*, ed. Cindy Ness, 131–45. New York: Routledge.

Secor, Anna J. 2002. "The Veil and Urban Space in Istanbul: Women's Dress, Mobility and Islamic Knowledge." *Gender, Place and Culture* 9 (1): 5–22. http://dx.doi.org/10.1080/09663690120115010.

Segal, Naomi. 1994. "Who Whom? Violence, Politics, and the Aesthetic." In *The Violent Muse: Violence and the Artistic Imagination in Europe, 1910–1939*, ed. Kana Howlett and Rod Mengham, 141–50. Manchester: Manchester University Press.

Shah, Benazir, Nazar Ul Islam, and Sherbano Taseer. 2013. "Lady Parts: More and More Women Are Finding Their True Calling. As Suicide Bombers." *Newsweek*, 15 September, at http://newsweekpakistan.com/lady-parts/.

Shapiro, Ian. 2007. "Review Symposium: Understanding Suicide Terror." *Perspectives on Politics* 5 (1): 133–7.

Shepherd, Laura. 2007. "Victims, Perpetrators, and Actors Revisited: Exploring the Potential for a Feminist Reconceptualisation of (International) Security and (Gendered) Violence." *British Journal of Politics and International Relations* 9 (2): 239–56. http://dx.doi.org/10.1111/j.1467-856X.2007.00281.x.

– 2009. "Gender, Violence, and Global Politics: Contemporary Debates in Feminist Security Studies." *Political Studies Review* 7 (2): 208–19. http://dx.doi.org/10.1111/j.1478-9299.2009.00180.x.

– , ed. 2013. *Critical Approaches to Security: An Introduction to Theories and Methods*. London: Routledge.

Simon, Jeffrey D. 1994. *The Terrorist Trap*. Bloomington: Indiana University Press.

Sixta, Christine. 2008. "The Illusive Third Wave: Are Female Terrorists the New 'New Women' in Developing Societies?" *Journal of Women, Politics & Policy* 29 (2): 261–88. http://dx.doi.org/10.1080/15544770802118645.

Sjoberg, Laura. 2007. "Agency, Militarized Femininity and Enemy Other: Observations from the War in Iraq." *International Feminist Journal of Politics* 9 (1): 82–101. http://dx.doi.org/10.1080/14616740601066408.

– 2009. "Feminist Interrogations of Terrorism/Terrorist Studies." *International Relations* 23 (1): 69–74. http://dx.doi.org/10.1177/0047117808100611.

– 2010. "Introduction." In *International Security: Feminist Perspectives*, ed. Laura Sjoberg, 1–14. Abingdon, UK: Routledge.

– 2011. "Conclusion: The Study of Women, Gender, and Terrorism." In *Women, Gender, and Terrorism*, ed. Laura Sjoberg and Caron Gentry, 227–40. Athens, GA: University of Georgia Press.

Sjoberg, Laura, and Caron Gentry. 2007. *Mothers, Monsters, Whores: Women's Violence in Global Politics*. London: Zed Books.

– , eds. 2011. *Women, Gender, and Terrorism*. Athens, GA: University of Georgia Press.

Sjoberg, Laura, and Sandra Via, eds. 2010. *Gender, War, and Militarism: Feminist Perspectives*. Santa Barbara, CA: Praeger.

Skaine, Rosemarie. 2006. *Female Suicide Bombers*. London, NC: McFarland.

Slee, Chris, Brian Senewiratne, and Vickramabahu Karunarathne. 2009. *The Tamil Freedom Struggle in Sri Lanka*. Broadway, Australia: Resistance Books.

South Asia Terrorism Portal. 2009. "Suicide Attacks by the LTTE." http://
www.satp.org/satporgtp/countries/srilanka/database/data_suicide_
killings.htm.

Speckhard, Anne. 2008. "The Emergence of Female Suicide Terrorists."
Studies in Conflict and Terrorism 31 (11): 995–1023. http://dx.doi.
org/10.1080/10576100802408121.

– 2009. "Female Suicide Bombers in Iraq." *Democracy and Security* 5 (1): 19–50.
http://dx.doi.org/10.1080/17419160902723759.

Speckhard, Anne, and Khapta Akhmedova. 2006. "Black Widows: The
Chechen Female Suicide Terrorists." In *Female Suicide Bombers: Dying
for Equality?*, ed. Yoram Schweitzer, 81–90. Tel Aviv: Jaffee Center for
Strategic Studies. http://www.isn.ethz.ch/Digital-Library/Publications/
Detail/?id=91164.

– 2008. "Black Widows and Beyond: Understanding the Motivations and
Life Trajectories of Chechen Female Terrorists." In *Female Terrorism and
Militancy: Agency, Utility, and Organization*, ed. Cindy Ness, 100–21. London:
Routledge.

Spivak, Gayatri Chakravorti. 2004. "Terror: A Speech after 9-11." *Boundary 2*
31 (2): 81–111. http://dx.doi.org/10.1215/01903659-31-2-81.

Stack, Alisa. 2011. "Zombies versus Black Widows: Women as Propaganda in
the Chechen Conflict." In *Women, Gender, and Terrorism*, ed. Laura Sjoberg
and Caron Gentry, 83–95. Athens, GA: University of Georgia Press.

Stack-O'Connor, Alisa. 2007. "Lions, Tigers and Freedom Birds: How and
Why the Liberation Tigers of Tamil Eelam Employs Women." *Terrorism and
Political Violence* 19 (1): 43–63. http://dx.doi.org/10.1080/
09546550601054642.

Standish, Katerina. 2006. "Human Security and Gender: Female Suicide
Bombers in Palestine and Chechnya." *Peace and Conflict Review* 1 (2). http://
www.review.upeace.org/pdf.cfm?articulo=73&ejemplar=13.

Stern, Jessica. 2003. *Terror in the Name of God: Why Religious Militants Kill.*
New York: Harper Collins Publishers.

Stone, Jennia, and Katherine Pattillo. 2011. "Al-Qaeda's Use of Female
Suicide Bombers in Iraq: A Case Study." In *Women, Gender, and Terrorism*,
ed. Laura Sjoberg and Caron Gentry, 159–75. Athens, GA: University of
Georgia Press.

Stowasser, Barbara. 1994. *Women in the Qur'an: Traditions and Interpretation.*
New York: Oxford University Press.

– 2001. "Old Shaykhs, Young Women, and the Internet: The Rewriting of
Women's Political Rights in Islam." *Muslim World* 91 (1/2): 99–120. http://
dx.doi.org/10.1111/j.1478-1913.2001.tb03709.x.

Struckman, Sara. 2006. "The Veiled Women and Masked Men of Chechnya: Documentaries, Violent Conflict, and Gender." *Journal of Communication Inquiry* 30 (4): 337–53. http://dx.doi.org/10.1177/0196859906290709.

Suhrke, Astri. 1999. "Human Security and the Interests of States." *Security Dialogue* 30 (3): 265–76. http://dx.doi.org/10.1177/0967010699030003002.

Sutton, Barbara, and Julie Novkov. 2008. "Rethinking Security, Confronting Inequality." In *Security Disarmed: Critical Perspectives on Gender, Race and Militarization*, ed. Barbara Sutton, Sandra Morgen, and Julie Novkov, 3–29. New Jersey: Rutgers University Press.

Sylvester, Christine. 2013. *War as Experience: Contributions from International Relations and Feminist Analysis*. London: Routledge.

Sylvester, Christine, and Swati Parashar. 2009. "The Contemporary 'Mahabharata' and the Many 'Draupadis': Bringing Gender to Critical Terrorism Studies." In *Critical Terrorism Studies: A New Research Agenda*, ed. Richard Jackson, Marie Breen Smyth, and Jeroen Gunning, 178–93. London: Routledge.

Talbot, Rhiannon. 2000–1. "Myths in the Representation of Women Terrorists." *Éire-Ireland* 35 (3 and 4): 165–86.

Thaindian News. 2008. "US Troops Arrest Pakistani Female Suicide Bomber in Afghanistan." 18 July. http://www.thaindian.com/newsportal/india-news/us-troops-arrest-pakistani-female-suicide-bomber-in-afghanistan_10073370.html.

Thakur, Ramesh. 2004. "A Political Worldview." *Security Dialogue* 35 (3): 347–8. http://dx.doi.org/10.1177/096701060403500307.

Thomas, Caroline. 2001. "Global Governance, Development and Human Security: Exploring the Links." *Third World Quarterly* 22 (2): 159–75. http://dx.doi.org/10.1080/01436590120037018.

Thomas, Caroline, and Peter Wilkin, eds. 1999. *Globalization, Human Security and the African Experience*. Boulder, CO: Lynne Rienner Publishers.

Thomas, Nicholas, and William Tow. 2002. "The Utility of Human Security: Sovereignty and Humanitarian Intervention." *Security Dialogue* 33 (2): 177–92. http://dx.doi.org/10.1177/0967010602033002006.

Thompson, Elizabeth. 2003. "Public and Private in Middle Eastern Women's History." *Journal of Women's History* 15 (1): 52–69. http://dx.doi.org/10.1353/jowh.2003.0037.

Tickner, Ann. 1991. "Hans Morgenthau's Principles of Political Realism: A Feminist Reformulation." In *Gender and International Relations*, ed. Rebecca Grant and Kathleen Newland, 27–40. Bloomington: Indiana University Press.

– 1992. *Gender in International Relations: Feminist Perspectives on Achieving International Security*. New York: Columbia University Press.

– 2001. *Gendering World Politics: Issues and Approaches in the Post–Cold War Era.* New York: Columbia University Press.

Tickner, Ann, and Laura Sjoberg. 2006. "Feminism." In *Theories of International Relations: Discipline and Diversity*, ed. Tim Dunne, Milja Kurki, and Steve Smith, 185–202. Oxford: Oxford University Press.

Tishkov, Valery. 2004. *Chechnya: Life in a War-Torn Society.* Berkeley: University of California Press. http://dx.doi.org/10.1525/california/9780520238879.001.0001.

Toros, Harmonie, and Jeroen Gunning. 2009. "Exploring a Critical Theory Approach to Terrorism Studies." In *Critical Terrorism Studies: A New Research Agenda*, ed. Richard Jackson, Marie Breen Smyth, and Jeroen Gunning, 87–108. London: Routledge.

Turpin, Jennifer, and Lester Kurtz, eds. 1997. *The Web of Violence: From Interpersonal to Global.* Urbana: University of Illinois Press.

Tzoreff, Mira. 2006. "The Palestinian Shahida: National Patriotism, Islamic Feminism, or Social Crisis." In *Female Suicide Bombers: Dying for Equality?*, ed. Yoram Schweitzer. http://www.inss.org.il/uploadimages/Import/%28FILE%291188302013.pdf.

UNDP. 1994. *Human Development Report.* New York: United Nations Development Programme.

UNICEF. 2015. "Northeast Nigeria: Alarming Spike in Suicide Attacks Involving Women and Girls – UNICEF." www.unicef.org/media/media_82047.html.

USA Today. 2009. "Female Suicide Bomber Kills 40 in Iraq." 13 February. http://usatoday30.usatoday.com/news/world/iraq/2009-02-13-female-suicide-bomber_N.htm.

Uvin, Peter. 2004. "A Field of Overlaps and Interactions." *Security Dialogue* 35 (3): 352–3. http://dx.doi.org/10.1177/096701060403500311.

Victor, Barbara. 2003. *Army of Roses: Inside the World of Palestinian Women Suicide Bombers.* New York: Rodale.

Von Knop, Katharina. 2007. "The Female Jihad: Al Qaeda's Women." *Studies in Conflict & Terrorism* 30 (5): 397–414. http://dx.doi.org/10.1080/10576100701258585.

Walby, Susan. 1986. *Patriarchy at Work.* Oxford: Polity.

Weber, Max. 1949. *The Methodology of the Social Sciences*, ed. and trans. Edward Shils and Henry Finch. New York: Free Press.

Weinberg, Leonard, and William Eubank. 2011. "Women's Involvement in Terrorism." *Gender Issues* 28 (1–2): 22–49. http://dx.doi.org/10.1007/s12147-011-9101-8.

Weinberg, Leonard, Ami Pedahzur, and Sivan Hirsch-Hoefler. 2004. "The Challenges of Conceptualizing Terrorism." *Terrorism and Political Violence* 16 (4): 777–94. http://dx.doi.org/10.1080/095465590899768.

Wendt, Alexander. 1992. "Anarchy Is What States Make of It: The Social Construction of Power Politics." *International Organization* 46 (2): 391–425. http://dx.doi.org/10.1017/S0020818300027764.

West, Jessica. 2004–5. "Feminist IR and the Case of the 'Black Widows': Reproducing Gendered Divisions." *Innovations: Journal of Politics* 5:1–16.

Wibben, Annick. 2011. *Feminist Security Studies: A Narrative Approach*. London: Routledge.

Wieringa, Saskia. 2006. "Measuring Women's Empowerment: Developing a Global Tool." In *Engendering Human Security: Feminist Perspectives*, ed. Thanh-Dam Truong, Saskia Wieringa, and Amrita Chhachhi, 211–33. London: Zed Books Ltd.

Wight, Colin. 2006. *Agents, Structures and International Relations: Politics as Ontology*. Cambridge: Cambridge University Press. http://dx.doi.org/10.1017/CBO9780511491764.

– 2009. "Theorising Terrorism: The State, Structure and History." *International Relations* 23 (1): 99–106. http://dx.doi.org/10.1177/0047117808100615.

Wilcox, Lauren. 2013. "Explosive Bodies, Bounded States: Abjection and the Embodied Practice of Suicide Bombing." *International Feminist Journal of Politics* 16 (1): 66–85.

Wilford, Rick. 1998. "Women, Ethnicity and Nationalism: Surveying the Ground." In *Women, Ethnicity and Nationalism: The Politics of Transition*, ed. Rick Wilford and Robert Miller, 1–22. London: Routledge. http://dx.doi.org/10.4324/9780203169582.

Williams, Michael. 2006. "The Hobbesian Theory of International Relations: Three Traditions." In *Classical Theory in International Relations*, ed. Jahn Beate, 253–76. Cambridge: Cambridge University Press. http://dx.doi.org/10.1017/CBO9780511491429.011.

Williams, T. 2009. "80 Are Killed in 3 Suicide Bombings in Iraq." *New York Times*, 23 April. http://www.nytimes.com/2009/04/24/world/middleeast/24iraq.html?_r=0.

Williams, Zoe. 2014. "The Radicalisation of Samantha Lewthwaite, the Aylesbury Schoolgirl Who Became the 'White Widow.'" *Guardian*, 27 June. www.theguardian.com/uk-news/2014/jun/27/what-radicalised-samantha-lewthwaite-77-london-bombings.

Wittgenstein, Ludwig. 1953. *Philosophical Investigations*. Oxford: Basil Blackwell.

Wood, Elizabeth. 2008. "The Social Processes of Civil War: The Wartime Transformation of Civil Networks." *Annual Review of Political Science* 11 (1): 539–61. http://dx.doi.org/10.1146/annurev.polisci.8.082103.104832.

Yaqoob, Salma. 2008. "Muslim Women and War on Terror." *Feminist Review* 88 (1): 150–61. http://dx.doi.org/10.1057/palgrave.fr.9400382.

Yeğenoğlu, Meyda. 1998. *Colonial Fantasies: Towards a Feminist Reading of Orientalism*. Cambridge: Cambridge University Press. http://dx.doi.org/10.1017/CBO9780511583445.

Yelenin, Semen, and Aleksandr Boyko. 2013. "Terroristka Ne Reshalas Yekhat v Moskvu." *Komsomolskaya Pravda*, 21 October. www.kp.ru/daily/26148.5/3037740/.

Yeliseyev, Stanislav. 2013. "Naida Asiyalova Sem Let Prorabotala v Moskve," 24 October. www.slon.ru/fast/russia/naida-asiyalova-sem-let-prorabotala-v-moskve-1009230.xhtml.

Young, Iris Marion. 2003. "The Logic of Masculinist Protection: Reflections on the Current Security State." *Signs (Chicago, IL)* 29 (1): 1–25. http://dx.doi.org/10.1086/375708.

Yuzik, Yulia. 2013. "Russia's New Black Widows: The Deadly and Mysterious New Breed of Female Suicide Bomber." *Foreign Policy*, 24 October. http://foreignpolicy.com/2013/10/24/russias-new-black-widows/.

Zedalis, Debra D. 2004. "Female Suicide Bombers." Carlisle: U.S. Army War College. http://www.strategicstudiesinstitute.army.mil/pdffiles/00373.pdf.

– 2008. "Beyond the Bombings: Analyzing Female Suicide Bombers." In *Female Terrorism and Militancy: Agency, Utility, and Organization*, ed. Cindy Ness, 49–68. London: Routledge.

Index

Palestinian Islamic Jihad (PIJ), 53, 76,
    78–80, 139
Palestinian-Israeli conflict, 49, 74–5,
    77–9, 157, 183
Palestinization, 49, 74, 183
Pape, Robert, 10, 18, 31, 33–4, 41,
    52–3, 63–4, 135, 190
patriarchy, 9, 110, 112–13, 120, 129,
    140, 154–5, 162, 175, 178, 207,
    215; indigenous, 162, 168, 174;
    orientalized, 22, 44, 110, 113–14,
    116, 123, 128, 133, 161–2, 166–8,
    170, 172, 175, 182, 185, 216–18
Pedahzur, Ami, 31, 51–2, 63, 145, 190
Prabhakaran, Velupillai, 56, 149, 151
problem-solving, 23–8, 31–2, 37,
    110, 120, 122–3, 125, 133, 135–7,
    153, 161, 163, 165, 170–3, 181,
    184–5, 187–8, 194, 211, 219–20;
    approach(es), 25–6, 29–30, 171–2,
    187, 189, 194, 207, 210, 216, 218;
    author(s), 20–1, 25, 27, 115–16, 128,
    142, 144, 169–71, 181, 186, 188, 191,
    211, 215, 218; discourse(s), 22, 181;
    literature, 20, 22–3, 26, 110, 113,
    122, 127, 133, 136, 145, 151–3, 162,
    166, 179–80, 216; representations,
    22, 161–2, 173, 217; scholar(s),
    22–3, 30, 159, 162, 165, 189, 191,
    221; scholarship, 21, 23, 26–7, 136,
    182; theory/theories, 20, 24, 26–9,
    47; understanding(s), 20

Qazi, Farhana, 7, 10, 122, 129, 136
Qur'an, 84, 170–1

race, 14, 22–3, 25, 39, 42, 111, 113,
    161, 174, 177, 179, 184, 193, 198–9,
    206, 220
Rajan, Julie, 14, 37, 46–7, 182

rape, 43, 61, 119, 123–4, 127, 142, 148,
    196, 204, 209
rational choice, 11–12, 30, 33,
    189–90
resistance, 12, 20, 26, 31–2, 37–8,
    41, 45–9, 52–3, 58, 65, 67–8, 74,
    80, 83, 140–1, 143, 149, 152, 174,
    176–8, 183, 189–90, 193, 201, 203,
    215
Russia, 3, 23, 42, 49, 67–74, 82, 140,
    168, 207, 213–14
Russian wahhabi, 73, 212, 216

sacrifice, 35–6, 46–7, 74, 80, 118, 131,
    169, 182; self, 10, 34–5, 53, 114–15,
    222
Said, Edward, 163–5, 182
Salafism, 82
Schweitzer, Yoram, 11, 18, 32, 77, 114,
    150, 211
sex, 15–16, 22, 34, 39–40, 42, 45, 112–
    14, 121, 123, 129, 138, 143, 156–7,
    161, 171, 179, 184, 206, 210–11
sexual purity, 58, 127, 157, 216
shahida, 77
Sharia, 170, 177, 212
Shepherd, Laura, 12, 39
Shia, 50–3, 82–4, 86, 90–1, 221
Sjoberg, Laura, 4, 12, 14, 16–18, 40,
    42–3, 46, 77, 81, 90, 107, 110–13,
    124, 126–7, 132, 136, 138, 153, 174,
    188, 197
social contagion, 145
Sokolov, Dmitri, 73, 212, 214
Somalia, 3, 49, 81, 98–9
Sri Lanka, 3, 42, 49, 55–62, 74, 82,
    124, 127, 129, 139, 157, 168, 179–80,
    193, 221–2
structure-agency, 21, 37, 108–10,
    125, 128